Writing Song Lyrics

Creative And Critical Approaches

Series Editor: Graeme Harper

Published

Amanda Boulter, *Writing Fiction*
Craig Batty and Zara Waldeback, *Writing for the Screen*
Chad Davidson and Gregory Fraser, *Writing Poetry*
Glenn Fosbraey and Andrew Melrose, *Writing Song Lyrics*
Jeremy Scott, *Creative Writing and Stylistics*
Kim Wiltshire, *Writing for Theatre*

Writing Song Lyrics

Creative and Critical Approaches

Glenn Fosbraey
Andrew Melrose

First published 2019 by
RED GLOBE PRESS

Red Globe Press in the UK is an imprint of Springer Nature Limited registered in England, company number 785998, of 4 Crinan Street, London, N1 9XW.

Red Globe Press® is a registered trademark in the United States, the United Kingdom, Europe and other countries.

ISBN 978–1–137–60538–2 paperback
ISBN 978–1–137–60554–2 hardback

This book is printed on paper suitable for recycling and made from fully managed and sustained forest sources. Logging, pulping and manufacturing processes are expected to conform to the environmental regulations of the country of origin.

A catalogue record for this book is available from the British Library.

A catalog record for this book is available from the Library of Congress.

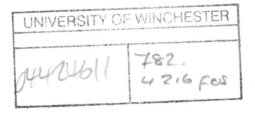

For Emily: my favourite artist and writer (GF)

For Diane, Abbi and Daniel and the house full of music, laughs, patience and guitars (AM)

Contents

Introduction

Despite straddling the high-culture cache of opera through to a nursery rhyme for children, song lyrics have never really been accepted as a major art form, like poetry, for example. They have always been the interloper on the literary list. But we think that's just fine because they are not literature (as we and Bob Dylan discuss in the coming pages). Sure, they get written down, pencilled in notebooks – typed even – just like poetry, but they are written to be sung over music, and that is the big difference. Thus they are there to be received, not by reading, but by listening. And although they can and often are read, this is a byproduct. Lyrics are an all-important part of that art form called songs, and this book is dedicated to that notion.

Do lyrics even matter?

Music is unique in that it is the only art and entertainment medium that we are constantly exposed to, even against our will. As I write this sentence, I sit in a café with Kelis blaring out of the speakers. If I walk into a shop; if I get a taxi and the driver has the radio on; if I'm watching TV and an advert comes on; if I go to a bar or a nightclub; if I walk into my child's bedroom; at a football match before the game and at half time; someone's ringtone next to me on the train: and all of it music and songs

I haven't selected, but I am hearing anyway. It's hard to imagine such a set of circumstances with books, poems or film. And with most of these songs come lyrics. Whether we like or loathe them, whether we choose to listen to them or not, we absorb them daily, along with their melodies, and inevitably we remember them, even if we choose not to. We belt them out at karaoke events; we sing along with thousands of others at gigs; we write them in love letters, texts, or tweets; we get them tattooed on our skin; we sing along in the car, hum them when walking – they are an intrinsic component in our cultural consciousness. Lyrics are an enormous part of our lives. The song lyric has come be such a strong part of art and culture, being ephemeral, throwaway, unforgettable and memorable all at the same time, it is like no other art form. It sneaks into our pores, our individual taste and our individual and collective identity at the same time. In short, the song lyric is perennially a vital part of modern culture.

Many words have been written dismissing the pop song lyric as 'disposable – or worse, as spiritually bankrupt' (Frisicks-Warren 2006: 2), and it has been posited that 'not all songwriters care equally about the words, and even those who do care are aware that part of the audience may not be bothered about the lyric' (Rooksby 2006: 97). Although 'literature, theatre, opera, and film are deemed to be capable of tackling the really heavyweight subjects with the requisite degree of chin-stroking gravitas ... the leftovers – the gently crooned "babies", the screamed "oh yeahs", the sundry other trifles and fripperies ... go to pop. At least that seems to be the critical and cultural consensus' (Thomson 2008: viii). But song lyrics are important to people, and this book is built on that premise. It may be the fact that they are so 'available' that their seriousness as an art form is downgraded, but this is a kind of cultural conceit. Never let their popularity deny their importance or their ability to touch people. Work is what we do, but art is who we are, and songs are right in the mix as far as that is concerned. Indeed, enter 'song lyric tattoos' into Google images, and see the millions of instances where lyrics meant so much to people that they got them permanently etched onto their skin; had them played at their weddings; christened them as 'their song' in loving relationships; attended their joy, their sorrow, their heartache – the list goes on and on. And it's not all just the good or emotional stuff. We know that Van Gogh cut his ear off, but he painted some of the most glorious works (and inspired a quite lovely song by Don McLean). The lyrics of Slipknot, Marilyn Manson, The Beatles, Ozzy Osbourne, U2, Judas Priest and many more have been cited in murder and suicide cases. Neil Young's lyric from 'Rust Never Sleeps' was included in Kurt Cobain's suicide note, and the lyrics of rapper Tyler the Creator were reason enough for the UK government to say he was 'rejected [entry to the UK] under the terms of Home Office policy on "behaviours unacceptable in the UK"' in 2015 (Shepherd 2015). The fact is, the song lyric is a part of our lives.

'The apparent paradox between music's impact on society ... and its lack of academic discussion is an ongoing debate, and one that needs to be given close attention if lyrics are ever going to become an appreciated academic form' (Fosbraey 2017: 59). This book aims to address this issue, and while acknowledging that 'pop songs are more tolerant both of banality and repetition than poems; more tolerant of filler syllables; more tolerant of meaninglessness, too' (Leith 2007), we discuss how what may seem throwaway and laborious to the songwriter may still be life affirming and vital to us, the listeners. And, indeed, on the flip side to this, what may seem like the greatest piece of art ever to a lyricist may be meaningless to us.

In a video for ShortList online magazine, Bill Bailey listed his 'Top 5 worst recorded songs ever'. Four of the five were on the list because of their lyrics: Des'ree's 'Life' (for its forced rhymes), Toto's 'Africa' (for its inaccuracies), Chris De Burgh's 'The Lady in Red' (for being 'toe-curling'), and Akon's 'Smack That' (for its 'charmless, horrible lyrics'). And yet ... 'Life' reached number 8 in the UK charts and was certified platinum in four countries. 'Africa' reached number 3 in the United Kingdom, number 1 on the U.S. *Billboard* Hot 100 and was certified gold in five countries; 'The Lady in Red' reached number 1 in 25 countries, including the United Kingdom; and 'Smack That' reached number 1 in 12 countries and was certified double platinum in the United States. We find similar situations when looking at any 'worst songs ever' posts, with lyrics being highlighted as major reasons for them being so 'bad'. And yet the fact that these songs still manage to sell in their millions is suggestive of the fact that when it comes to commercial success, lyrics are a matter of personal taste.

An indication of how important the lyrics are to a song can perhaps be found via its production. It's rare in pop music, but if we're faced with a single, lone voice singing a capella, all we have to focus on is what that voice is saying. Everything beyond this is distracting us from the words alone, even if the arrangements are enhancing them and making them more powerful. Or even if we are faced with an acoustic guitar and a vocal, and the guitar isn't doing anything particularly intricate beyond playing chords, we could hypothesize that we're supposed to pay great attention to the lyrics. See Bob Dylan, Joni Mitchell, Paul Simon and Nick Drake for examples (and include Billy Bragg, if we exchange acoustic guitar for electric, who took up the mantle of the balladeers). In rap music, a lot of the backing is simplistic; a basic beat and bass line, so we are focussing on the lyrics. Then we go all the way to the other extreme with acts whose production is so detailed and busy that the words are way down the list of priorities. This would explain how so many lyrics that are considered 'bad' are to be found in songs that have sold in enormous quantities: they simply weren't the writer's/producer's priority. There is nothing wrong with this, but by using lyrics as filler in this way, the writer is missing an opportunity to use music as a communication device, missing out on writing lyrics that convey a message or impact people's lives. 'Bad' lyrics won't harm a song's commercial success, but they have less potential to 'speak' to people and have an influence on their lives. Although of course defining 'bad' in this context is still a matter of individual taste, which is too important not to matter. Even writing this book we have disagreed.

Glenn's way of looking at the importance of lyrics is to use this analogy (his apologies in advance):

> It was my wife's smile that first attracted me to her, but it was her personality that made me love her. In my opinion, this can also be applied as an analogy for how I bond with songs: the initial attraction is the *sound*, the melody, the production, the singing, etc., but the deepest bond comes via the *lyrics*; that's what forms the long-term connection and, indeed, the love.

Andrew's way is different (again, apologies in advance):

> I grew up in a small, rural and cold coal mining community south of Edinburgh. One Christmas when I was around the age of 10, three or four of us got cheap guitars as presents. In no time we were a band called

Scot Free, which became Southpaw, and in learning the lyrics to sing, I suddenly realized they were the stories of life. I then started writing my own because I wanted people to see I had a life too. Songs brought joy; the band brought loads of laughs (and girls – did you think it was only Bruce Springsteen?), but lyrics let me know what a big and wonderful world it is that I lived and continue to live in.

But it is probably also a fact that on another day we might find other reasons, other moments, other parts of our timelines in the speed bumps of the roads we have travelled. The simple fact is that there are a number of reasons why we find lyrics important. What is more important is what you feel about them. What are they to you? If you can answer that question, you are more likely to become the writer you want to be, if you are not already. So think it through – what do lyrics mean to you and why are they important to you?

And on writing the book, we should say that although there has been a great deal of collaboration and editing of each other's contributions, our individual expertise is different. So early on in the writing, we decided to divide up the sections. Glenn wrote Part 1 and Andrew wrote Part II, and unless it is otherwise discussed hereafter, when the first person pronoun *I* is used in Part I and the rest of this chapter, it is Glenn speaking; and in Part II it is Andrew; and when *we* is used, it is usually to include you as the reader, though sometimes we include ourselves and/or all of us as a co-conspirators as songwriters. Either way, the book has been written with this 'informal' narrative voice because such a tone is extremely important to the art form of songwriting, itself.

So why don't we just write instrumentals?

It could certainly be argued that there are situations where lyrics are *less* important than melody, rhythm, production, vocal ability and a range of other factors. On one hand, in folk music 'there can be no doubt that the words of the song are all-important; the tune takes second place' (Zuckerkandl 1973: 114). On the other hand, one would be hard pressed, for example, to say that he or she listens to Daft Punk for their lyrics, and yet a number of their tracks (at least the tracks beyond debut album *Homework 1997*) do contain lyrics. This reveals that even where lyrics are not the focus or selling point of a song, most pop songs still *need* lyrics in order to function, however (seemingly) meaningless or banal they may be. Will.i.am still writes lyrics for the verses of his songs, even though (as we'll see in a moment) he dismisses their importance. Why would he be this dismissive? His music – *most* music which becomes a song – needs words so we can engage, so we can remember the melodies better. The lyrics may be subordinate to the tunes, but surely this is no reason to simply chuck them in for the sake of it. Of course, other artists might be popular *because* of their lyrics, not despite them. I certainly appreciate Bob Dylan way more as a lyricist than I do as a melody writer, but the opposite is true for Paul McCartney. If lyrics weren't important, why would Bernie Taupin have rewritten 'Candle in the Wind' following the death of Princess Diana (although I am not so sure he improved the original song)?

I could fill the next 50 pages with quotes about the power of words, but in the interests of brevity (and everyone's sanity) I'll settle for one from the international speaker and author Yehuda Berg:

> Words are singularly the most powerful force available to humanity.

And if we combine the power of words with the power of music, it leads us to a combination that brings meaning, hope, passion, enlightenment, wonder and humour to millions of people every year.

Instrumental music can entertain us; it can make us feel emotion; it can allow us to reflect; it can even persuade us to physically react by dancing or grimacing or smiling. But though there may be a melody in existence that we can say 'sums up our lives', the addition of words persuades us of a certain viewpoint or makes us re-evaluate our outlook on life; or can make us laugh or feel disgusted or like we're not alone. Lyrics can achieve all of these things and more. When Eminem utters the line 'They say music can alter moods and talk to you', he may well be referring to musicality when talking about altering moods, but he must be referring to lyrics when he says they 'talk to you'. Without lyrics, how, for example, was John Lennon going to put across his 'give peace a chance' message? Even if the rest of the lyrics in that particular song were randomly thrown together, that one refrain, 'Give peace a chance', conveys a message that music alone couldn't. And how do we give a social commentary like Plan B's 'Ill Manors' (2012) without lyrics? How do we convey feelings of loss, alienation, inadequacy, dissatisfaction without lyrics? How would Rage Against the Machine, well, rage against the machine on 'Killing in the Name' without being able to put their message into words? How could Weird Al Jancovic make his parody songs without the words to lampoon in the first place?

How could we address complex themes like war, racism, suicide and peace without using words? The *how* questions could go on and on – and you will have your own. Indeed, the *why* questions are there too. Why lyrics? The most useful answer is that, though they can be heard by millions, they actually speak to us as individuals – and as a songwriter that will be your challenge.

But speak to the artists, and it's a common consensus that lyrics are the 'grind' of songwriting; the hard part, but the necessary part. We hear so many artists bemoaning the fact that they need to write lyrics, but they still acknowledge the *need* to write them. So will anything at all 'do' when we write them? Looking at some of the most popular songs in history, the answer would appear to be yes. Critically acclaimed lyricist Jarvis Cocker says of writing lyrics: 'You don't really want to do the job but because a song isn't really a song until it's got some lyrics, it's down to you to write them' (Cocker 2012: 1).

Some writers suggest that lyrics aren't particularly important, with Charli XCX saying about Will.i.am that in the verses they should just say random words as 'nobody listens to the verse' (Robinson 2017).

And others attach so much importance to them that they write 'in blood, not ink' (Self, 2011: 103).

But none can argue that they aren't a basic part of our everyday life. Let's expand on this.

Songwriters use lyrics in different ways. To some writers, lyrics are used as a way to express their feelings or as a kind of therapy, like Ian Curtis, where 'all he was unable to express on a personal level was poured into his writing, and so his lyrics tell much more than a conversation with him could' (Curtis and Savage 2014: xi).

Some, like Mike Skinner, write simply to entertain:

What it all comes down to for me is this: you want to entertain people as effectively as you can, so you strive to make the three minutes they spend listening to your song as worthwhile as it can possibly be.

(Skinner 2012: 119)

Some lyricists write to explore specific themes and enforce change, like Morrissey, who 'has used the three-minute pop song to embrace society's outsiders and tackle taboo subjects' (Devereux, Dillane and Power 2011: 10). Some aim for simplicity and clarity, like Paul Simon, who says that 'the easier it is for people to understand, the better it is' (Simon 2011: xvii). And others prefer ambiguous songs with multiple meanings. As Neil Finn says, 'For a lyric I just think it's that thing of opening doors and let[ting] people walk in whatever door they wish' (Finn 2017).

But all know songs *need* lyrics one way or another, and so too, it seems, do millions of people throughout the world.

Following a talk I gave at the Hampshire Writers Society in 2016, I was asked to come up with my top five ever lyrics. They were as follows:

'November Spawned a Monster' - Morrissey
'Kathy's Song' – Simon and Garfunkel
'This Is Hell' – Elvis Costello
'Common People' - Pulp
'Brain Damage' – Pink Floyd

When it came to writing this book, it got me thinking about whether my list would've been different had I been asked for my favourite ever *songs*. The answer would almost certainly have been yes, with that list looking something like this (my top five today; tomorrow it will likely vary, like most self-respecting musos):

'Strawberry Fields Forever' – The Beatles
'Don't Dream it's over' – Crowded House
'Dosed' – Red Hot Chili Peppers
'Give Me Novocaine' – Green Day
'I Get Around' – the Beach Boys

If someone were to ask me who I thought were among the *worst* lyric writers of all time, I'd most certainly include Red Hot Chili Peppers among them. For reasons, and an impressive array of horribly forced rhymes, see 'Rollercoaster of Love' and 'Dani California', songs that give the impression of being improvised in the vocal booth. And even 'Dosed', which makes it into my top five songs list, includes the baffling line 'Show love with no remorse and/Climb on to your seahorse,' where one can almost imagine the scenario:

> **Anthony Keidis:** 'Guys; I'm laying down vocals in 5 minutes and I still haven't finished the lyrics! Quick: anyone got a rhyme for 'remorse'?
> **Flea:** 'Um … seahorse?'
> **Anthony:** 'Good enough!'

'I Get Around' wouldn't win any awards for its lyrics either: 'We always take my car 'cause it's never been beat/And we've never missed yet with the girls we meet' (with *yet* pronounced as 'yit' in order to internally rhyme with *it's*). And 'Give Me Novocaine' is hardly poetic.

Okay, so that Red Hot Chili Peppers skit was just a bit of fun, but if I were to go through the list and analyse what it was that I loved about these songs, it'd look like this:

> 'Strawberry Fields Forever' – The Beatles – lyrics (especially the lines 'Always, no, sometimes think it's me/But you know I know when it's a dream/I think, er, no, I mean, er, yes, but it's all wrong'); dreamlike singing and production
> 'Don't Dream It's Over' – Crowded House – melody (especially chorus)
> 'Dosed' – Red Hot Chili Peppers – melody; production; the fact that it instantly reminds me of a certain time in my life
> 'Give Me Novocaine' – Green Day – melody; slide guitar
> 'I Get Around' – Beach Boys – melody, vocals

So what does this say about music, lyrics and us? In my case, it means I can love songs whose lyrics aren't my favourite part, but I couldn't love a song where I disliked the lyrics or disagreed with the author's moral code. I think most of us have two selves: one which needs stimulating on an intellectual level (the Morrisseys, the Waters, the Simons) and one which just wants to be entertained, even if the lyrics somewhat pass us by (the Chili Peppers, Green Day, the Beach Boys). The important thing to note about our listening (and this will also be important for our writing) is for those times when we are inspired, captivated, impressed, awed and so on by a lyric, what is it that has left such an impact? Is it the imagery? The wordplay? The use of rhyme? The symbolism? The singer's biography? Its cultural significance? The way it seems to capture our own lives in song? The way we would like to be? The life we would like to have?

Exercise

Make you own 'Top 10 songs' and 'Top 10 lyrics' list, making sure to add in your reasons for liking them.

Lyrics versus Poetry

This is addressed later in Part II of the book, but it is important to stress a couple of things: firstly, that the song lyric has long been regarded as the poor cousin in the literary canon, and this book is intent on challenging this idea.

> For a songwriter, you don't really go to songwriting school; you learn by listening to tunes. And you try to understand them and take them apart and see what they're made of, and wonder if you can make one, too.
>
> Tom Waits

The following chapters look at this issue in depth because Tom Waits's advice isn't the last word on this. Rikki Rooksby (2006: 96) writes:

> Lyrics are words whose full effect depends upon music. A lyric is a set of words intended to be sung, and to be supported by music. A lyric happens in time, so a listener cannot on first hearing ask the singer to stop and go back a line; reading a poem you could. Poems communicate ideas and feelings by word alone, straight off the page. This is crucial. Music is so potent it can lend banal and clichéd words an expressiveness they could

never have in a poem. Delivered by Aretha Franklin, Levi Stubbs, Sam Cooke or Jeff Buckley, the most pedestrian phrases can still 'work'. The music can compensate for lack of style and substance in the lyric. Poetry has nothing to rescue it in the same way. The music can compensate for whatever profundity or style is missing from the words. Music can excuse or even temporarily revive clichéd words and images.

Other critics also draw attention to the differences between lyrics and poetry, with Lars Eckstein (2010: 23) stating, 'Lyrics are not poetry, and their study therefore requires a different set of analytical tools from that which is conventionally applied to poetry'; Remnick (2011: xvi–xvii) saying, 'Even the best songs … are utterly linked to the melodic, harmonic, and rhythmic qualities that go along with them'; and Gottlieb and Kimbal (2000: xxiv) asserting that 'reading song lyrics is very different from reading a poem. A lyric is one half of a work, and its success or failure depends not only on its own merits as verse but on its relationship to its music.'

What this book will do

This book will give readers the opportunity to explore song lyrics from both critical and creative perspectives, allowing them to analyse existing artists while creating and reflecting upon their own work. Among other things, the chapters in this book include discussions on the following:

- The notion that lyrics are a co-collaborative process between writer and listener
- The link between formula and generic expression, and commercial success
- How lyrics can persuade us to do certain things (including buy records!)
- How, even though they may appear 'real', all lyrics include some degree of artistic manipulation
- Meaning being elastic and dependent on the listener
- How literary criticism, associated more with novels and poems, can also be applied to 'read' song lyrics

- How the use of the first-person pronoun *I* doesn't necessarily indicate the writer's voice or opinions
- How we can analyse a song by looking at nothing but what's contained within its lyrics
- How a song can be analysed using the song itself as merely the starting point for a wider discussion
- How minimal lyrics can equal maximum impact
- How nonsense can have meaning
- The extent to which the writer should consider the listener
- What songs *are* discussing, what they *should* be discussing and what they should *refrain* from discussing
- How biographical awareness of the author can be used to increase emotional impact

In addition, the book discusses the process of writing lyrics.

Although there are times when the characters and opinions of the authors make an appearance, most of this book is objective, both with regards to what we *like* and what we consider, in our very subjective opinions, to be *good*. Unlike other books on the subject, our place as authors is to offer a discussion on the topics contained within, observing what writers have done in the past, what techniques they have used in their songs, what impacts this has had on the listener, what is common, what is rare, what has been successful in terms of sales, what subjects can be talked about in our lyrics, how we can use what has been before to shape new material, and so on.

Part I

Foundations

1

How do we listen?

Defining what the 'text' is when we talk about pop songs

In conducting close critical readings of any text, be it a poem, a novel, a play or so on, we have the opportunity to look at both the text itself and at what lies beyond it; lyrics are no different. This methodology offers great benefits to us in our analyses and in aiding our understanding of the meaning, historical, critical and cultural context of the lyric. You might be asking, how important is this? Well, insofar as the lyricist is a writer just like other writers, I contend that it deserves the same critical consideration.

Nevertheless, given the nature of popular songs, in whatever genre (see below) deciding what constitutes 'the text' needs a different approach from literature. In a novel, for example, we can *see* what the text is: whatever appears within the pages, perhaps including the front and back covers, blurb and author bio if applicable, but the text is defined as the words of the novel itself. Everything is contained in the words, sentences, paragraphs, chapters and so on that make up the pages of the novel. The same is true for a poem. With a song, however, there are other factors to consider. The song is a combination of music and lyric, both of which can be read as well as heard; and then there is the accompanying material that surrounds the delivery. Should the 'text' include cover art, information found inside the sleeve or booklet, including lyric transcriptions (for hard copy) or website (for download/streaming). Should 'text' include music video? And to what extent should we allow these factors to influence our readings of the song? Once information is obtained, it's hard to ignore or dismiss. If we have seen the music video for a song, it is likely to influence our perception of the song. Who can separate Robin Thicke's 'Blurred Lines' (2013) from its video now; or Queen's 'Bohemian Rhapsody' (1975), which was a seminal breakthrough in song delivery via video for television?

In this book the 'text' when we are talking about popular music is the song itself– the song coming out of speakers or headphones, without any other factors interfering with the experience. Imagine tuning a radio dial or getting Spotify, iTunes, or some such to randomly select you a song. You hear the song for the first time, don't know who performed or wrote it, and have no knowledge of its music video or artwork. This is, perhaps, popular song analysis at its purest. From a straight gut reaction, we might mishear the lyrics; we might think the singer is female when he is a male, black when she is white, in his twenties when the singer is in his sixties, and it's all relevant because what we are doing is processing what we don't know alongside what we do. Such reactions, whether fact or error, still make for an analysis, after all it's our *first*. Put yourself into this position and think about the time you stumbled across a much-loved song in this way. Later, when we find out more about the song and bring in the artist's info, appearance or biography, our perspective will change, whether we want it to or not. This later analysis is also valid, but very different from the first. The first draws entirely on two things:

1. reader response (*our* reaction to the music based upon our own experiences), and
2. (which carries on from this first point) a quasi-structuralist criticism where we judge the song based upon what's been before (but only what *we* have heard before, up to that point) and also the cultural context in which it is delivered and received. When we start to bring factors outside the text into our analyses, we will likely come up with a reading that is completely different to one that looks *only* at the text.

Now that we've defined what we mean by the text, we can begin to think about how to analyse it.

What do we look for in a song?

Although it could certainly be argued that many very successful songs have lyrics which don't contain a great deal of depth, it doesn't mean that lyrics are unimportant. Although these songs may prioritize the hook, the big chorus, the production or vocal acrobatics above the actual lyrical content, there are many, many others whose lyrics are intended to be front and centre.

Sometimes, a couple of lines and a general theme are enough to carry a song, regardless of what the rest of the lyrics are doing. Take Pharrell Williams' 'Happy' (2013) as a prime example. At the time of writing, it was the biggest-selling single of the decade so far. The song revolves around the simple refrain 'I'm happy' and the repeated instruction for the listener to 'clap along'. That the listener may not understand or agree with what they're clapping along with – and with instructions including clapping along 'if you feel like a room without a roof' and 'if you feel like happiness is the truth', this may well be the case – is irrelevant as they're essentially clapping along to agree with the hook 'I'm happy'. The rest of the lyrics' function is only to back up the general feel of being happy, and once again, the fact that they include lines which stray into the nonsensical – 'I'm a hot air balloon that could go to space/With the air, like I don't care, baby, by the way' – doesn't impact on the song's overall appeal. It can, indeed, be summed up by its one-word title. All Pharrell Williams had to do was to make it sound convincing. Although there is obviously nothing wrong with this as a writing technique, and no one can argue with Pharrell's success, this isn't what some writers want to be doing. As with most art forms, different people seek different things. In literature, some writers want to write page-turners that hit the top of the bestsellers list, and others want to create something profound that will last forever in the memory. Some film directors want to make a rip-roaring blockbuster simply to entertain, and others want to make art-house films to move their audience and make them question themselves and the society they live in. And so it is with songwriting. For every writer who wants nothing more for his lyrics than for them to be part of a whole package of entertainment within a song, there is the lyricist who wants her words to be meaningful, impactful and profound. For every Black Eyed Peas ('The beat bump bumps in your trunk trunkas/The girlies in the club with the big plump plumpas' [2003]), there's a Joni Mitchell ('We're captive on the carousel of time/We can't return we can only look behind' [1970]). For every Girls Aloud ('Don't hit my what/Come hit my spot/Don't pop the lock/Don't hit my what/Come like my spot/Let me give it to ya/Break it down, Mr. Shock' [2008]), there is a Leonard Cohen ('As he died to make men holy, let us die to make things cheap' [2016]). And so on. And that's not to rubbish any artists or the style they choose to work in; it's merely to observe that different lyricists have different goals in mind when they sit down to write (which we will explore later through our discussions of formula and persuasion).

The type of lyricist you're going to be will depend greatly on what kind of listener you are. Don't really pay much attention to lyrics and just want something (anything) to sing along to? Fine – no problem. The likelihood is, then, that your main focus won't be on lyrics when you're writing a song, and you'll just write whatever words fit the melody and don't sound *too* awful. Love lyrics and pore over the transcripts in search for meaning? You'll likely spend a lot of time on your lyrics and fill them with hidden messages. Love lyrics because they help you get to know the artist? You may be drawn to self-confessional lyrics where you lay yourself bare on the page. Love wordplay, clever rhyme and poetic language, but aren't fussed over what they mean? You might find yourself writing lyrics that are aesthetically pleasing but have no underlying message. Love lyrics that make a bold statement, be it political, social, racial or sexual? Then maybe that's what you should write about. Not that as a lyricist you should ever limit yourself to one particular style, of course, but spending a few seconds thinking about your relationship with lyrics in your life so far could be quite revealing about what you want to do with your lyrics, be it making an empowering statement about feminism or selecting words because they rhyme and sound good.

Exercise 1

Think of your top five songs of all time, and make a few notes about *why* they're your favourites.

Now think of your top five sets of *lyrics* of all time, and consider what it is about their words you love so much.

Lastly, compare the two lists and, if there are differences, think about the importance you attach to lyrics and the importance you attach to the other aspects (melody, singer, production, etc.)

Exercise 2

To flip things around, make a note of the five songs that you dislike the most. Note your reasons. Do they have to do with the overall sound (production)? The lyrics? An annoying earworm melody that you can't shift for days after listening? The artist themselves?

Exercise 3

Nick Hornby wrote a wonderful book called *31 Songs* (2014), where he wrote a personal essay (about 1,000 words each) on 31 of the tracks that he had the biggest connection with and his relationship with them. Choose one of the songs from your first top five list and do something similar. At what point in your life did you discover the song? Did you buy it, hear it on the radio, see its music video on TV or stream it? Was the attachment instant, or did it take awhile? Are any specific memories associated with it? Did it lead to your liking more songs from the same artist, and similarly, did it open gateways to other types of music? Apart from the song itself, is there anything else that you associate with it (e.g. music video, artist interview, gig, album cover, etc.)

After this short series of exercises, you'll start to discover more about yourself as listener, and this will have an impact on what kind of writer you'll be, whether it's through directly aping a particular style or simply being drawn to specific subjects or themes and allowing these to emerge via osmosis into your lyrics.

Starting to analyse

Listen to a song of your choice, and consider the following questions:

Which perspective is used (first, second or third person)? Is there more than one?

Which tense is used? Is there more than one?

Who, if anyone, is being addressed?

How many 'characters' are present in the song?

What kind of emotional impact does it have on you?

What emotional impact do you think the writer is trying to have on you?

Is the writer trying to persuade you of anything?

What, if any, 'meaning' do you take from the lyrics?

Are any words difficult to follow? If so, which ones?

What conclusions do you draw of the lyricist?

Does the song remind you of anything else you've heard before (either in terms of the sound, melody, vocal or lyrics)? If yes, what do the 'other' songs mean to you, and what memories or emotions do you attach to them?

Does there appear to be any metaphor, simile or symbolism present in the lyrics?

When you listen, who are you seeing as the 'I' character?

When you listen, who are you seeing as the 'you' character (yourself or another)?

To what extent does the song 'speak to you' about your own life?

To what extent does the song 'speak to you' about someone else's life? And who might that be?

From this list of questions, which involve looking *inside* the text (just at the music and lyrics), and which require you to look *outside* (beyond just the music and lyrics).

2

Author, intention, biography

Historically, in music criticism the author's intention has been central to us being able to 'understand' the lyrics. As Hopps says,

> Never is the reliance on author's intention more prevalent than it is in reading pop music, and it is commonplace for 'commentators [to] read the lyrics literally, as transparent disclosures of the singer's biography. (2009: 9)

On 23 April 2016, Beyonce's album *Lemonade* was released, with the song 'Sorry' (2016). It includes the line 'He only want me when I'm not there/He better call Becky with the good hair.' The reaction on the internet was immediate and widespread, with articles in *Vanity Fair, Hello, Independent, NME, Daily Mirror, Daily Mail*, MTV, *Metro, Vogue, Cosmopolitan*, NBC News, CNN.com, BBC.co.uk, *Daily Express, Daily Star*, and *Huffington Post* (to name just some), all of which ran stories that sought to discover the identity of the 'Becky' character. Indeed, a Google search of 'Becky with the Good Hair' on 6 July 2017 brought with it 2,480,000 results. Why, though, do we immediately assume there is weight and meaning and reality to the line in 'Lemonade', instead of thinking that Beyonce may simply have been floundering for a rhyme with 'there' and plumped for 'hair', then worked in a random female character to fill the line? Beyonce certainly has form when using perfect rhymes in songs, so it's not too much of a leap. Look at it this way:

9

if Stephen King had written a 'Becky with the good hair' into his new novel, would it have caused this furore?

The Beyonce 'Lemonade' saga continued, with speculation around new Jay-Z album '4:44', where, apparently, 'instead of raving about the music and collaborations, fans appear to be more interested in the fact he addresses his rocky relationship with Beyonce' (Shenton 2017).

> This desire to discover more about an artist is nothing new, of course, with fan clubs and band newsletters having been around for decades, but this kind of instant access to biography, and the ease with which it can be obtained is relatively new . . . [and] knowing what they look like, how they speak, how they interact with their fans, even elements of their personal lives becomes part of the listening experience.
>
> (Fosbraey 2017: 59–60)

Such readings are limiting what we as critics and writers can actually 'get' from a song, and with the explosion of social media and the ease of sharing information (and rumour) quickly and often anonymously, attaching writers' personal life to the songs they write is now more convenient than ever.

This might be suggestive, of course, that it's merely representative of the reality TV, celebrity-obsessed times we live in (and, most importantly, the relationships of said celebrities), but critics and fans alike have been looking at song lyrics in this way for decades, at the expense of the more in-depth attention we might afford, say, to literature or poetry. After all, no one was clamouring to find the identity of Brady Hartsfield when, in June 2016, bestselling author Stephen King released his novel *End of Watch*, for it was just assumed that he was a fictional character.

Again, there's this contrast between how we look at other art forms. Why is one art form assumed to be purely fictional, with its names and characters nothing but inventions of the author's imagination, but another is assumed to be a personal revelation?

But we should be careful when looking for meaning to occur via the author's intentions.

The difference between how we may choose to read songs and what the writer's own intention was can be shown via two podcasts, the first which discusses the Nirvana song 'Heart-Shaped Box' (1993), and the second where Weezer songwriter Rivers Cuomo talks about how we wrote the song 'Summer Elaine and Drunk Dory' (*Song Exploder* podcast 2016).

In *The Great Albums* podcast, the presenters dissect each song, trying to interpret the lyrics based almost entirely on what they think the songwriters may have intended them to mean. In their 'Nirvana – In Utero' broadcast, for example, while discussing the song 'Heart-Shaped Box', one of the presenters posits that he 'can never figure out what it's really *about*'. He then asks how the other presenters 'interpret it' (*The Great Albums* podcast 2017).

This technique of 'analysis', where the songs are looked at in terms of their 'aboutness' is common (you need only type 'song meanings' into a search engine to see just *how* common), but it's also restrictive, ignoring what's actually contained within the song in its efforts to immediately look beyond it to the artist's intention.

If we now look at the *Song Exploder* podcast, where Rivers Cuomo talks about his songwriting technique for the song 'Summer Elaine and Drunk Dory', we can immediately see how futile a search for such authorial meaning may actually be. In writing the song, Cuomo uses a technique where he draws phrases from a spreadsheet he has created that contains lines of 'things that I want to say, or things that I've read in a book, or heard on a TV show or a movie' or 'really cool lines' taken from his 'stream of consciousness' journals. The spreadsheet results in 'a couple of thousand lines . . . tagged by how many syllables each line has.' Having written the vocal melody for 'Summer Elaine and Drunk Dori', and knowing how many syllables he needed for each line, Cuomo then searched the spreadsheet for lines that would fit. The result was a song where 'it sounds like something happened in my life and I observed it and then I wrote a song about it, and it's coherent, there's a beginning, middle, and end, and it's totally not the case at all; each line is from a completely different place and I reassembled them in an order that suggests a story that never happened' (*Song Exploder* podcast 2016).

The important thing to note here, though, is that just because Cuomo didn't intend for there to be a meaning to the song doesn't mean there wasn't one. As Levitin points out, 'because the meaning is not perfectly defined, each of us as listeners becomes a participant in the ongoing process of understanding the song. The song is personal because we've been asked or forced to fill in some of the meaning for ourselves' (Levitin 2009: 31–32). More on the role of the listener in creating meaning later.

Fact versus fiction

> All art . . . including that which affects to speak most directly and in the most heartfelt way, is a matter of contrivance and manipulation.
>
> (Hopps 2009: 84)

John Hiatt said, 'People always think these songs are autobiographical. And they're not, although I certainly draw from life experience. But it's fiction, for God's sake' (Zollo 2003: 649), and this is a very relevant point in all artwork, much less fiction. Although many artists see songwriting as a way to vent, confess or talk about their personal lives, this doesn't mean that the lyrics they are producing are accurate reflections of truth. Lyrics are an art form, and art means manipulation. Even if lyricists want to give a 'warts and all' account of what it's like to be them, a number of factors prevent them from being able to achieve this. Firstly, the length of the average pop song immediately limits how much material can be included in a song. Is three minutes enough to tell us everything, or does it necessitate an editing or paring down of the material? It might be argued that the moment a lyricist starts to recognize the form they're writing in, and the conventions associated with it, total truth is compromised. When we also consider how many writers will look for a particular syllabic count in their lines, or seek end or internal rhymes, or a particular rhythm to their words, total truth is getting further and further away. What we can be left with, then, is an artistic impression of the truth; it's an oil painting rather than a high-definition photograph. However, this should not negate the point that the line between truth and fiction is very fine. And indeed a lot truths are made up of many composite ideas and many truths that come together in one lyric.

David Byrne, singer and songwriter for acclaimed band Talking Heads, plays down the trueness of biography in song:

> In the West . . . it's assumed that everything one utters or sings (or even plays) emerges from some autobiographical impulse. Even if I choose to sing someone else's song, it's assumed that the song was, when it was

written, autobiographical for them, and I am both acknowledging that fact and at the same time implying that it's applicable to my own biography. Nonsense! It doesn't matter whether or not something actually happened to the writer – or to the person interpreting the song.

(Byrne 2012: 155)

In his career, John Lennon used two different writing techniques: experience and projection. He claims that in The Beatles:

the only true songs I ever wrote were 'Help!' and 'Strawberry Fields' . . . They were the only ones that I really wrote from experience and not projecting myself into a situation and writing a nice story about it . . .'

(Wenner 2000: 10)

He even went as far as to say that he'd 'have a separate songwriting John Lennon who wrote songs for the sort of meat market [that were] just a joke' (Wenner 2000: 84). Of course, it has been reported widely that Lennon was notoriously fickle about truth telling and would often just say things for effect, so who knows what the truth really is? On the album *Plastic Ono Band*, he wrote mainly from experience, saying that 'it's real . . . It's about me' (Wenner 2000: 10), but was it really?

Sticking with The Beatles for a moment, Paul McCartney comments that 'George Harrison once said he could only write songs from his personal experience, but they don't have to exist for me. The feeling of them is enough' (Miles 1998: 316). Isn't this a fantastic statement? He is writing truths, but not necessarily his own, and it's the wonderful thing about being an artist – that ability to write about the human condition, not just your own. As critics, though, are we to take these statements at face value? Who's to say some of Lennon's biography didn't unconsciously seep into his 'meat market' songs? Or that Harrison's 'personal experience' songs didn't start off that way but then end up, during the editing process, to resemble blurry depictions of them?

Let's look at the song 'Things the Grandchildren Should Know', by the band Eels (2005d). It is a song which, on the surface at least, does seem to be straight autobiography. The lyrics to this song, and many of their others, appear to be confessional insights into the life of songwriter and singer Mark Everett, and this technique is probably most pronounced here, where Everett is self-evaluating and looking back over his life. What we can't ignore as critics, however, is that what Everett is giving us is what he wants us to see; what he feels comfortable divulging to us, and he's doing so in about four minutes (instrumental outro excluded). In contrast, the audiobook of Everett's biography, incidentally of the same name as this song's title, clocks in at over five hours. Obviously the pop song's lyrics can never run to such lengths, and we could put across a strong argument that any autobiography is simply a brief, artistically manipulated version of the author's life that picks and chooses the most entertaining stories. But this means that any such autobiography in lyrics has gone through an extreme editing process, leaving us with only the barest of bare bones. 'Things the Grandchildren Should Know' thus relies on a prior knowledge of both author and previous lyrical subject matter to make the song have real emotional connection and reaction. It can be contended that it wouldn't have nearly the same impact on a listener who wasn't aware of his biography or previous songs, including the tear-inducing 'Dead of Winter' (1998a) ('the saddest song I ever wrote'; Everett 2008: 143), 'Elizabeth on the Bathroom Floor' (1998b), or 'Going to Your Funeral Part 2' (1998c). For those that *are* aware of Everett's biography, however, the final verse of the song 'Things the Grandchildren Should Know' contains a positivity long-time followers always hoped he would achieve: 'So in the end I'd like to say that I'm a very thankful man . . . I had some regrets, but if I had to do it all again, well, it's something I'd like to do' (Eels, 'Things the Grandchildren Should Know' 2005d).

This song, appearing as the final track on a double album, although seemingly providing a great optimistic note to finish on, takes on a rather ominous tone when considering the line 'I thought I'd better tell you before I leave'. Taken at face value, this could refer to the writer/narrator simply leaving the conversation (between himself and whoever he is relaying this story to), but taken in the context of his personal history, combined with the lyrics on other tracks that precede it on the album, like 'I've got something, maybe I should tell you/I could check out at any given time (Eels, 'Check-Out Blues' 2005a); 'I'll go none too bravely into the night/I'm so tired of living the suicide life' (Eels, 'Suicide Life' 2005c), and 'I don't want to live in a world you've left behind' (Eels, 'The Stars Shine in the Sky Tonight' 2005b), and also taking into account that the songs often talk about his life in the past tense, the lyrics could be read as a suicide note. Stretch our research further and we'll see that

Everett also starts his autobiography listing the different methods he had considered for committing suicide.

So, without looking at the author's role in this song, his personal history, his previous work and the songs that preceded it on the album, we're left with a completely different reading to what we get if we do consider all these things. And that is the power the author can have over our interpretations of songs. And it should be reiterated that just because a song can be read like a tragic novel or a reflective movie does not mean its content is necessarily true.

Similarly, with Morrissey, Hopps suggests that the line:

> 'the heart feels free' in the song 'Dear God Please Help Me' is so moving 'because it represents the latest stage in a long and elaborate drama – which is the life and work of Morrissey – and is therefore densely resonant with what has preceded it.
>
> (Hopps 2009: 13)

the key word here is *suggests*. Hopps doesn't know this at all; he is compiling what he knows to make an unconfirmed assessment, and in fact, Steven Patrick Morrissey has made a career out of creating a character called Morrissey to lead us down these roads. David Bowie was notorious for this, as Ziggy Stardust and the Thin White Duke (e.g.) but you only have to google his television interview with Michael Parkinson, 'David Bowie talking about Yorkshiremen' to see the mask revealed.[1] It is as much a case that the artist is making his own persona a story. And let's face it: we have all done that at some time in our lives.

Lyricists continually blur the lines between fact and fiction, character and self, admitting 'truths' as they reveal their own personalities, but retreating as they write words or phrases that fit the song, but not necessarily their biographies personalities or, indeed, reality. In 'Common People,'

> Cocker claimed to have forgotten the girl's real identity but admitted to half-truths in his autobiographical lyrics. She may not have studied sculpture, but the line scanned better. And, although it implies that she wanted to bed him, he resorted to poetic license to enhance the narrative. (Dimery 2013: 731)

---

[1] https://www.youtube.com/watch?v=P4wqgLU3YK8.

Kurt Cobain stated in his journal that he used 'bits and pieces of others' personalities to form (his) own' (Cobain 2003: 95), and in the song 'Something in the Way', which was thought to be biographical due to a story he used to tell about living under a bridge (later dismissed as a fallacy), distorted his own biography to make for a good narrative (Cross 2002: 57). In the songs '97 Bonnie and Clyde' (1999a), 'Kim' (2000) and 'Hailey's Song' (2002a), Eminem takes certain parts of his real life, like the fact that he's called Marshall, has a wife called Kim and a daughter called Hailey, and various other biographical details, then mixes this real narrative with a fictional one. In these songs it's clear that Eminem hasn't actually killed his wife in real life. And of course, if we applied the same belief logic as truth and took an artist's biography in a song literally, we would see Eminem currently serving a life sentence for murder – which we can agree would be absurd.

Adele's seemingly super-personal tale of heartbreak, 'Someone Like You' (2011), was written 'in Los Angeles with professional songwriter Dan Wilson (Hodgkinson n.d.), suggesting that the words may have originally been broadly autobiographical but were tailored to work as well as possible in the medium of song, possibly meaning they were broadened to be less specific to Adele and more generic to a wider audience.

Thus, relying on biography to find meaning in songs can be limiting to us as readers and can also be limiting to us as writers. As writers, it leads some to assume that we need to 'bare all', and to value truth over storytelling, artistry and aesthetics as 'a simplistic creative process wherein authors simply recycle their own life experience in each text they create . . . [leading a reader to overlook] . . . what is special or unique' (McCaw 2008: 74).

Of course, that's not to say we should ignore the author. Firstly, given the way our minds work, it would be near impossible to go against this habit of a lifetime of linking lyrics to their singer (though not necessarily their author), but secondly, it can elevate a work to allow for more emotional impact upon the listener.

3

The role of the listener

These days we are hard-wired as cultural consumers to look for meaning and significance in everything we do. Electronic media, television, even old-fashioned magazines and newspapers demand it of us, and we consume trivia as 'news', however spurious or vacuous it may be. It stands to reason, therefore, that we often look on this surface for meaning and significance in art, too. But this is really doing it a disservice.

Meaning in any art form is dependent on the consumer (listener, reader, viewer, etc.), but if you plan to be a serious artist, in this case a lyric writer, meaning deserves closer attention than it often receives. This is perhaps most obvious, and where meaning is most fluid, in pop music, where the listener is always an active participator. This is due, in main, to the fact that song lyrics and their delivery haven't got the time to lay out a full story in the way other mediums do. The songwriter provides a template onto which the listener places an interpretation of what the full text might look like, fleshing out character, setting, plot and eventually meaning itself. Within any song, as the writer has only a short time to work with, there will invariably be 'gaps'; gaps in the story, gaps in the character, gaps in the settings and gaps in time itself. Any fiction will have these gaps – it's what prevents a story going on forever – and it's up to the writer to select what he or she feels are the most crucial sections

and include these in the finished product. That's why in a novel we sometimes cut from two characters preparing to, say, drive from Southampton
to Edinburgh, to them arriving at their destination. Unless the eight
hours in the car are crucial to the plot (it may be the case, of course,
where the characters uncover vital information about each other during
conversation), those hours will be cut – deemed as unnecessary by the
author – dead time that would bore the reader with its lack of pace and
story arc.

In song, there may well be more gaps than there is actual text, and many
are reliant on the listener's active participation and collaboration. Music,
more than any other medium, requires the listener to 'intervene with' the
lyrics, expanding the story, creating meaning and interpretation, fleshing
out character, taking emotional prompts from the lyric and reacting
accordingly during instrumental breaks. In this way, listeners are as vital
to the creation of meaning within songs as writers themselves. Despite
the enormous amount of opinions to the contrary (see the Introduction),
song lyrics don't need to have a single agreed meaning in order to have
an impact or be successful. In fact, it could be argued that 'meaning' is
something impossible to define, dependent as it is on the listener's own
collaboration with the song. The suggestion is to read between the lines,
read the silences, read the unsaid, the innuendo, the implied and the
lyrical story.

'Finding' meaning in a song is dependent on a number of different
factors but will always culminate in the level of participation carried out
by the listener and his or her desire to find depth in a song. This will differ
from person to person, with some listeners satisfied with taking lyrics at
face value, viewing them simply as words whose function is to provide
something to sing along to, and others not satisfied until they find some
kind of deeper meaning to the song (if indeed it exists – for some listeners
it will, but not for others). Whether this is by looking at the author's
biography and applying it in order to gain the 'window into the writer's
soul' approach, or it's using the lyrical 'prompts' to apply the words to
their own lives, or it's manipulating phrases to find some kind of spiritual
enlightenment through metaphor or hidden message.

'If we acknowledge that the role of the reader (or in our case, the
listener) is "relevant to an understanding of texts . . . [and that to read

is to] collaborate in a process akin to a performance" (McCaw 2008: 71), it allows us to see how the songwriter's intention is not necessary in order for us to form a bond with a particular song, and we need look no further than ourselves in order to analyse' (Fosbraey 2017: 62). In fact, it 'authorizes and encourages readers to begin where, really, readers must always begin: with an individual response' (Lynn 1994: 52). David Byrne even goes as far as to say that 'it is the music and the lyrics that trigger the emotions within us, rather than the other way round. We don't make music – it makes *us*' (Byrne 2012: 155).

If we have a prior opinion of an artist, it can affect the way we listen to his or her music. Have you ever heard a DJ introduce a song on the radio, and then you switched straight over because you didn't like the singer or band? That's us allowing our preconceived ideas of an artist to influence our relationship to a song, to the extent where we're not even willing to *listen* to it. Other reactions will be less extreme, but we may be more inclined to dismiss or dislike a song where we've already formed a negative relationship with an artist. On the flip side of this, if we've already bonded with an artist, we may be more inclined to give his or her music time to grow on us, as we *want* to like it. There are a number of artists whose albums I will buy without hesitation, and although I may not end up liking them, I will certainly give all the songs a fair chance before coming to that conclusion. If I'm not invested in the artists, I may not listen quite as many times before coming to a verdict.

As well as bringing in our own preconceived ideas of the artist, a lot of our emotional connection with a song arises from our own personal experiences. If the lyrics are about a break-up, we apply our own experiences of break-ups, whether they are ones we've been through ourselves, witnessed in friends, or seen or read about in films or books. If we've not personally experienced a break-up, we will respond to the lyrics through indirect means, drawing upon what we've seen second-hand rather than what we've been through ourselves. This reaction can be equally as powerful, as 'the very thought of things can generate emotions' (Cave 2009: 10) but it will lead to a different reading and interpretation from that of someone who has been through a break-up personally. Similarly, those who have been through a break-up recently may read the song differently to those who went through one some time ago; likewise for those whose break-up was amicable and those whose break-up was not, and so on. Each variable is dependent on the listener's life experiences prior to and post (in this analogy) break-up. The different types of possible interpretations using this kind of reading are infinite, and our own individual responses to songs are subject to change as we grow older.

How we choose to believe whether or not writers are being realistic and/or authentic in their writing is dependent on three different factors. Firstly, it will depend on the specific language they use and how persuasive an argument they put across; secondly, it will depend on their biography (or, more importantly what we *know* about their biography); and thirdly, it will depend on the extent to which we've experienced similar things ourselves.

Fish notes that we need to ask ourselves of a text, 'What does this do?' – with *do* equivocating between a reference to the action of the text *on* a reader and the actions performed *by* a reader as he negotiates (and, in some sense, actualizes) the text' (Fish 1994: 2–3). 'In this formulation,' he says, 'the reader's response is not *to* the meaning; it *is* the meaning' (Fish 1994: 3).

So, we need to look for particular sensations the song makes us feel (e.g. 'the shivers'; anger; adrenaline; happiness; sadness etc.), then try to isolate the specific areas of the song that elicited these reactions. If there are no reactions to the song, this also needs to be noted, for absence of reaction is still a response and is therefore worthy of further analysis. We need to ask ourselves why there's been no reaction, and to compare and contrast this with our overall relationship with music. Do we normally react to music? If so, do we react differently to different songs? What is it about this one that makes us so apathetic? Most people will experience some kind of reaction, even if it is boredom, so a complete lack of response is a valuable area of analysis. Without first acknowledging our personal relationships with a song, we are less likely to be able to form a more objective analysis later on.

Hearing a song is a personal experience; no one else can hear it for us. So our first reaction, our early reading and analysis, is fundamental to our understanding and the way in which we create meaning from it. Hence understanding what our relationship to the song is becomes essential to our reading of it. Of course, such relationships, and therefore reactions, will depend on whether we are coming to it new or have heard it before. An analysis of this kind will vary a great deal from person to person. Any meaning taken from a song can also be dependent on other factors, such as that person's age, upbringing, music taste, political mindset, social status and a whole host of other factors. When we listen to music, we are often drawing upon a pool of thousands of previously heard songs in order to make sense of this one.

If we've heard a song before, we come to it with a massive amount of preconceptions, and we will naturally judge anything new against what we've already heard. Hawkes suggests, 'When we think we are seeing objects in the material world, we are really seeing only our ideas, or concepts' (Hawkes 1996: 61), and the same can be applied to how we 'see' music. What Hawkes is implying is that we bring what we know to that which we don't in an effort to understand it.

In his essay 'Against György Lukács', Bertold Brecht reasoned:

> With the people struggling and changing reality before our eyes, we must *not* [italics mine] cling to 'tried' rules of narrative, venerable literary models, eternal aesthetic laws. We must not derive realism as such from particular existing works, but we shall use every means, old and new, tried and untried, derived from art and derived from other sources, to render reality to men in a form they can master. (1977: 81)

Brecht wrote that in the 1977. Imagine what he would think now in our modern, electronic, information age of new technology. Brecht's idea is still valid and can be extended to speak for the newness of a song, even though it may allude to the ever-sameness of songs that came before. So understanding and analysing what has gone before is crucial to producing the new.

Juslin and Sloboda take this further by saying, 'Music, like odours, seems to be a very powerful cue in bringing emotional experiences from memory back into awareness. This is not surprising, for two reasons: first, music is quite a pervasive element of social life and accompanies many highly significant events in an individual's life . . . Thus there are many associations between musical elements and emotionally charged memories (Juslin and Sloboda 2001: 369).'

In learning the songwriter's trade, it helps to try to work out your critical relationship with a song you've already heard. For example, you could access memories linked to the first or early hearing and ask yourself whether these have had any impact on the way you perceive the song. Firstly, ask yourself if your emotional connection is coming from a particular, specific memory (an Individual Interpretation, such as 'my first day of university') or a more generic one, based on a number of memories that have fused together to form a broad outline of emotion (a cumulative interpretation, e.g. 'summer 2008') and, indeed, what the overall feeling is attached to such memories (anticipation, fear, sadness, happiness, remorse etc.). If the memories are happy ones, perhaps we are all more likely to look back on the song with fond memories, even if we don't actually *like* the song itself. If they're sad ones, perhaps we might be inclined to think negatively of the song, even if it's something we know we should like. We also need to acknowledge that our relationship to songs can alter over time. In researching this book, I looked back through every 'Now . . .' album that had been released since I was aware of music (not necessarily 'into', but aware of) and highlighted the songs I knew. I found myself feeling affection for those songs that reminded me of happy times in my life, even if the songs themselves weren't to my taste and, perhaps most surprisingly, ones that I remember detesting at the time! In these cases, then, I have two very different reader-response interpretations of the songs, both from myself but at very different stages of my life. It is clear, then, that memory and the passing of time can have a significant impact on how we react to songs. 'Our knowledge emanates from our perspective: it is inextricably situated in time and space, and we must try to resist the temptation to view our own ideas as though they were absolute or eternal' (Hawkes 1996: 67). Lots of songs carry emotion purely because of the context in which they are encountered. The lyrics may have no particular significance at face value, but they can take on meaning by proxy because of the emotions being experienced at the time of listening. This kind of 'emotional osmosis' allows us to personalize our own meanings and interpretations, which may deviate from the author's original intention. Therefore, that a song, or indeed an album, may be read or judged in a personal context, tells the song-writer a great deal about the art form, and also about art and public perception.

I feel emotional attachment to most of the songs on Green Day's *American Idiot* album, but relate to pretty much none of the lyrics. All attachment arises through what I bring to the table myself, based on the memories of where I was in my life when I first listened to it, and this attachment makes the lyrics have a significance to me as an individual, as I merge them with my memories.

Meaning and significance can come to us without us even trying. Thus it's good to consider this issue. If you see it working for yourself, you will begin to understand the reception or understanding of your songs by others.

Exercise

Write your 'soundtrack', pinpointing songs that define (or are most prom-inent when you recall) certain periods of your life. Consider whether you consciously chose said soundtrack – or if you even like the songs! This shouldn't be a 'favourite' songs list, but one that has contributed to the soundtrack of your life in some way. As John Berger (2016: 96–8) said in *Confabulations*, for example:

> The song I most remember my mother singing is 'Shenandoah' . . . [she] sang it to me when I was one or two years old . . . and I was aware of it being there – like a shirt in a wardrobe for special occasions.

My own example will be of little significance to anyone except myself, but I'll jot a few down by way of illustration anyway.

Song	Event/time/ experience	Emotions then	Emotions now	Means of listening	Opinion on song now	Image attached	Favourite artists at the time
'A Groovy Kind of Love' (1988) Phil Collins version	Age 5. Mum singing to me after it had been on TV	Close-ness with mother	Nostalgia/ Sadness	TV/sung to me	Wouldn't choose to listen	Mum singing it to me in lounge	–
'Stars' – Simply Red	First football match	Excitement	Nostalgia	Tannoy at White Hart Lane	Wouldn't choose to listen	View of pitch from Lower West Stand, White Hart Lane, UK	–
'Love Is All Around' – Wet Wet Wet	Emigrating	Excite-ment/ Sadness	Nostalgia	TV/Sister playing	Will listen if on	General Summer montage/packing up house to move abroad	–
'Free as a Bird' – The Beatles	The song that got me 'properly' into music	Joy	Nostalgia	TV/CD single	Probably not in top 50 Beatles songs	Watching video in lounge	Queen

(continued)

(continued)

Song	Event/time/experience	Emotions then	Emotions now	Means of listening	Opinion on song now	Image attached	Favourite artists at the time
'So Young' – The Corrs	Summer when I got 4-track and started recording	Excitement	Excitement/ Inspiration to go and write and record	Music TV	Will listen if on	Music TV, watched while having break in between recording	Beatles/ Rolling Stones/ Chemical Brothers
'When You Say Nothing at All' – Ronan Keating	Summer after finishing GCSEs	Happiness/ fun/relief	Nostalgia: Happy memories of that summer	Music TV	Wouldn't choose to listen	Generic images of that summer	Beatles/ Crowded House
'Teenage Dirtbag' – Wheatus	6th form College	Confused (who isn't at 16?)	Nostalgia/ Happy memories of college	Music TV/ Sung by fellow students	Have always loathed it!	Music room in college	The Smiths/ Weezer/ Pink Floyd
'Galvanize' – Chemical Brothers	At nightclub while at University	Confused (who isn't at 21?)/ Drunk	Fun/ Freedom	Nightclub	Wouldn't choose to listen.	Nightclub	Green Day/ Eminem/ Beach Boys

So, the tracks that define these various parts of my life, from the ages of 5 to 21, aren't ones I would go out of my way to listen to, and none would make it into my top hundred songs list if I wrote one. It's also worth noting that absolutely none of the lyrics 'spoke' to me at the time (except, perhaps, the Phil Collins (1988) which my mum sang to me: 'When I'm feeling blue/All I have to do/Is take one look at you/Then I'm not so blue'; but technically that's the lyrics speaking to her rather than me). So all meaning, attachment, emotion is coming from my own personal situations, and I'm merely attaching songs to them. Thinking about the songs you are writing, then, are you making this connection with your own memories unconsciously, or projecting onto others (see the ideas on biography above). Either way, what this establishes is that the art of songwriting is about making connections. Knowing what some of those connections are becomes important – especially in the life of listeners. As Berger (2016: 99) also reports the 'Man in Black', Johnny Cash, saying, 'I could wrap myself in the warm cocoon of a song and go anywhere; I was invincible.'

Other connections can be made directly through the lyrics themselves, of course, but again this can occur due to what the listener brings to the lyrics in terms of meaning and emotional attachment. Sometimes a song will be so 'to the point' that it almost seems to have been written to sum up your own life. As I have shown, you can become immediately connected with the song because it resonates directly with your life. As Denora says, 'Music provides a device of prosthetic biography' (Denora 2006: 143).

An example of this is The Smiths' 'These Things Take Time' (1984), where the lyric 'Oh the alcoholic afternoons/when we sat in your room/ they meant more to me than any/than any living thing on earth' (The Smiths 1984). This describes almost exactly the days of my adolescence (and I am assuming that of many others likewise), drinking and listening to music in the living room of my best friend. Even the first line of that song 'My eyes have seen the glory of the sacred wunderkind,' have a direct emotional connection, where, having grown up a Spurs fan and heard/ sung the lyric 'My eyes have seen the glory of the cups at White Hart Lane' many times, I form an attachment to the lyric and therefore emotionally bond with the song. My memory of listening to that actual song is non-existent, perhaps because my emotional attachment has been achieved directly through the lyrics rather than through emotional osmosis.

If you haven't heard the song before but have a knowledge of/familiarity with the artist or genre, consider your relationship with them, too. For example, if you have heard of the artist and have liked their previous work, are you more likely to open yourself up to liking the new song? And on the flipside of this, if you have already formed a negative attitude towards them, are you more likely to close yourself off to the possibility of liking it?

While this way of looking at songs is probably more useful to us as critics than as lyricists, thinking about lyrics as being open-ended and subject to multiple interpretations can actually be quite liberating, much in the same way as blurring the lines between fact and fiction can be. Why not slip in an ambiguous phrase here and there? Why not put together unconnected but aesthetically pleasing phrases like Cuomo suggests? Why not use foreign, slang or nonsense words if they sound right at that point in the song? Hopps says that Morrissey's songs:

> often play with meanings – staging a mobility, heterogeneity, or reflexivity – and are shaped as much by aesthetic concerns as they are by a desire to express or represent a state of affairs outside themselves.
>
> (Hopps 2009: 96)

He is absolutely not alone in this. Seek out others, get a feel for what it means; it's all a good lesson in learning your craft.

The absolute extreme of this technique is where the vocal remains, but all words are cut, leaving only vocal sounds rather than lyrics. Take a look at Pink Floyd's 'The Great Gig in the Sky', one of many highlights on *The Dark Side of the Moon* album. Over Richard Wright's beautiful chord sequence, we have the female vocal of Clare Tory, a session vocalist who was brought in to provide backing vocals on other tracks and improvise a lead vocal on this. The vocal sounds range between 'oohs' and gut-wrenching wails, producing an emotional impact that it would have been hard to create through standard lyrics. This 'free' vocal, or vocables, allowed for an expression that is as core as it can possibly be and goes beyond language and understanding to something far more fundamental. Combined with the mood created through the piano melody and the production, this makes for quite an experience as a listener, but it couldn't be sustained over an album. Not only would the intensity and novelty be lost, but as listeners we are encouraged to bond with the song on a different level (as we will discuss later).

Another example of artists that detach themselves from imposing 'any of their own conceptions of the music's content or subject matter onto the listener' (Hayden 2014: 11) comes via the band Sigur Rós. Often singing in an imaginary language, 'Hopelandic', with their album Sigur Rós created a world in which 'any subjective, extra-musical content . . . is erased. This is done by removing any/all semantics from the album, be it in lyrical content, song titles, or overall concept . . . Removing the band as speakers creates a gap, and it is understood that this gap is to be filled by the listener' (Hayden 2014: 11–12). As a lyrical technique, it has more to do with the fantasy genre in literature than the usual literary realism, and there is a whole different discourse around that, which can't be explored in depth here.

It doesn't take much understanding of Roland Barthes (1977) to recognize the 'author is dead' idea. Even with positive connotations, most writers can acknowledge their importance when the song is taken over by the listener. Most writers, songwriters included, create work with an objective in mind, and if that goes beyond the simple desire to entertain, they will likely have something that they are eager to put across to the listener. To consider that this may be lost in translation and those carefully crafted lines misinterpreted is the price any writer pays for going public with their work. And indeed, the more successful writers become, and the more people their songs reach, the more likely it is that different interpretations will be attached to their work. One of the main attractions of music is its ability to personally move, speak to and touch people en masse, and yet still remain able to connect to them as individuals.

So what kinds of thing can we look for with reader response interpretations and how can our findings affect our readings of songs?

Shared social history

Although we're all living different lives and have different opinions about the world around us, if we're living at the same time period as other people in a similar environment, then we have a shared social history with them. Jung refers to a collective unconscious, and Émile Durkheim to a collective consciousness, and it is not difficult to see how they function in a social, critical and cultural context, especially in this worldly twenty-first century where news media keeps us up to date almost as events are unfolding. And as a result, this particular time and environment we occupy will impact upon how we view the past, present and future, both regarding our political views and our opinions on art and entertainment as fashions and popular opinion change. Music is subject to these shifts in fashion just as much as clothing and other consumable goods because they are all connected to the way we interact. Look at the way coffee shops have begun to take over the world: who would have thought that? And indeed it's hard to avoid the influence Starbucks is having on music, with their playlists.

In musical terms, think about the way it has changed, the reverb-soaked snare sounds of the eighties, or the Spector Wall of Sound from the sixties, the punks of the seventies, boy band love ballads of the nineties, and the auto-tuned vocals of the 2000s. The huge rise and development in country music, which has come a long way from the rhinestone cowboy. What is fashionable today becomes passé tomorrow as new sounds become the 'in' thing and the older sounds often only become fashionable again when they're old enough to be retro and ironic (the sixties revival in the Britpop era, or the eighties resurgence of the last few years is evidence of this). Lyrics, although not necessarily as subject to ageing as the sound of a song, are also susceptible to changes in listeners' outlook as the decades pass. The Sir Mix-a-Lot song 'Baby Got Back' (1992), which sold over 2 million singles in its year of release and was seen as light-hearted and amusing (amusing enough, it would seem, to be aped on an episode of *Friends* for comedic effect), was viewed offensive enough by Nicki Minaj for her to record the song 'Anaconda' (2014), which many critics say subverts the objectification and male gaze of the original track.

Listeners today, where opinions on sexual equality have developed considerably since the 1960s, would be entitled to view the following songs with dismay, but listeners at the time may have been inclined to accept them as being representative of the common opinion towards women at the time:

Dusty Springfield, 'Wishin' and Hopin'' (1964): 'Do the things he likes to do/Wear your hair just for him.'

Jack Jones, 'Wives and Lovers' (1964): 'Day after day/there are girls at the office/And men will always be men/Don't send him off with your hair still in curlers/you may not see him again' and 'Don't think because there's a ring on your finger, you needn't try anymore.'

Ray Charles, 'I Got a Woman' (1958): 'She knows a woman's place is right there now in her home.'

Rolling Stones, 'Some Girls' (1978), the lyrics go through varies nationalities and races of women and objectify them, including the lines 'black girls just want to get fucked all night' and 'Chinese girls are gentle/they're really such a tease/you never know quite what they're cookin'/inside those silky sleeves.'

Guns N' Roses, 'One in a Million' (1988): 'Immigrants and faggots/They make no sense to me/They come to our country/And think they'll do as they please/Like start some mini Iran/Or spread some fucking disease/They talk so many God damn ways/It's all Greek to me.'

Peter Sellers and Sophia Loren, 'Goodness Gracious Me' (1960), a duet between a patient and her doctor, with Sellers acting the role of an Indian doctor

Any song from the past that we're listening to today is being filtered by us through what we know of the past and how our present has informed those opinions. We can look upon these lyrics as misogynistic or bigoted today because our culture's acceptable norms have changed. And just as we might not forgive our ancestors for historical atrocities because 'it was acceptable at the time', we are unlikely to respond positively to songs which include lyrics that don't fit with our modern-day code of conscience. Hamilton notes:

> Historicism shows . . . that the historical character of interpretation allows us as critics continually to refocus a present that is always changing, always sliding out of focus again. We should therefore expect the process of understanding the past to be as unending as the future.
>
> (Hamilton 1996: 18)

The examples above are extreme cases of how time can alter our reactions to songs, but our reactions to anything that was recorded in a time before we were born may be viewed completely differently than someone who lived in those times (positively or negatively). Those of us who weren't around when the Sex Pistols released 'God Save the Queen' (1977b) may acknowledge its cultural impact, but we can't *feel* it because we weren't there, experiencing the actual culture of the time. It's important in an analysis, therefore, to research the culture and context around the time the song was written and released, to examine whether the intervening years have influenced our view of it and, if they have, to what extent.

Even how we view the present is dependent on a number of factors, including our peer group, our education, which media we choose to read or be influenced by, the entertainment we ingest and indeed what we've experienced in the past that has led us to this point in time and these present opinions. But this is also governed by other factors like location. Understanding what has become known as Madchester or the Liverpool scene or Northern Soul means more than just locating the music and the songs. The whole context becomes crucial to the cultural experience.

Transferable lyrics: Context of utterance

Searle and Vanderveken suggest the term *context of utterance* is necessary in critical thinking because, 'the same sentence can be uttered in different contexts to perform different illocutionary acts':

> For the purposes of formalization a context of utterance consists of five distinguishable elements and sets of elements: a speaker, a hearer, a time, a place, and those various other features of the speaker, hearer, time, and place that are relevant to the performance of the speech acts.
>
> (Searle and Vanderveken 1985: 27)

To explore this, let's take a look at the song 'Don't Dream It's Over'. The song was written by Neil Finn and originally released by the band Crowded House in 1986, reaching number 2 on the Billboard Hot 100 in the United States. Over the years, it has become synonymous with high emotion and has subsequently been attached to a number of different events and causes, including Concert for Linda (McCartney); the Princess Diana tribute CD; humanitarian aid in Gaza and Syria and, most recently, by Ariana Grande and Miley Cyrus, firstly in 2015 to raise money for Cyrus's Happy Hippie Foundation (which benefits LGBT and homeless youth) and then again in 2017 at the One Love Manchester concert (raising money for those affected in the Manchester Arena bombing).

Songs like these are examples of where the context of utterance has changed the interpretation of the song on a number of occasions. The actual semantics are overruled and replaced by a broader interpretation: one which focuses in on particular words to create a generic 'feel' that can be applied to most emotional situations. If we took all the lyrics at face value, we would find they didn't really fit some of the circumstances they were applied to: in the case of the One Love Manchester concert in particular, the repeated utterance of the refrain 'Don't dream it's over' isn't exactly a morale-boosting message (if we were applying it directly to the circumstances surrounding the concert, it could easily be taken as a rather grim assertion that terrorism isn't over). But the focus, and therefore the appropriateness, comes via the line 'They come, they come, to build a wall between us, We know they won't win' (Crowded House 1986). Every other lyric within the song is almost rendered meaningless due to this one, which becomes the focus, and the song takes on new meaning in every situation it is placed. In Finn's performance of the song at the Concert for Linda, the focus would be on the refrain itself, suggesting that even though Linda has died, she will be remembered, so we are told in 'Don't dream it's over'. Sung by Finn at Crowded House's Farewell to the World concert in 1996, which was billed as the band's last before breaking up, the refrain is a consolatory message to the fans that the band may reform. Thus we can see three different applications of the same lyric to form very different messages.

Take a look at this excerpt from Carless and Douglas' work on song and audience response:

It's an Oasis gig, a high point in the career of one of the most popular British bands towards the end of the 20th century. One hundred and twenty thousand fans face the stage at Knebworth Park as, returning to the stage for encores, the band start up the song 'Champagne Supernova'. Midway through, in unison, over 100,000 people raise their arms to the skies and sing the words back to the band.

'Don't you tell me,' says Noel Gallagher, the band's songwriter and guitarist, some time later in an interview, 'that song doesn't mean anything.' He's annoyed at comments made by one 'expert' critic who voiced his opinion that the song's lyrics are meaningless. With cool clarity and insight, the songwriter simply points back to those who were pointing at him, the 120,000 fans who bellowed out the song: 'Looks like it means something to them!'

(Carless and Douglas 2011: 439)

Gallagher, who has dismissed intended meaning in his lyrics time and time again is aware of the idea of transferable lyrics, and how, even if he himself didn't consider them to be meaningful, others might. Gallagher would find another of his songs, 'Don't Look Back in Anger', whose lyrics he previously dismissed, taking on an extra poignancy 21 years after its initial release, like 'Don't Dream It's Over' in relation to the Manchester Arena bombing of 2017.

The moment a crowd of Mancunians spontaneously broke into a rendition of the Oasis song Don't Look Back in Anger has been shared around the world, cementing the song as a symbol of Manchester's resilience in the face of tragedy.

(Perraudin and Halliday 2017)

Once again, the relevance of this situation to the lyrics (and vice versa) only applies to the refrain 'Don't look back in anger'. Which of course reveals how potent a good hook can be.

There have been a number of instances over the years where, following an artist's death, some of his or her songs have become more poignant. Eva Cassidy's version of 'Somewhere Over the Rainbow' had massive emotional impact on listeners, for example, and much of this is due to the fact she had died by the time her version was widely released. Cassidy's version would have been beautiful anyway, given her voice and the arrangement, but armed with the knowledge of her death, lyrics that previously seemed a little twee suddenly become haunting and take on a gravity and significance that may not have been present in previous versions of the same song. Similar things occur with Charity singles, too. In cases where previously released songs have been rereleased to raise funds for certain causes. 'Ferry Cross the Mersey', originally written by Gerry Marsden of Gerry and the Pacemakers and released by the group in December 1964, was rerecorded by various Liverpool artists in 1989 in aid of those affected by the Hillsborough football stadium disaster earlier that year. Although the song obviously wasn't written about the disaster, the lyrics could quite easily be attached to it anyway, especially the opening lines, 'Life goes on day after day/Hearts torn in every way', so the emotion we feel is coming from applying the knowledge of Hillsborough to those lyrics, bringing external factors into the song to create emotion. Taken by itself without this knowledge, it's a fairly generic line that doesn't carry much emotional weight.

Gottschall says, 'A writer lays down words, but they are inert. They need a catalyst to come to life. The catalyst is the reader's imagination' (Gottschall 2013: 6). Although this quote references literary fiction, it can also be applied to the importance of the listener in bringing a song to life. That isn't to say that writers are powerless in how their words are interpreted; they just don't have total control and can't possibly take into account every single possible reading, as they haven't lived the lives of all their listeners. As discussed, lyrics can be interpreted in any way imaginable, with the lyrical content twisted beyond all logic. To what extent, then, are writers responsible for the words they use, and to what extent are they able to persuade the listener to draw the conclusions they want them to?

4

Intertextuality and Allusion (the role of one text on another)

Intertextuality

> The term intertextuality describes how texts interact with other texts. In particular, it stresses the idea that texts are not unique, isolated objects but are made out of numerous other texts, some known to the new text producer and some not directly known. Allusion is a form of intertextuality that works mostly though verbal echoes between texts. However, texts may also interact with one another through other kinds of formal and thematic echo, as well as by recycling the voices and registers of other literary texts and general culture in which they exist.
>
> (Montgomery et al. 2013: 166)

Intertextuality can refer to situations where the readings of texts are broadened beyond what's self-contained in the actual text itself to incorporate wider influences (including texts that have been before). 'Roughly, intertextuality is a blanket term for the idea that a text communicates its meaning only when it is situated in dialogue with other texts' (Gracyk 2001: 56). If we start by looking at the 'text' as other songs, we can note a number of different ways in which a text can be imported into another.

Cover songs

'Covering' a song can be as straightforward as taking the original and recording it again with exactly the same melody, lyrics and arrangement (see Robson and Jerome's (1995) and Gareth Gates's (2002) versions of 'Unchained Melody' e.g.), but most covers change something about the original, bringing new life and meaning to it. An example of this is Johnny's Cash's 2002 cover of the Nine Inch Nails song 'Hurt'. Written by Trent Reznor to conclude the 1994 *Downward Spiral* album, the Nine Inch Nails version included discordant guitar, tape interference and vocals buried under walls of distorted guitar, and mirrored the song's lyrics about self-hatred, self-harm and drug addiction. Cash's version changed the arrangement completely, with a clean piano and guitar, and haunting vulnerable vocal. Combined with the 'heart-wrenching music video that spoke about the transience of life, the gracelessness of death, the Ozymandian crumbling of an oeuvre and the decline of a genre, an era and an attitude' (Hooton 2015), the song becomes as different from the original as it's possible to be. The line 'What have I become' is changed from referring to a man ruined by drugs to a man ruined by age, 'Everyone I know goes away in the end' no longer refers to abandonment, but to old friends dying off. Add to this the fact that Cash would die just seven months after the song's release, and we are presented with a tear-jerking emotion in this song that wasn't present in the original.

Sampling

Sampling involves importing sections of existing songs and placing them in new ones. These imports can range from riffs (see MC Hammer's 'U Can't Touch This' (1990), Puff Daddy's 'I'll Be Missing You' (1997), or Rihanna's 'Wild Thoughts' (2017)) to vocal samples, where the meaning of the initial lyrics are often changed (see Jay-Z's 'Hard Knock Life (Ghetto Anthem)' (1998) for a good example of this, where he imported a song from the musical *Annie* into a hip-hop song, or Eminem's 'Stan', where an innocuous Dido lyric becomes something much more sinister when placed in its new text and context.

Spoof

A number of spoof songs can only really work if we have prior knowledge of what is being spoofed. Weird Al Yancovic's 'Smells Like Nirvana' (1992), for example, relies heavily on the listener being familiar with the fact that the original song, 'Smells Like Teen Spirit' (Nirvana 1991) contains unintelligible lyrics when he sings 'What is this song all about?/ Can't figure any lyrics out/How do the words to it go?/I wish you'd tell me, I don't know'. The spoof even stretches to lampooning the 'Smells Like Teen Spirit' music video and the *Nevermind* album cover; again, the humour relies on the audience's awareness of the originals.

Concept albums

Allen notes that 'meaning becomes something which exists between a text and all the other texts to which it refers and relates, moving out from the independent text into a network of textual relations'. (Allen 2000: 1) In its narrowest form, this 'network' can be within the other songs on a concept album, and in its broadest, a link to an entire genre. In concept albums, one 'text' (one song) relies on the other songs on the album in order to communicate meaning. A friend of mine once said he was trying to get into Pink Floyd and, after listening to their songs on shuffle, couldn't really bond with the songs, least of all those from *The Wall* (1979). Taking the odd song from *The Wall* and listening to it in isolation from its surrounding tracks is to miss a huge amount. Pink Floyd famously won a court case against record label EMI, preventing them from selling downloads separately, meaning that their albums were to be taken as complete pieces of work, where each song impacts upon the others preceding and following it. The importance of the other songs is perhaps most evident on *The Wall*, and much of its impact comes from the listener taking in the whole experience and going from A to B with the protagonist. Ironically, one of the only singles Pink Floyd ever released, 'Another Brick in the Wall (Part 2)' (1979b), is perhaps unique in that it is most reliant on other tracks to show its full context.

As its title suggests, 'Another Brick in the Wall (Part 2)' is only a section of a much larger narrative, (including Parts 1 and 3) and needs to be experienced alongside the whole of sides 1 and 2 of the album (disc 1 and two on the CD release) for its proper story to be revealed in full. Taken on its own, we see a commentary on the education system, but don't get a real insight into the character who's narrating it, or the overarching storyline. The title and line 'another brick in the wall' is a pretty major clue towards that, particularly the use of the word *another*, and the word *part* in the title itself. As we look at the other songs on the album, we see that overall, the 'bricks' are metaphors for traumatic experiences in the narrator's life, with each contributing to the narrator's spiral into madness:

- His dad's departure in 'Another Brick in the Wall (Part 1)' (1979a) – 'Daddy's flown across the ocean/Leaving just a memory'
- An unhappy school life in 'The Happiest Days of Our Lives' (1979g) – 'When we grew up and went to school/There were certain teachers who would hurt the children any way they could'
- A rejection of education on 'Another Brick in the Wall (Part 2)' (1979b) – 'We don't need no education'
- Inherited insecurities from his mother in 'Mother' (1979g) – 'Mama's gonna make all of your nightmares come true; Mama's gonna put all of her fears into you'
- Subsequent struggles with masculinity in 'Young Lust' (1979i) – 'Will some woman in this desert land/Make me feel like a real man'
- An increasing mental instability in 'One of My Turns' (1979f) – 'Nothing is very much fun anymore . . . And I can feel one of my turns coming on'
- A break-up in 'Don't Leave Me Now' (1979h) – 'Ooooh babe, don't leave me now/Don't say it's the end of the road'
- A rejection of everyone and everything in 'Another Brick in the Wall (Part 3) (1979c) – 'I don't need no arms around me/I don't need no drugs to calm me/I have seen the writing on the wall/Don't think I need anything at all'
- A culmination with the final track on side 2 (CD disc 1) with 'Goodbye Cruel World' (1979e), where our narrator seals himself off from the outside world completely

Texts beyond song

We can also use intertextuality to describe the deliberate transferring of one text into another via the songwriter's much loved technique of being directly inspired by or 'borrowing' pre-existing material. This can include inspiration via theme and/or character from external, non-musical texts (e.g. Led Zeppelin's 'Ramble On' [1969b], Kate Bush's 'Wuthering Heights' [1978], Dire Straits' 'Romeo and Juliet' [1980], Gordon Lightfoot's 'Don Quixote' [1972]); taking direct lines from external, nonmusical texts (e.g. The Libertines' *Up The Bracket* album (2002) – a Tony Hancock phrase; Blur's 'Tender' (1999), with its opening line taken from the F. Scott Fitzgerald novel *Tender Is the Night* (1934); Morrissey's 'The National Front Disco' (1992), with its title taken from a line in Bill Buford's book *Among the Thugs* (1992)

But is such intertextuality 'borrowing', 'stealing' or simply inspiration? 'Asked why his 2001 album *Love and Theft* relied upon Junichi Saga's book *Confessions of a Yakuza* and Henry Timrod's US civil war poetry, Dylan said, "I'm working within my art form . . . It has to do with melody and rhythm, and then after that, anything goes. You make everything yours. We all do it."' (Sherwin 2017)

Revisiting the Oasis song 'Don't Look Back in Anger', Noel Gallagher talks about how he 'borrowed' a phrase from a John Lennon recording for one of the lyrics: 'Somebody gave me . . . a cassette of John Lennon speaking into a tape recorder about his memoirs . . . and one of his lines was *the brains I had went to my head*. I'll have that, thank you very much' (Rachel 2013: 469). And of course many of us will recall the 'kitchen sink drama' play by John Osbourne, *Look Back In Anger* (1978).

By making **intentional** allusions, the author invites the reader/listener to look at both old text and new, and so needs to be aware of any inter-pretation that may be made as a result of this interaction.

This does of course rely on the reader/listener noticing the allusion in the first place, but 'spotting an allusion is not so dependent on the chance of having read and remembered something as this suggests. It is often possible to detect the presence of an allusion because it stands out in some way from the text that surrounds it – perhaps through some

difference of style or register' (Montgomery et al. 2013: 165). Any interpretation of this nature first relies on our need to first know that the 'text'
we're listening to has taken on elements of another. I'm sure at one point
or another we've heard a song and only realized months later that it's a
cover version. In these instances, then, a reading based on the 'transferring of texts' is impossible.

The effect of bringing one text into another

In The Divine Comedy's 'Eye of the Needle' (2001), Neil Hannon's
lyrics seem to be questioning his (religious) faith on a very personal level.
Depending on our knowledge of the Bible, the title itself (also repeated as
a refrain throughout the song) may have offered immediate significance
when taken with the lyrical content. To others, it would have passed
them by and only taken on extra meaning when they became aware of
the context in the New Testament:

> I tell you the truth, it is hard for a rich man to enter the kingdom of
> heaven. Again I tell you, it is easier for a camel to go through the eye of a
> needle than for a rich man to enter the kingdom of God.
> (Matthew 19: 23–26)

If we then revisit Hannon's lyrics, particularly the chorus – 'The cars in
the churchyard are shiny and German/Distinctly at odds with the theme
of the sermon/And during communion, I study the people/Threading
themselves through the eye of the needle' – the song takes on a significance
beyond a man questioning his faith. But depending on our awareness of
the external text being alluded to, our reading of the song will vary.

Hopps suggests that the questions we need to be asking when thinking
about the transfer of one text into another are these:

What is the effect of bringing one text into another?
What kind of status does the 'imported' text have?
What happens to the voice?
To whom does it 'belong'?

What of its original context does it bring with it, and what does it leave behind?

[And] with respect to the singer's use of personae and his speaking with a voice which is other than his own, what are the implications of this ventriloquism? (Hopps 2009: 8)

Add to this my own question: how does the process impact our reading of the new text and subsequent rereading of the original (now I've heard that, I'll never look at the original in the same way again).

If we apply these questions to 'Eye of the Needle', we may come up with useful answers:

What is the effect of bringing one text into another?

In this instance, in one phrase it sums up the lyrics from the chorus and externalizes the confusion that Hannon is feeling, taking it beyond introspection into a criticism of the wider world.

What kind of status does the 'imported' text have?

Anything from the Bible is going to bring with it a certain gravitas, and when placed in this song's narrative, it adds an authority, too.

What happens to the voice?

It becomes broader, not just focussing on the plight of one man, but the plight of anyone struggling to balance material wealth with faith.

To whom does it 'belong'?

The song itself very much 'belongs' to Hannon, even with the borrowed phrase, as he is using it to summarize/reinforce his own points.

What of its original context does it bring with it, and what does it leave behind?

Given its original context, the imported phrase can't directly comment on twenty-first century life, but its general meaning and its reference to the broad 'rich man' can be applied to any modern setting. It leaves behind, when taken with the rest of the song, a rather damning verdict on modern life.

And with respect to the singer's use of personae and his speaking with a voice which is other than his own, what are the implications of this ventriloquism?

Those quoting New Testament verse are usually either clergymen or those with faith, so for him to use the phrase while questioning his own faith implies a hypocrisy perhaps – and perhaps even a blasphemy. If we delve a little deeper, we will see that Hannon's father was a bishop, which makes the 'preaching' element to the use of the phrase more poignant. Is he therefore appropriating the phrase directly from the Bible itself or from his father?

'How does the process impact on our reading of the new text and subsequent rereading of the original?'

Personally, it added an extra 'level' to the lyrics and made me question my own morals.

5

Perspective

Song lyrics offer the writer the flexibility to routinely shift/switch between different points of view in a short space of time without it seeming jarring. This section of the chapter looks at examples of different uses of perspectives in song and the impact they have on the listener. Here, we take a look at the different perspectives songwriters may use in their writing and what impacts they can have on an audience.

First person

The first-person perspective in song lyrics is by far the most common. If we look at the number of songs that use first-person pronouns, we'll see that it's a startlingly high statistic. In both the top 10 biggest selling songs of all time and the top 10 biggest selling songs of the twenty-first century, personal pronouns were used 100 per cent of the time. In The Beatles' catalogue of 237 original compositions, 87 per cent used personal pronouns. To further the examples, they were also used in 91 per cent of Simon and Garfunkel songs, and 92 per cent of Smiths and Morrissey songs.

The first-person narrative can be split into two different components; the first-person direct (via the word *you*), or the first-person indirect (directed to a named person).

First-person direct

I've always thought that the starting point for any true analysis on pop music should come via The Beatles; not because of any personal preference toward their music, but because of their pioneering spirit in the art of songwriting. Because their output was so vast and so varied across a short space of time that we can actually track their development as writers, as they were essentially learning on the job, experimenting with different lyrical musical and lyrical styles and pushing themselves creatively to cover new ground. The sheer amount of written material that has been dedicated to their songwriting craft also allows us access to a wealth of different opinions, including those of The Beatles themselves, particularly Paul McCartney, who, in Barry Miles' *Many Years From Now* (1998), dissects a great number of Beatles songs in detail, talking about the writing process and what The Beatles were hoping to achieve.

With regard to perspective, or point of view in song, we can see that in The Beatles their early work differs from their later work not only in terms of the overall sound but in the lyrics, too. Early Beatles songs were very simplistic in their lyrical content, with most dealing with straightforward narratives told in the first-person direct address style, which includes an unspecific 'you' ('I love you', etc.). We can even see this through many of the titles from those early years:

'I Want to Hold Your Hand'
'P.S I Love You'
'From Me to You'
'I Want to Be Your Man'
'I'll Get You'

and within dozens of lyrics, for example,

'It's you, you you you' – 'Hold Me Tight' (1963c)
'You know you made me cry' – 'Not a Second Time' (1963e)
'Close your eyes and I'll kiss you' – 'All My Loving' (1963b)
'Since you left me, I'm so alone' – 'It Won't Be Long' (1963d)
'I'll be here, yes I will, whenever you call' – 'All I've Got to Do' (1963a)

We can actually track the shift in the perspectives The Beatles were using by looking at their UK singles releases, where they used a first-person direct address perspective on their first seven singles, but only one out of the next seven.

In their early songs, Paul McCartney says, he and John intentionally – somewhat calculatingly – tried to inject personal pronouns into as many of the early lyrics and song titles as they could. They took seriously the task of forging a relationship with their fans in a very personal way' (Levitin 2009: 32–33). In the words of McCartney himself, 'The early stuff was directly relating to your fans, kind of really saying "please buy this record"' (*The Beatles Anthology*, 1995).

Famously, The Beatles stopped touring in 1966 to concentrate on their studio work, so it could be surmised that the shift away from direct address coincided with the shift away from such a close relationship with their fans. One hundred and twelve Beatles songs in total are written in this first-person direct address style (or at least include elements of them; as we'll see later, songs can shift between multiple perspectives), with many of them occurring in their first few years as recording artists.

Even in these simplistic early songs, though, Lennon and McCartney were still trying to play around with perspective, perhaps most notably with 'She Loves You' (1964), which does include direct address: 'You know it's up to you/I think it's only fair'. But unlike with previous songs, where the direct address is to the love interest, this is to a third party, and the narrator (the 'I' character) is acting like a friend acting as a go-between in a spat between lovers.

So what is the effect of this direct address technique on the listener?

As we've already seen, as the individual listener has a role to play in creating meaning within a song, the effect of the direct address will differ from person to person, but most will attach a face to the 'you', because that's just the way we are as people (if I said to you 'think of a person', you'd at least have *some* kind of image, right?)

Some will suspend disbelief completely and hear the *you* directed squarely at them, so when McCartney sings 'I love you', they'll believe he is singing the song *to* them and *for* them, ignoring the impossibility of such a thought. When we hear the singer use the word *you*, we are complicit in a dialogue, and this explains why so many people feel such an emotional connection with lyrics, even though, on a conscious level, we are well aware that, unless we personally know the singer or the singer is using *you* to describe an audience en masse, the *you* cannot possibly refer to us personally. How many times have you heard someone say, 'Those lyrics really spoke to me,' or 'It feels like they're singing just to me'? Rarely, if ever, will these statements be attached to poetry or prose, because the act of reading is less natural to us than the act of listening – purely because we learnt to do one long before we did the other.

Some listeners won't be quite so directly involved but may inhabit the song to the extent where they think, 'This character could easily be me' (Pattison 2009: 136).

Others will attach an external *you*, imagining either a generic person or someone they either know personally or are aware that the songwriter knows personally. This is where the writer's biography once again becomes significant, for we are more likely to attach the *you* to a specific person if we know the writer is romantically attached to that person (in today's transparent world of pop-star romance, it doesn't take much research to find out who is apparently dating whom).

Exercise

Analyse yourself as a listener, and take a moment to think about how you picture this *you* character when you listen.

First-person indirect

'Norwegian Wood' (1965a) – 'I once had a girl, or should I say, she once had me'
'Here, There and Everywhere' (1966a) – 'To lead a better life, I need my love to be there'
'Lovely Rita' (1967b) – 'Lovely Rita, meter maid/Nothing can come between us'

'Martha My Dear' (1968a): 'Martha, my dear, though I spend my days
   in conversation'
'Something' (1969b): 'Something in the way she moves/Attracts me like
   no other lover'

Excluding the use of *you* and directing the song at a particular person or people (even if it's as broad as *he, she, they*, etc.) can offer the listener the opportunity to 'see into' the life of the writer, to observe as the writer speaks to someone else, but it may not have the same impact as a direct address, and the listener may not feel quite attached to the narrative as a result.

Overall, the first-person perspective has the potential to 'take us into a character's own story and into their confidence as if writing a confessional memoir (Burroway 2007: 45). Writing in the first-person perspective, as well as allowing for intimacy, also enables us to inhabit different characters and tell their story for them.

There are examples where first person can be seen as a negative in songwriting, especially if it is an internally looking first person. Damon Albarn observed that 'young artists generally just talk about themselves; they don't talk about what's happening out there. It is the selfie generation in every sense of the word' (Batchelor 2015: 23).

But first person allows us to inhabit a song if we sing along with it, and singing along is a big part of our bonding with a song. During this process, as the *I* is now coming out of our mouths, it becomes attached to us, just as we so often attach it to the singer. So, as well as the use of *you* speaking to us, any narrative written in the first person can also speak to us, and songwriters can use this to their advantage, making the *I* generic enough to allow it to transfer to another in this way. Other first-person songs are too specific to manage this. Taking a look briefly at Tori Amos's harrowing 'Me and a Gun' (1991), it is evident immediately that her first-person narrative can't be so easily transferred (e.g. 'It was me and a gun/And a man on my back'. Whether or not we attach this narrative squarely to Amos's life and therefore decide she is the *me* (there is plenty of evidence to suggest it is at least semi-autobiographical) or apply the 'death of the author' analysis (Barthes 1977), such utterances belong to the song's narrator and can't really be transferred to an external body unless that person has had similar experiences.

Including speech from third parties (lyrics in speech marks)

Something that doesn't always come across clearly in songs is where the writer wants to include a voice beyond that of the narrator's. In literature, this is easy enough, as the moment we have text within speech marks, we know another character is talking. In a song, this isn't always obvious unless another singer is introduced for these parts; or we have a transcript of the lyrics where we can *see* the sections which are in speech marks; or, as is the case with Joni Mitchell's 'A Case of You' (1971a), such a section is pre-empted with 'you said'. It's worth noting, however, that even in such circumstances, although we're aware where the new voice *begins*, we're not always sure where it *ends* (again, unless we're looking at a transcript).

Despite the many techniques utilized in their songs, this is one The Beatles rarely used. An example is in 'She's Leaving Home' (1967c), where Paul sings the majority of what is a third-person narrative (e.g. 'She goes downstairs to the kitchen, clutching her handkerchief') and John represents the parents' perspective through the call-and-response lines in the choruses, with his lines bracketed in the transcript included with the album, and the narrator's un-bracketed.

There is a section, however, in the second verse, where there isn't this separation, and Paul emerges from the third-person narrative to sing from the perspective of the mother: 'Daddy our baby's gone/Why should she treat us so thoughtlessly?/How could she do this to me?' This is neither speech-marked in the transcript of the lyrics included with the album, nor is it sung by a person outside the original narration, but Paul does introduce it by singing, 'She breaks down and cries to her husband' before the 'Daddy, our baby's gone' line, so we know where the mother's perspective starts. What is unclear, however, is where it ends. These lines are followed by the chorus, including John's 'call and response', but this time, we're not sure whether Paul's sections are from the mother's perspective or the narrator's. If it's from the mother's, then John may be representing the father, and this becomes a conversation between the two of them rather than a conversation between both of them and an unseen narrator. If we look at it this way, it does have a substantial impact on our reading of the song. Through the line 'She's leaving home, after living alone, for so many years', the mother now appears to be looking inward and blaming herself rather than merely questioning her daughter's decision to leave, and the father is trying to persuade her that they did all they could and were not responsible. By the next verse, we are clear that the third-person narrator has returned, as it includes information that the mother couldn't/wouldn't know:

> Friday morning at nine o'clock she is far away
> Waiting to keep the appointment she made
> Meeting a man from the motor trade

However, this 'alternative' reading we have explored above demonstrates the significance that points of view can have in our reading of a song.

Second-person narratives

It is worth noting that the difference between a second-person narrative and the first-person direct address narrative previously discussed is that an *I* character is absent throughout.

As we've seen, second-person **utterances** are common in song lyrics, but maintaining a second-person narrative throughout the duration of a song is much rarer. Examples of this technique can be found in Beatles songs:

> 'Tomorrow Never Knows'
> 'For No One'
> 'Lucy in the Sky with Diamonds'
> 'Baby, You're a Rich Man'
> 'Magical Mystery Tour'

'Lucy in the Sky with Diamonds', and 'Tomorrow Never Knows' are, perhaps, two of The Beatles' most intriguing songs lyrically, but if we look at the albums they're on and the percentages of the songs on these albums that use first person, we can see they're anomalies.

Writing in this perspective can be difficult as it can come across as preachy, and/or 'instruction-manual-esque', with the writer 'telling' us a story rather than showing it to us through either (apparent) personal experience or detached narration. Although we preach, mantra-like to our creative writing students that they should 'show, not tell', song lyrics are different from literature, of course. 'Telling' may be an example of poor technique in a novel. In songwriting, which is more instantaneous, it can work because it forces listeners to engage as they are the front and centre as the main character in the song. The writer also needs to beware of telling people things they already know.

Third person

In literature, the third person is the voice with the greatest range of effects, from total objectivity to great intimacy, and is broken into three techniques:

The **omniscient** narrator, who may know anything past, present or future and is free to tell us readers what to think or feel

The **limited omniscient,** who may go inside the mind of one or two characters and observe from the outside

The **objective**, who may know no more than the person observing the scene (Burroway 2007: 46)

In lyrics, it allows the songwriter to take a step back from the events they are commenting on, perhaps allowing them to seem more objective as they are (seemingly) not passing judgement by involving themselves in the narrative. A third-person perspective can be just as subjective as a first, of course, and it can be edited and 'stacked' in a certain way so that a single, clear point of view is visible, but to an audience, it may *seem* less opinionated. If we're writing about big topics like war or racism, for example, this could be a good way of presenting the information without seeming preachy. One of the most powerful songs I've ever heard is 'Strange Fruit' (1939) by Billie Holiday, a protest song described as 'the most vivid symbol of American racism, a stand-in for all the more subtle forms of discrimination affecting the black population' (Lynskey 2011). The third-person narrative allowed Holiday to take on the role of a haunted observer, someone that had been there and experienced it and was telling us what she had seen, but most importantly, by keeping herself out of the narrative, it became a problem that was everyone's, not just hers. It was her story to tell, but it wasn't just *her* story.

Third-person narration is exemplified in these Beatles songs:

'Being for the Benefit of Mr. Kite'
'The Fool on the Hill'
'Ob-la-di, Ob-la-da'
'Maxwell's Silver Hammer'
'Mean Mr. Mustard'
'Rocky Racoon'

Interestingly, if we look at Wayne Booth's work on the narrator, we see another difference emerge between literature and lyrics.

> A major legacy of Booth's is his separating out of 'reliable' and 'unreliable' narrators – the former, usually in the third person, coming close to the values of the 'implied author'; the latter, often a character within the story, a deviant from them. (Selden and Widdowson, 1993: 20)

If we apply this theory to lyrics, where, as we've seen, the *I* is more commonly associated with author rather than character, it's evident that most see first person as the 'reliable' narrator. So what does third person offer in lyrics? It's rare (as evidenced by the first-person pronoun stats earlier), but when used, what function does it fulfil? And should we as writers try to use it more often?

Switching perspectives

Some songs use a variety of techniques. Take David Bowie's 'Repetition' (1979), which includes third-person narrative 'with the focus on one character, from whose point of view the events are related' (Birkett 1998: 76):

And he could have married Anne with the blue silk blouse

Third person (one character addressing another):

'Can't you even cook?'

Second person (placing the reader into the action as a character):

Johnny is a man/And he's bigger than you

Then third-person omniscient narrator, which offers the 'repetition' suggested in the title, revisiting the first verse to tell the story from a more distanced perspective:

Well Johnny is a man/And he's bigger than her

This 'switching' technique could work in a number of ways depending on how the reader chooses it interpret or inhabit the text, but one of the ways it could function is that by starting off in second person, Bowie immerses us in the narrative, and makes us *experience* the domestic violence, before switching to third person to *show* it to us, making us both suffer and watch.

The song also includes lines which could be taken from multiple perspectives:

And the food is on the table/But the food is cold/Don't hit her

This could either be a third-person narrative, where the author emerges as a character to pass opinion, or third person from a character's point of view, where he's speaking to himself.

Rage Against the Machine's 'Killing in the Name' (1992) switches from the second person of 'and now you do what they told ya (now you're under control)', to the first person of 'Fuck you, I won't do what you tell me'. The second-person sections occur earlier in the song and are delivered in a low-key, almost whispered fashion, and the first-person sections occur at the climax of the song, where they are screamed by singer de la Rocha for maximum impact. In this particular song, then, it could be said that the second person is being used to speak directly to the audience, almost mocking them and encouraging them to look inward and self-analyse. The first-person sections, then, although attached to de

La Rocha in the first instance, actually become a rallying cry of defiance when sung by an audience, with the *I* becoming them. The audience therefore inhabit the first-person section and become active in the song, rather than passive.

The fourth wall

Some writers will give the impression the song is aimed at an individual, sometimes named, as in these examples:

'Kathy's Song' – Paul Simon
'Hey there Delilah' – Plain White T's
'Isobel' – Dido
'Iris' – Goo Goo Dolls

And sometimes, the individual is an anonymous 'you', as in the examples listed here:

'You're So Vain' – Carly Simon
'Go Your Own Way' – Fleetwood Mac
'I Wanna Be Your Boyfriend' – the Ramones
'The Way You Move' – Outcast

Some writers even anticipate where the song will be played (e.g. gigs, nightclubs) and tailor their lyrics accordingly for maximum potential of interaction, for example:

'Independent Women Part I' – Destiny's Child
'Cha Cha Slide' – DJ Casper
'Senorita' – Justin Timberlake
'Dance the Night Away' – Jennifer Lopez

Some lyricists often embrace the fact that they're aware of an audience and include them in the song by addressing them directly, drawing attention to the song's artificial status and 'playing' with the listener.

Although associated mostly with theatre, the 'breaking of the fourth wall', or deliberately drawing attention to the fictional status of a song can also be present in music. The breaking of the fourth wall in theatre means that deliberate attention is drawn to its fictional status and the fact that we are watching a stage play rather than real life.

The breaking of the fourth wall in song means that deliberate attention is drawn to the fact that we are listening to a song and that it is both fictional and manufactured.

Much theatre relies on the audience suspending disbelief to the extent that they see neither stage nor actor, but an invented reality. To generalize, the audience don't want the actors or writers or directors to be present when watching a play; such an intrusion shatters the invented reality the play is designed to create for the audience to receive.

> We know that fictional entities are indeed fictional and lack existence; yet, paradoxically, we experience emotions towards them . . . It has been suggested that fiction leads the audience to have the fear, the pity, the joy – and so on – at real people (not the fictions) who have the relevant characteristics. The causes of emotions need not be the objects at which the emotions are directed.
>
> (Cave 2009: 9)

In pop music, a great deal of the time we *want* the artist to be present; we *want* to hear the person behind the music (either through voice or content); we *want* to know what we're hearing has come through Kanye West's studio experimentation (2010) or from Adele's heartbreaks or Eric Clapton's guitar. As discussed elsewhere, the absence of such knowledge can also work, but as a listening experience, it's far more common for us to know who is behind the music.

Although the sheer existence of music draws attention to its creation, we still see often see it as true and as a window into the soul of its creators. We suspend disbelief in that we hear the vocal as a whole rather than a series of takes glued together; we hear the guitar played live rather than overdubbed in a control room; we hear a whole rather than the sum of its parts. And unless we were present in the recording of the songs, this is all we can do. The breaking of the fourth wall in song occurs when a writer draws attention away from the unified whole to one of these parts. Most often this is the act of songwriting itself, but it could be a reference to the singing or playing, too. Perhaps the artist most famous for playing with his listener's reactions is Eminem.

Eminem is not only aware of the fact he's writing for an audience, but he also plays with them, encouraging them to react and interact with his lyrics, even guessing how they're going to react, almost daring the listener and critic to draw conclusions, and he toys with them accordingly, as in the following examples.

- Guessing what they think of him and speaking from *their* viewpoints:

  Man I'd hate to have it as bad as that Mr Mathers claims he had it/I can't imagine it, that little rich poor white bastard/Needs to take some of that cash out of the bank and take a bath in it/Man if I only had half of it/Shit, if you only knew the half of it. ('Evil Deeds', 2004)

- Having the last line revert back to his own (or at least the own narrator's) voice:

  Now you probably get this picture from my public persona/That I'm a pistol-packing drug-addict who bags on his momma. ('Sing for the Moment', 2002b)

- Directly questioning the power an artist is perceived to have over a listener:

  They say music can alter moods and talk to you/Well can it load a gun up for you, and cock it too? ('Sing for the Moment', 2002b)

- Inviting criticism by flouting his position as a 'role model' and *telling* the listener to act in a certain, irresponsible way:

  Follow me and do exactly what the song says: smoke weed, take pills, drop outta school, kill people and drink/And jump behind the wheel like it was still legal. ('Role Model', 1999c)

- Blurring the lines between artist and character:

  A lot of people think that what I say on records or what I talk about on a record, that I actually do in real life, or that I believe in it . . . Well, shit . . . if you believe that then I'll kill you. You know why? 'Cause I'm a *criminal*. ('Criminal', 2000a)

Eminem even references his own songs, shown through the 2013 song 'Headlights', where he refers to previous songs in which he has mentioned his mother, especially 'Cleaning Out My Closet' (2002c). If this knowledge weren't there, his forgiving her wouldn't have nearly so much emotional impact.

Breaking down the fourth wall in this way can create a very close bond between artist and listener, and further reinforces our previous statement that pop music can be a collaborate process.

Tenses

Deciding which tense to write a song in and whether to stay in the same one for its duration or to use multiple tenses is another important decision a songwriter needs to make.

The past tense can offer depth to a song, allowing the writer to build complicated narratives and characters that would be too confusing if told in the present tense. Past tense can also reflect on past events with a trustworthy, objective eye. The present tense can be great for offering immediacy, as if we're experiencing the events with the narrator as they unfolding in real time. It is also a good way of bringing the past into the present, to show that the events are still relevant to today's world.

Börjars and Burridge (2010), note that 'there is no future tense in English, even though there are of course many ways we can talk about the future' (132). They posit that:

> since present tense seems to be able to refer to present time, future time and timeless statements, it might seem most appropriate to refer to this verb form as the NON-PAST, rather than the present, tense. However, for the sake of simplicity, we will go on referring to it as present tense, but keeping in mind that tense and time need not correspond. (132)

The Kinks' 'Village Green' (1968) is told mainly in the present tense ('It's been a long time since I last set eyes on the church with the steeple') but shifts to past tense via flashbacks, for example:

'Twas there I met a girl called Daisy/And kissed her by the old oak tree

This technique gives the impression of our narrator walking round his old village and memories coming back to him as he shows us around. Even though the song involves past tense utterances, the narrative itself is in the present, as a narrator is telling us a story in the present. Think about having a conversation with a friend where you're talking about the past. The events being discussed are in the past, but the utterance itself is occurring in the present.

Blur's 'Essex Dogs' (1997) uses:

Past tense ('I remember the sunset and the plains of cement'), *reminiscing about how the town **was***

Present tense – here and now ('In this town cellular phones are hot with thieves'), *showing us what it **is** like **now***

Present tense – future projection ('You'll catch the flu or you'll catch the city'), imagining the effect the town **will have** on the 'you' character. *Having already given past and present accounts, we view the narrator as a trustworthy authority, so this line takes on significance even if, taken at face value, it's nonsensical.*

Gorillaz's 'Fire Coming Out of the Monkey's Head' (2005) uses:

Past tense ('Once upon a time at the foot of a great mountain'), *giving the impression of a folk tale being recited around a campfire. The non-emotional narration adds an eerie element to the story.*

Present tense ('Falling out of aeroplanes and hiding out in holes') *bringing the song into the present, thereby showing that the story is still alive or is still having an impact.*

Dixie Chicks' 'Long Time Gone' (2002) uses:

Past tense ('I caught wind and hit the road runnin'') *setting the scene and gives us context*

Present tense – here and now ('My daddy sits on the front porch swingin''), *showing how things are at the moment: the status quo.*

Present tense – future projection ('Yeah, I'm gonna be a star'), *predicting the future, setting out goals. Shows a nice contrast between the narrator and her past and shows a positivity going forward.*

6

Looking at and looking beyond

The type of analysis where we look at the song using nothing but what is contained within the music and lyrics is known as 'close reading', where 'the emphasis of the criticism, the analysis of the words on the page, all starts (and often ends) with those words' (McCaw 2008: 43). Close readers, McCaw argues, 'work up a reading of the text through a tight focus on the specific details of language, often with no reference at all to anything beyond the text (e.g. the life of the author, the politics of the time of publication, its place in literary history)' (McCaw 2008: 44).

Close reading allows us to look at songs in a greater depth than a number of critics have previously, as it doesn't focus on lyrics as a 'window into the soul of the author'.

Roland Barthes (1977) coined the phrase 'death of the author' as part of the discussion of the role we apply to an author when analysing a text. 'The notion of the author's "death" is not, of course, to be taken literally. By announcing the death of the author Barthes was attempting to kill off a tendency in literary criticism and educational institutions to use the notion of an author, and his or her supposed intentions, to limit interpretive possibilities in reading' (Montgomery et al. 2013: 176). We can apply this same technique. If we take the Leonard Cohen song 'Suzanne', for example, 'the immediate temptation for any analysis . . . would be to discover who this character is outside the song, and what she meant to Cohen' (Fosbraey 2015: 63). Close reading suggests that we resist this temptation and look at what the character means within the context of the song and no further.

Close reading has the potential to be limiting because it can inhibit creativity as we try to find the 'right' interpretation and attempt to 'solve' the lyrics as if they were a maths problem or puzzle.

Different songs will benefit from different kinds of analysis, and this may depend on the extent to which the song is dependent on what is contained within its lyrics themselves rather than the external factors. We will see in a moment that a song like Elvis Costello's 'Kinder Murder' (1994b), where there is a strong narrative and use of character, will benefit from a close reading analysis but offer little extra by expanding our analysis into biographical or cultural information. Nicki Minaj's 'Anaconda' (2014), on the other hand, offers us little via a close reading analysis, but an enormous amount if we apply a wider cultural analysis. Other songs, as we've seen via our discussion of 'Things the Grandchildren Should Know', are as reliant on the author's biography as they are on the actual words contained within the song.

Things we might consider in Elvis Costello's 'Kinder Murder' while staying within the text itself

The title

> The first thing that might be considered is the title . . . Its relation to the rest of the text is important (does the title refer to a person, a place, a symbol or a well-known phrase, for example) . . . Considering whether the title is primarily denotative (as in descriptive) or connotative (that is, suggestive and allusive) is useful but it is also important to consider the range of meanings that a title could have because there may be more than one.
>
> (Childs 2008: 107)

The title of 'Kinder Murder' could be described as connotative because it offers a play on words, with three possible, separate interpretations of the word *kinder*, none of which are definitive:

1. Kinder: showing the quality of benevolence. 'Kinder Murder' taken literally would suggest killing someone in order to be generous or merciful. The word *kinder* also suggests we need something to compare it with; it begs the question 'Kinder than what?' and needs us to fill in the blank in the sentence 'This murder is kinder than . . .' The phrase is a very odd juxtaposition between two dissimilar images.
2. Kinder: phonetically the same as *kinda* as in 'sort of' or 'type of' (this interpretation only really applies if we're just *listening* to the song without seeing its title or lyrical transcript, as it's clearly not written that way. This interpretation would suggest that the events in the song's narrative all amount to a kind of murder, perhaps referring to the characters themselves or the decline of society.
3. Kinder: German for 'children'. This interpretation, with the song title now being 'Children Murder', would fit the line 'The child went missing and the photo fit his face', *but* its pronunciation involves a different vowel sound on the *i* to what Costello sings.

A title like this creates intrigue in a listener and gets us interested before we've even heard a single note.

The significance of the opening line

Childs states that the 'first line or sentence . . . serves as a prelude to the rest of the text' (Childs 2008: 108) and suggests that we ask ourselves: 'Does it orient you by giving information? Does it throw you into the narrative as though you had entered a story in the middle?' (Childs 2008: 108). Our first line in 'Kinder Murder' is 'Here in the bar, the boys like to have fun'. The use of the word *here* gives us a location to inhabit and places us directly in the action, allowing us to be there in the bar, watching 'the boys'. Depending on how we read the song, this opening line either starts the linear narrative of the story or serves as a present-day narrative from which we branch off into flashback, turning it into the *final* action in the song's timeline as it is the only event in the present, meaning it's the most recent. The use of the word *bar* in the same sentence as *boys* means we can't apply the most common meaning ('young males') and must therefore look upon it as a group of young men. So the title and the first line are very allusive and ask more questions than they answer ('What *is* a "kinder murder"?'; 'Where's the bar?' 'Who are the boys?'), serving as 'lyrical hooks' for the listener and mirroring the opening of the first page of a novel, whose job it is to draw the reader in to the rest of the work.

Perspective

The song is all in the third person, using an omniscient narrator who can see into the minds of the characters. Burroway suggests, 'This kind of narrator is free to tell us readers what to think or feel' (Burroway 2007: 46), and although the majority of the song is spent merely observing, the narrator does seem to become active in this way during the 'Kinder Murder' refrain and (possibly) during the 'She should have . . .' sections, although the latter could just as easily be attached to Jimmy (the fact that these lyrics aren't put in speech marks, however, keeps things ambiguous). Where the third-person omniscient narrator is passive (observing), we are given the feeling of objective truth, almost like a documentary, where the narrator provides us with all the facts without emotion or personal attachment. This, in turn, allows listeners to draw their own conclusions. Even though the characters don't directly speak themselves, we hear their voices through the narrator, giving us the impression we are seeing multiple perspectives, even though, in reality, they've been filtered through the lexicon of our narrator, the equivalent of interviews in documentaries going through an editing process, even allowing them, perhaps, to be misquoted and/or taken out of context. The times where the narrator emerges and becomes active could be taken in different ways, depending on which of the three proposed interpretations of the title/refrain we go with and whether we attach the 'could have/should have' sections to the narrator or Jimmy.

Tenses

The word *here* in the first line and subsequent present-tense utterances during the first two verses and refrain (with use of *there's, spitting, see,* and *it's*) suggest that the following past-tense verses are either flashbacks, or these initial sections are being given prominence as they are the catalyst for everything that follows. The repeated use of the present-tense refrain 'It's a Kinder Murder' certainly implies that although the event of the kinder murder itself may have occurred in the past, it's still relevant and therefore needs to be given present status.

Idioms, slang, ambiguity and confusion

There is a lot of confusion in the song, and neither the characters, events or order in which they occur is clear. The song is almost willing the listener to come up with contrary interpretations, and the ambiguity could itself serve as an over-arching metaphor, suggesting that life is complicated, never clear-cut or easy to figure out. A number of idioms, euphemisms and slang phrases are used, each of which offers multiple interpretations, meaning it's impossible to come up with a definitive reading of the song. One particular example comes via the line 'All the family pride in the little ram-rider', where we have two idiom phrases that are hard to decipher. At first glance, though, even if we don't unpick these phrases any further, the words *family* and *little* stand out, suggesting a child. This is further reinforced by the actual use of the word in the next verse.

Without wandering too far outside the text itself, which must at all times remain our focus, here I will take *family pride* in the most literal possible sense, which is that it is the pride of the family as a whole (with *pride* taken in the 'gratification' sense rather than as a group of lions – although this could spawn an interesting reading!)

Ram-rider is harder to define without some degree of research, but even the words themselves (when separated from their hyphenated state) can conjure up images of aggression or force (*ram*), and sex (*ram* and *rider*), so even a surface reading could provide some kind of significance. If we *do* dig a little deeper, however, we find that *ram-riding* is a euphemism for 'public humiliation' (Holder 1995: 305). If we put all our suppositions together, then, including what we've previously gleaned from the song, we are left with two possible interpretations:

1. The public humiliation refers to the 'would-be teenage bride', and the 'family pride', a positive image juxtaposed against the negative image of humiliation, shows how it's impacted the family of the girl.
2. The public humiliation refers to a child that was conceived at the perimeter fence, born to an underage teenage mother out of wedlock. The 'family pride' could be an ironic statement, referring to how the girl's family's pride was misplaced, or it could be genuine, referring to a new mother's pride in her child, despite others thinking the whole situation is a public humiliation.

Characters

What characters do we have?

- The boys
- Stonewashed damsel
- 'He'
- 'Her' (in silhouette)
- 'She'
- Jimmy
- 'Her' no. 2 (perimeter fence)
- Officer
- Would-be teenage bride
- Child
- Best friend
- 'Her' no. 3 (owner of the handbag)

Due to the ambiguity of the song, it's unclear which of the characters above are the same and which are separate. This will vary depending on which interpretation we apply, but I will edit this list in accordance with my own:

- Jimmy
- Jimmy's best friend
- The boys (which include, at minimum, Jimmy and his best friend)
- Stonewashed damsel

- Officer
- Child

Jimmy is the only person in the song given a name, suggesting he is its focal point and subject. 'In a sentence, the subject is the "doer", often the instigators of an action expressed in the verb string' (Börjars and Burridge 2010: 79).

Jimmy is the subject of every sentence he's directly named in, instigating the action: '**He took** her down to the perimeter fence'; '**He was back** in half an hour'; '**he said** he left her senseless', etc.

The 'stonewashed damsel' is 'a patient', affected by another participant (Börjars and Burridge 2010: 79), whether it's having words **put into her mouth**, being **taken** down to the perimeter fence or being **left** senseless. The woman's remaining nameless (a patient to Jimmy's agent) and being 'taken' like an object are symbolic of her disposability to Jimmy, the song, and if we're to take it even further, society itself. Where she is the subject, she is still kept characterless, firstly by never being named, secondly by being objectified and thirdly, through what is presumably Jimmy's voice *telling* her what she could or should have done. 'She could have kept her knees together/Should have kept her mouth shut'.

The effect of all this is to portray the male subject (Jimmy) as all-controlling, and the female subject (the stonewashed damsel) as disposable and meaningless, no more important than the clothing she wears.

The child is largely symbolic in the song, an innocent in a narrative which describes some unsavoury aspects of life. It's not characterized and is easily dismissed by Jimmy, just as the stonewashed damsel is.

The best friend serves as little more than a bit-part character, existing only to play his part in the 'wager' and to provide the car.

There are further cues within the song which provide us with more information to 'flesh out' these characters, and this is perhaps most evident with the stone-washed damsel. If we consider this phrase as a cue to evoke some kind of imagery in the listener, we might come to the following conclusion:

The word *damsel*, meaning 'a young, unmarried woman', may link this character with the 'would-be teenage bride' later in the song, and she could possibly be the same 'her' who 'could have kept her knees together/Should have kept her mouth shut' and was taken down to the perimeter fence. The word *damsel* is often used in the phrase 'damsel in distress', which could suggest that the stonewashed damsel is in need of rescuing from something or someone.

Having explored the word *damsel*, we can now focus on *stone-washed*. We can take this phrase one of two ways. In the first, we can assume it is metaphorical and refers to the jeans the woman is wearing, making the line become 'there's a young, unmarried woman wearing stone-washed jeans'. In the second interpretation, we could consider the appearance that stone-washed jeans suggests – a worn-out look – and apply that to the 'damsel', making the line become 'there's a worn-out young, unmarried woman'.

The sound of the song

The instrumentation, melody, structure and the way certain lines are delivered are all available to us in a close reading analysis, as the 'text' can be extended to include all musical elements.

Think about the way the music becomes more or less aggressive, depending on which lyrics are being sung, and the way Costello delivers different lines in different ways; for example, there is a harmony on the refrain 'Kinder Murder', drawing further attention to it by making it more melodic and therefore more memorable.

The 'should have kept her knees together' sections have a desperation to them. And the way he delivers the word *knickers* is with a leery, lecherous snarl.

Looking beyond the text itself via Nicki Minaj's 'Anaconda' (2014)

'Anaconda' is a prime example of a text which offers little when using only close reading techniques, but actually becomes quite significant when applying a wider analysis that looks not only at the text itself but what has been before it, what has *influenced* it, what conventions it draws upon and what significance it might have in terms of its impact on culture.

If we focus on the lyrics of 'Anaconda' and nothing else, we are faced with a fairly basic first-person narrative from a narrator (understandably perceived to be female by most listeners because of the female vocalist) who speaks about past relationships, drug taking, money, violence and physical appearance. A series of forced rhymes seem to dictate the narrative rather than the other way round (e.g. *rifle* and *Nyquil, cocaine* and *romaine, kill* and *pill, Troy* and *Detroit, motorcycles* and *'Eiffels'*) and periods where actual words aren't even used (e.g. Dun-d-d-dun-dun-d-d-dun-dun) all succeed in giving the impression that the lyrics have been written in haste and are largely forgettable and unimportant (perhaps adhering to the Will.I.Am. school of thought from the introduction of this book). If we look back over her body of work leading up to the song (which we can do now that we're not limiting ourselves to close reading), Minaj seems to have a penchant for lyrics that appear to be written for no other reason than to rhyme and fit a syllabic count, for example:

'Where Them Girls at?' (Guetta 2011a): 'Just the other day me go a London, saw dat, kids down the street/Paparazzi, all dat/hey, hey, what can I say/Day day da-day day day day'.

'Turn Me On' (2011b): 'D-d-d-d-don't let me die young, I just want you to father my young/I just want you to be my doctor, we can get it crackin' chiropractor/I, I, I, I, I, I, I know you can save me/And make me feel alive'.

'Check It Out' (2010): 'Da done done/The sun done/Yep the sun done/Came up but we still up in dungeon/Da done done/Yep in London'.

'Pound the Alarm' (2012a): 'Skeeza, pleeza, I'm in Ibiza'.

'Va Va Voom' (2012c): 'Boom, boom pow, this thing so bingo/Wondering if he could understand my lingo'.

With Minaj using this technique of structuring the songs so the words are chosen for their sound and ability to rhyme, it makes any search for direct biographical meaning difficult, as the shape of the words dictate the story, not the other way around. This applies to all lyrics, of course; they all have an artificial nature due to the fact they have to be written (and edited) to fit into such a short format in the first place, but it applies more to writers like Minaj whose lyrics are *so* forced and manipulated.

If we pick through 'Anaconda', we can see where words exist purely for their aesthetic value (rhythm or rhyme):

'Boy toy named Troy used to live in Detroit' (tough to tell which way round the rhymes came, but at least *some* of these words exist purely for their function of rhyme. As such, if we were looking for 'a window' into the life of Minaj, we must discount this line as offering anything significant, as the truth (if there was any in the first place) has been distorted.

'Was in shootouts with the law, but he live in a palace/bought me Alexander McQueen, he was keeping me stylish' (rhyming couplet where the pronunciation of 'stylish' has had to be twisted almost the point of it being unrecognizable in order for it to achieve the rhyme. Does this suggest that the word *stylish* was so important that it had to be included at all costs? Or that Minaj came up with the word *palace*, which is a clichéd way of demonstrating wealth, and had to find something that rhymed with it, this opting for *stylish*, which was the closest she could come? After all, what other simple image could she have used to replace *palace*? Once more, then, the only thing that stands out here as not being totally manufactured is 'Alexander McQueen' as any designer with a similar syllabic count would have served the same purpose here, and McQueen probably isn't the most recognizable of names).

More significance comes when we begin to look *outside* the lyrics and consider their place in the wider world of pop music. Restricting ourselves only to what's contained within the lyrics themselves wouldn't allow us to identify the fact that large sections of the song are sampled from an existing track, Sir Mix-a-lot's 'Baby Got Back' (1992), or discuss the subsequent implications of a female artist using such samples. We would also be unable to consider the video's impact on the lyrics – a video which is, arguably, more famous/infamous than the song itself.

Such is the importance attached to the music video of 'Anaconda' that it's near impossible to find any kind of review/analysis of the song that ignores it. A Huffington Post article, for example, even when setting out to 'take a deeper look into Nicki's lyrics' (Mueller 2014), talks almost exclusively about the video, for example:

> She entices with whipped cream and a maid costume, only to slice a banana into pieces (I'll let you figure that one out on your own). She shows a sense of power, a power that she wants to reclaim for women, especially women of color.

So ingrained is the music video into popular culture that there have been numerous instances where a video has either led to the success of a song or become *more* successful. So any time we conduct a full in-depth analysis into a song, and it *has* a music video (this would include pretty much every 'single' released today), we must include the music video in this analysis, as once it is made, it is as inseparable from the overall music package as lyrics are from melody, and melody is from production.

Stephen Greenblatt suggests that the following questions be asked in order to look at the types of cultural commentary present in texts:

1. What kinds of behaviour, what models of practice does this work seem to enforce?
2. Why might readers at a particular time and place find this work compelling?
3. Are there differences between my values and the values implicit in the work I am reading?
4. Upon what social understandings does the work depend?
5. Whose freedom of thought or movement might be constrained implicitly or explicitly by this work?
6. What are the larger social structures with which these particular acts of praise or blame that is, the text's apparent ethical orientation – might be connected? (Greenblatt 1995: 226)

If we apply these questions to 'Anaconda' and compare the answers with what we would get if we limited our reading to just the lyrics (close reading only), we see the very different results:

	Close Reading Only	Wider Research
What kinds of behaviour, what modes of practice does this work seem to enforce?	Female violence; crime pays; body image is important.	Women are in control of their own sexuality and in control of men.
Why might readers at a particular time and place find this work compelling?	We are used to the elements of structural criticism (length, production, content, language). Being 'compelled' may depend on our knowledge of the song 'Baby Got Back'.	It may be viewed as the ultimate feminist statement in an age where female equality is widely discussed in popular culture, and the objectification of women is still ongoing in many societies. Sexual empowerment (lap-dancing scene and chopping up of phallus-shaped banana).
Are there differences between (i) my values and (ii) the values implicit in the work I am reading?	Listeners may be against body shaming, and drug or violence glorification. The song appears to condone all three.	Some of us might be against using the female body to sell records. The female body can be used as its owner sees fit, and that is the true meaning of feminism.
Upon what social understandings does the work depend?	The listener understands the culture of referring to drug dealing and guns in pop music. There are issues with 'female size' within culture.	'Baby Got Back' was a misogynistic song. Females are overtly sexualized in pop music under the male gaze.

In conclusion, to limit ourselves to a close reading analysis of this song would be to miss everything that is important amount it, including a backlash at the objectification of women (including passing judgement on historical objectification via the subversion of 'Baby Got Back'), a commentary on female empowerment and a rejection of the male gaze. *All* of these factors occur outside the lyric and are thus unavailable to us if we're limiting ourselves to close reading.

7

Persuasion and Emotion

Music and emotion

For a number of years now, I have started my Composing Song Lyrics classes (at the University of Winchester) by discussing The Beatles' 'Yesterday' (1965b), and it's a good way to introduce here some of the themes we'll be discussing in this book.

To begin with, I talk the students through the origins of how the song was written, beginning with Paul McCartney's now legendary anecdote about how he woke up with the melody in his head and spent the next few weeks playing the song to others to figure out where he'd heard it before. So I play an instrumental version of the song, where the melody line is played in piano. The next step was for McCartney to sing nonsense lyrics while he tried to write lines he was happy with, giving it the working title of 'Scrambled Eggs'. I play the students a recording of this version of the song, which involves a vocalist singing the rather mundane ode to eggs. Once again, the melody is lovely, but the words . . . the words offer no emotional attachment as there is nothing we can really 'grab onto' in the song to get emotional about.

The next step is to play the finished version with McCartney's final lyrics. I would posit, a prime reason this song has been so successful is the sheer accessibility of the lyrics; they are generic enough to be applied to most people's lives if they've experienced any kind of loss, heartbreak or setback. It doesn't matter if it's not the kind of scenario McCartney was thinking of when he wrote it; it's open to listeners to apply their own experience and thus their own emotion. This created mood, combined with the melody with shades of sadness and the bittersweet, generates the combination that has made it the world's most covered pop song. Once again, it is very much an appeal to emotion; not designed to inform, but to persuade listeners to further bond with the melody, which in turn persuades them to further bond with the lyrics.

To finish off the exercise, I give the class some background information about the (apparent) meaning McCartney worked into the lyrics, to attempt to push the emotion even more. This will naturally get a bigger reaction from those who have experienced the loss of a relative, but it will still create emotion among those who haven't. For the first time, we are looking into factors beyond the song (or the composition of the song) and searching wider for an interpretation, even if our research begins and ends with the author's biography, which will be the case for most people when it comes to analysing popular music. This research, uncovering as it does McCartney's personal experience with loss, make us believe what he's saying (they're not just empty words now; they have significance and gravitas), and as we're now more invested in the singer of the song, our emotional attachment lifts again, as we now feel emotion for McCartney *and* for ourselves with our own thoughts on loss, heartbreak or remorse now established.

This brief introduction underlines how lyrics can elicit an emotional reaction from a listener, and begins the discussion of both the writer's role in this process and the listener's. If we take this slightly further, it could be argued that if songs are designed to get a *reaction*, then they can also be used to persuade, whether that's through persuading us to listen again (and subsequently buy), to bond with the artist and listen to/buy more of her work, to subscribe to a certain way of life, or to agree with the lyrics' political statements. Even the most avant-garde work, which seems to exist purely for art itself, persuades us merely through the fact of its own existence to reject the mainstream and think for ourselves. A number of these factors may be accidental, but if we break songwriting down to its most fundamental functions, which are to (i) get someone to listen, then (ii) get them to listen again and again, the act of injecting hooks (be they musical, rhythmic or lyrical) is a deliberate act to achieve this. We need to discuss how a set of lyrics can *persuade* us to act or feel a certain way as well as to what extent the persuasion is based on the lyrics themselves and to what extent it is based on outside factors. 'Persuasion is interactive and attempts to satisfy the needs of both persuader and persuadee' (Jowett and O'Donnell 2006: 1).

Exercise

Work though a song of your choice, looking at the basic means of creating emotion. Start off with the melody, and jot down some notes on how that makes you feel. Then look at the lyrics (without considering the artist or any story surrounding the song) before bringing backstory and biography into your analysis.

The main objective of any type of music, from classical to industrial, to jazz, to hip-hop, is to get a reaction from the listener. Taken a step further, it could be said that music is designed to *persuade* us to act in a certain way, whether it's the beat persuading us to dance; the infectious melody persuading us to hum along; the lyrics persuading us to *think* about certain issues, to bond with the artist, to emotionally react or to find meaning in a song. Above all else, songs need to persuade us to listen to them more than once and persuade us to *buy* them.

When it comes to art, music is one of the quickest, most effective mediums for making us feel emotion – a fast-track route to our hearts, and a fast track route to make us react mentally or physically. From rousing music at the start of football matches 'chosen to gee-up home players and supporters, while sending visitors into paroxysms of fear and doubt' (Gale 2012), to nursery rhymes sung softly to settle upset babies, music, more than any other medium, has the power to change our emotional state within just a few bars.

Emotion in pop music can be achieved through a variety of different means and often relies on a mixture of different methods in order to gain the desired response. On TV programmes like *Britain's Got Talent*, or *The X Factor*, when we see an artist with an emotional backstory, the sequence will invariably be scored with a song that heightens our feelings of sadness, compassion or pity. Such musical 'prompts' (as that's essentially what they are: prompts for us to feel a certain way) are usually instrumentals and demonstrate that impact melody can have on us. Today, where music videos are arguably as important to the success of a song as the song itself, the video can provide an extra emotional nudge that isn't necessarily present in the music or lyrics. In Britney Spears' music video 'Everytime', 'the video's narrative does not simply illustrate the lyrics of the song, or necessarily even amplify them, but, more complexly, it recasts them through their visual narration and in doing so affects their meaning' (Railton and Watson 2011: 57). As if to prove the impact of this heightened emotion caused through visual means, the song is included in Capital FM's '11 most emotional sad songs GUARANTEED to make you cry' (Capital FM 2015), a list that focuses almost entirely on the emotional impact of the accompanying music videos while largely ignoring lyrics.

Emotion and the listener

Our emotional connection to a song can come via two means: (i) through ourselves, or (ii) through the artist. The second involves a knowledge of the artist and some kind of connection with him or her, but the first requires only our own experiences. In order to emotionally connect in this way, we switch the lyricist's experiences with our own, applying our own experiences to either fill in the gaps or to eradicate any inconsistencies, and this is often how we can be persuaded to react to a song.

> Persuasion has the effect, when it is successful, of resulting in a reaction such as 'I never saw it that way before.' What happens is that the recipient of the persuasive interaction relates to, or contrasts the message with, his or her existing repertoire of information, beliefs, attitudes, and experiences.
> (Jowett and O'Donnell 2015: 37–38)

> Of the three elements in speech-making – speaker, subject and person addressed – it is the last one, the hearer that determines the speech's end and object. The hearer must either be a judge, with a decision to make about things past or future, or an observer.' – Aristotle.
> (Roberts 1995: 2159)

Who are we writing for

As a songwriter, one of the first decisions it's necessary to make is to figure out for whom you're writing the song and *why* you're writing it.

Most of the answers I receive are 'I write for *me*, of course, and I do it for the pure love of music and art.' But do take a few seconds to think deeply about this.

Critic Wayne C. Booth once observed of literature, 'True artists, we have been told again and again, take no thought of their readers. They write for themselves. The true poet writes to express himself, or find himself . . . and let the reader be damned' (Booth 1961: 89)

Never has this been less the case with an artist who knows his music is going to be heard by millions. Of course he is writing with the reader in mind, even if he is doing so subconsciously. Paul Weller suggests:

> it's important to be honest and reflect how you feel but it's also important to try and include the people that listen to your record . . . otherwise you're just writing for yourself.
>
> (Rachel 2013: 194)

If you do believe you're writing *purely* for you and you alone, are you not going to perform it, record it for others to hear it, play it to anyone? Then ask yourself again, are you really doing so with no consideration for who might hear it when it's finished? Because the moment a songwriter is thinking other people may hear their work, then it could be argued she's no longer writing only for herself.

Are we consciously (and, indeed, unconsciously) making decisions based on how an imagined audience will react? And do such decisions vary if we are aware of particular people who will be listening? And will they vary still further if we seek approval from such people or are extremely sensitive to their opinions? *Why* you're writing a song may indeed be simply because you love the process of writing, but consider why this is the art form you've chosen through which to express yourself rather than, say, poetry, prose or painting. Do you feel you can naturally express yourself better in a music form? Is it because it's a format you're most familiar with and therefore feel most comfortable with? Is it a method of artistic expression that is more immediate than a short story or poem?

It's also worth considering whether you're writing a song to get a particular reaction or end result from an audience, be it praise, validation, shock or simply persuading them to buy your music. A songwriter shouldn't feel guilt or 'impurity' if they're writing for this reason. It's likely that most songwriters are seeking some kind of *external* reaction, and the tortured artist sitting alone in a cellar, burning the recordings the second they're made may indeed exist, but is in a massive minority compared to those writers who want their music heard. Even Nick Drake, an artist famous for recording in secret before presenting the master tapes to the record label and disappearing again, sought fame:

> He was very agitated, very nervous, twitchy. He sat down and he immediately launched into this kind of tirade about his career, about money and basically it was accusatory. And he said, "You told me I'm great, but nobody knows me. Nobody buys my records. I'm still living on handouts from the publishing company. I don't understand. What's wrong?
>
> (Dann 2006: 179–180)

How can we be persuaded?

A listener can be persuaded to feel a certain way because of the words and phrases a writer uses.

This section looks specifically at the way lyrics can be used to try to inform; encourage a dialogue (between both the writer and the listener(s), and the listener and other listeners); or persuade us into thinking or acting a certain way. In order to do this, lyricists draw on a variety of techniques, including perspective (discussed in the next chapter), narrative content and, perhaps most importantly, rhetoric. 'Rhetoric is, as simply defined as possible, the art of persuasion: the attempt by one human being to influence another in words' (Leith 2012: 1)

At its root, rhetoric is broken down into three fundamental modes of persuasion. According to Aristotle, 'The first kind depends on the personal character of the speaker [ethos]; the second on putting the audience

into a certain frame of mind [pathos]; the third on the proof, or apparent proof, provided by the words of the speech itself [logos]' (Shabo 2010: 8).
    To give a little more information:

Ethos: The speaker emphasizes the strength of his or her own moral character and experience in order to establish personal credibility.

Pathos: emotion. An attempt . . . to elicit an emotional response from the audience.

Logos: reason, logic . . . the use of rational analysis and persuasive language.
(Shabo 2010: 8)

Although written to apply to oration, we can use these modes in our attempts to analyse popular music, for every song that has ever been written contains one of these devices. It's immediately evident from these definitions; however, although pathos can be created *without* lyrics (note how certain pieces of classical music elicit emotional reactions purely through melody), only songs with lyrics can draw upon ethos and logos.
    We find pathos in lyrics where we are persuaded to emotionally react or connect with a song without thinking too deeply about why we are doing so. This is very much a reaction of the heart over the head. Arguments that involve pathos often incorporate vivid descriptions and images, carefully selected words linked with the desired emotion (positive or negative), and make us feel a particular way toward a certain person or group of people (pity, anger, love, etc.). Although these kinds of reactions are also dependent on the listener's participation and how open they are to reacting without thinking too deeply, the lyricist can provoke a reaction like this through the words they use in their songs. Want to make people happy? Use positive language. Want to write a tear-jerker? Pepper your lyrics with sad words that tug at the heartstrings. Want to shock? Swear or use disturbing imagery. Want to rally or anger? Use words that show unfairness, injustice or oppression. With most songs, we get a general feel for their desired reaction of pathos by going through the lyrics and picking out some of the nouns and verbs they're using:

Desired Reaction	Song	Phrases Evoking Pathos	Words Evoking Pathos
Happiness/ positivity	Destiny's Child (2001) – 'Happy Face'	'I'm living, I'm able, I'm breathing, I'm grateful'; 'Everything's gonna be alright, everything's gonna be okay'	*Sunshine; shining; beautiful; grateful; blessings*
Sadness/ negativity	Toni Braxton (1996) 'Un-break My Heart'	'Without you I just can't go on'; 'I cried so many, many nights'	*Pain; hurt; cried; tears; cruel; sad*
Shock	The Sex Pistols (1977a) – 'Bodies'	'She was a no one who killed her baby'; 'Die little baby screaming/Body screaming fucking bloody mess'	*throbbing; mess; screaming; dragged; killed; fucking*
Anger	Rage Against the Machine (1992) – 'Killing in the Name'	'And now you do what they told ya'; 'now you're under control'; 'You justify those that died by wearing the badge, they're the chosen whites'	*Died; justified; burn; crosses; killing*

Looking at the Sex Pistols' song 'Bodies', it is evident that our reactions of shock are coming solely from the language utilized by its lyricist, John Lydon, rather that a response to any character or story. The narrative in the song is sketchy, with its direction often dictated by its rhyme scheme (e.g. 'She was a case of insanity/Her name was Pauline she lived in a tree'), and the characterization is very limited. In a feature film or novel, our emotional responses are often based upon a building of our relationship with the plot of characters, but in songs there is no time, so this technique employed by Lydon of maximum impact in minimum time is very effective in putting across an overall feeling, even if the message itself is open to interpretation. Part of the Sex Pistols' success revolved around their ability to shock, and this song certainly delivers.

The rest of the songs in the table employ similar techniques, but to elicit different reactions. It doesn't necessarily matter if we're invested in the narrator's story; the language used pushes us to experience particular emotions, regardless of storyline.

Songwriters are able to employ varying degrees of subtlety in their language when trying to express emotion in a song. Taking expressions of love for example; some go for the direct route, like Dolly Parton's 'I will always love you', and some like Mike Skinner, go for a more indirect approach. Skinner says that with The Streets' song 'Dry Your Eyes' (2004), 'The emotion that is at the heart of the story is never explicitly described. There's no mention of love; it's only pointed to by physical actions' (Skinner 2012: 112).

Although this song avoids explicit mention of the word *love* itself, it *does* express a deep suggestion of the emotion, most evident for me in the verse that was cut in the Radio Edit, where Skinner sings:

> I'm not gonna fuckin', just fuckin' leave it all now/'Cause you said it'd be forever and that was your vow. (The Streets 2004)

The repetition of the crass *fuckin'*, which seems out of place in a song talking about love, combined with Skinner's spoken word delivery, give a realism to this line, as though it's a conversation and Skinner is so emotional about the situation that he is struggling to put into words what he means. A lot of us will have been in similar situations and experienced that, so this lack of eloquence can have a real emotional impact, even though the likelihood is that Skinner was distant from the song's narrative and therefore its sentiment is manufactured.

With the use of character in a song, and its subsequent appeals using the rhetorical mode ethos, our 'hopes of stirring the audience to anger or pity depend on the extent to which they are prepared to identify with the anger or pity you yourself seem to feel' (Leith 2012: 48–49) (with the *you* referring to the writer). As with pathos, the way listeners bond with the artist/writer is reliant on their own reactions, but if writers want to be trusted or appear genuine or authoritative in what they're saying, they'll need to put this across in the language they use, instead of simply relying on the fact that the listener will be aware of the artist/writer's biography and/or public persona. This is perhaps most prevalent in rap, which 'is often more or less . . . a constant discussion of what the rapper is about to do, his credentials for doing it, 'shout-outs' to the crew with whom he intends to do it and 'disses' to members of enemy crews who propose trying to prevent him (Leith 2012: 86).

Artists within this genre are always striving for authenticity, and although the accumulation of money is a popular subject, it's important for rap artists to speak about how they weren't always wealthy. Cash Money and Young Money Entertainment are two of the genre's major record labels, featuring artists like Nicki Minaj, Drake and Lil Wayne (three of the biggest artists in the genre at the time of writing), and Lil Wayne mentions the word *money* in 11 of the 15 songs on his *Tha Carter IV* album and even states: 'I do it for the money, man' in the song 'Blunt Blowin'' (2010). But these artists have made sure to recount times when they weren't wealthy, reinforcing the fact that they are genuine and have faced a struggle to get where they are. Examples come in Nicki Minaj's 'I'm the Best' (2010b): 'I remember when I couldn't buy my mother a couch/Now I'm sitting at the closing, bought my mother a house' and Drake's 'Started from the Bottom' (2013): 'Boys tell stories about the man/Say I never struggled, wasn't hungry, yeah, I doubt it/Started from the bottom now we're here'. But pick any of the major rap artists, and you'll see a similar trend: Eminem, Jay Z, Rick Ross, Kendrick Lamar, Nas – all include rags-to-riches stories to show their authenticity.

Authenticity isn't just limited to rap, of course, and many pop artists are aware of how their success can make them seem distant to their fans. Leith notes that Jennifer Lopez's song 'Jenny from the Block' was written because 'sensing that her keeping-it-real appeal was on the wane, she sang a song that's one long desperate assertion of ethos' (Leith 2012: 49).

Problems arise, then, when artists that sing (and indeed boast) about enormous wealth then try and speak to the listener on a more realistic level. If we contrast Nicki Minaj's lines from 'Did it on 'Em' (2010a), 'Louis Vuitton everything, bitch!/Gucci – we don't fuck with it, it's too cheap, motherfucker!' and 'Monster' (2010c): '50k for a verse, no album out!/Yeah my money's so tall that my Barbie's gotta climb it', with (2012b) 'Starships': 'Jump in my hooptie hooptie hoop I own that/And I ain't paying my rent this month/I owe that' (with *hooptie* being a slang term for a 'beat-up car'), it's tough for the singer to lend any authenticity at all to the song, as the previous lyrics render the possibility of owning an old car and owing rent as highly unlikely. Taken along with the rest of the song's lyrics, though – 'Let's go to the beach, each' and 'Now everybody let me hear you say ray ray ray/Now spend all your money 'cause they pay pay pay' – it's debatable whether the lyrics mattered to Minaj at all.

I wonder, when Jessie J now sings the song 'Price Tag' (2011) live, belting out its chorus, 'It's not about the money money money/We don't need your money money money/We just wanna make the world dance/ Forget about the price tag', whether she feels a pang of insincerity, with the song having sold over a million copies in the UK.

This begs the question of whether writers should be looking at writing about money at all if they are signing with major labels and looking to be successful. It also begs the question of whether they should even consider such a thing or should just write whatever they want.

It all depends on what the song is trying to achieve. In Jessie J's case, this song may well be a mantra to many people who reject capitalist society and materialism, but should the conversation be led (as that's what a singer is doing: leading conversation, beginning the discussion) by someone who is a *part* of this capitalist structure?

On the Student Room Chat board, the question of Jessie J's hypocrisy was raised, with a comment taking the argument beyond this one song and into music as a whole: they're all hypocrites/don't take anything they say seriously/especially if they make money from what they're saying [*sic*] (Student Room Chat 2014).

Certainly not the most eloquent way of putting across a point, and definitely not the most accurate when it comes to punctuation, but it does raise an interesting point nonetheless in that it poses the question of whether an artist can ever really speak their mind if money is at stake.

> Anyone who claims to not care about money must be a monk, a trust-fund kid, or a complete liar. Money makes the world go 'round, and while there's no disputing its hold over mankind, it means different things to different people. Cash can represent freedom, victory, power, validation, and security. It can be a means to an end or the be-all, end-all of one's existence. It can't buy you happiness, but it might get you a date on Friday night.
>
> (Partridge 2016)

We won't spend too much time here talking about this one topic, but it needs to be recognized how certain writers working in certain genres will tackle the subject differently. It's more common in hip-hop, for example, to talk about opulence and extreme wealth than it would be in punk, where the notion of wealth is linked to 'selling out'. In 1977, when The Clash were signed to major record label CBS, some people believed they had 'sold out', with one critic going as far as to say that 'punk died the day The Clash signed to CBS' (Doane 2014: 42).

As we'll see in our subsequent discussions of formula and generic subject matter, a great number of songs deal with basic subjects like love or loss, so for us to trust that the lyricist has experienced these things and therefore can speak with authority isn't much of a leap as the majority of us will have experienced this, albeit it in different ways. It is harder, however, if we are going to discuss more complex themes where authority and authenticity can be challenged. This might encourage artists to play it safe so as not to invite criticism in this way by sticking their heads above the parapet, or even to appear to be too eloquent as it might alienate fans. Burroway notes that 'we have tended to equate eloquence with arrogance at best and dishonesty at worst, preferring people who, like you know, well, kinda couldn't exactly, like, say what they mean' (Burroway 2007: 49). We need only to look at Taylor Swift's 'We Are Never Getting Back Together' (2012b) for a great example of this:

> Huh . . . so he calls me up and he's like, 'I still love you'
> And I'm like, 'I just – I mean this is exhausting, you know?
> Like, we are never getting back together
> Like, ever.

Authenticity may not be about truth: it may be saying what you want to say because that's what fits the song, rather than worrying about how it'll be interpreted or how you're manipulating biography. If an artist wants to avoid questions of authenticity, then the easiest way to do it is to write about their lives, limiting their utterances to things we know it's likely they've experienced (love, loss, breakups, parties) as opposed to those things someone in their position is unlikely to have experienced recently (money issues, hunger, losing a job etc.). Even if we come to the conclusion that the lyricist is writing in character and not speaking directly from their own experience, the same rules apply to lyrics as they do to literature and script: unless the writer is being deliberately abstract, what is being presented to us has to be believable, and even if we can't relate to it personally, there has to at least be the *potential* for us to relate to it – some generic human qualities. Artists can show they are authentic to a certain place (e.g. South London in Stormzy's 'Shut Up', or California in Katy Perry's 'California Gurls'); culture (e.g. 'Fun Lovin' Criminals', er . . . fun-loving criminal antics in 'Scooby Snacks'); lifestyle (e.g. the 'party' lifestyle in Miley Cyrus' 'We Can't Stop' or Charli XCX's 'After the After Party'); experience (e.g. drug addiction, first-hand experience in the Red Hot Chili Peppers' 'Under the Bridge' or second-hand in Neil Young's 'The Needle and the Damage Done'.

Authenticity can occur in a number of ways outside the lyrics themselves and includes accent, appearance and public persona, but regarding the words themselves, one of the best ways artists can appear authentic is through the vocabulary they use.

Plan B's 2012 song 'Ill Manors' (2012) is an angry backlash at the media and government for the apparent demonization of council estate residents, including 'chav hate', which, 'as it began to emerge as a force in mainstream culture in 2004 . . . found support in the mainstream press' (Jones 2012: 113).

> 'For those of its readers who were bewildered by the chav phenomenon, the *Daily Mail* published a handy "A to Z" of chavs. "A" was for "A-Level" – "Something no Chav has ever possessed." "U" was for "Underage": "What every Chavette is at the time of her first sexual experience." . . . And, of course, chavs were to be taunted for their low-paid jobs. "What do you say to a Chav when he's at work? Big Mac and fries, please, mate."
> (Thomas in Jones 2012: 113–114)

Plan B (aka Ben Drew) needs to show authenticity in this song to situate himself as an insider (and therefore authority on the subject), and an alternative voice to what listeners might have previously heard about the 'chav phenomenon'. Drew does this in a number of ways; taking on the perspective of the 'outsider/snob' by speaking in their voices,

'Let's go on an urban safari' (which suggests those living in such areas are a different species), and 'Oi look, there's a chav', which makes them look narrow-minded, misinformed and ridiculous. Drew then includes himself as part of the council estate lifestyle by using the pronouns *we* and *us* and goes on to vilify the print media and government, referring specifically to David Cameron's comments 'Hug a Hoodie' ('He's got a hoodie on give him a hug/On second thoughts don't, you don't wanna get mugged') and 'Broken Britain' ('There's no such thing as broken Britain/We're just bloody broke in Britain). It's the language Drew uses that is perhaps most important in this song though. Firstly, he selects words and images that show he is well informed about the politics and culture of the time: 'Eco-friendly government', 'Built an entire Olympic Village without pulling down any flats', 'Who closed down the community centre?', 'Let's go looting', 'Here's a charge for congestion, everybody's gotta pay/Do what Boris does . . . rob them blind,' 'What needs fixing is the system/Not shops down in Brixton', 'Riots on the television'. Secondly, he uses a great deal of slang terms that show how he is 'real', an authentic insider source rather than an objective bystander:

buns the herb – smokes marijuana
burbs – suburbs
ill – awesome
shanks – homemade knife
tools – weapons
manor – territory or turf

It's worth noting here as well that Drew could well be *overusing* this kind of terminology to mock those who think this is the way that all council estate residents speak. The line 'We're all drinkers, drug takers/ Every single one of us buns the herb' certainly appears to have a degree of eye-rolling, 'yes, of course we all do that' about it, as Drew reads/hears yet another generalization about his lifestyle.

As we'll see in the chapter on formula, a great number of songs deal with basic subjects like love or loss, so for us to trust that the lyricist has experienced these things and therefore can speak with authority isn't much of a leap, as the majority of us will have experienced this, albeit it in different ways. It is harder, however, if we are going to be discussing more complex themes where authority and authenticity can be challenged. This might encourage artists to play it safe so as not to invite criticism in this way by sticking their heads above the parapet. Even if we come to the conclusion that the lyricist is writing in character and not speaking directly from personal experience, the same rules apply to lyrics as they do to literature and script: unless the writer is being deliberately abstract, what is being presented to us has to be believable, and even if we can't relate to it personally, there has to at least be the *potential* for us to relate to it; some generic human qualities.

Appealing to the intellect, logos, in contrast to pathos, is where we react with the head rather than the heart. Logos in popular music is the device with the least power of the three modes, as we tend to think with our emotions when it comes to music. In speech, an orator wishing to appeal to the intellect will use statistics, technical language, and draw upon reliable sources to evidence a depth of research. Even in songs like Paul Hardcastle's '19' (1985), which presents statistics and evidences a level of research, the argument it's making isn't well-rounded, or even concluded, so we are urged to react with emotion to the information presented to us.

A major strength of pop music is its ability to make a powerful point without having to make a huge amount of sense. Take the song 'Meat is Murder' (The Smiths 1985), for example. It could be argued that pathos and ethos are present, but logos is absent. The production of the song, most notably the sound of the saws and the heifer cries, makes us feel either repulsed or saddened, and the use of words such as *slice, die, unholy, stench*, and of course *murder* are also meant to gain some kind of emotional response. Ethos is delivered via us buying into every word Morrissey is saying because we know his credentials as a dedicated vegetarian, but there isn't an argument that appeals to the intellect, even though it *seems* as though there is. This line, which is probably the most powerful in the whole song, 'It's death for no reason, and death for no reason is *murder*', doesn't actually make sense, so the whole song relies on ethos and pathos to get its message across and has been enormously successful in doing so.

If we are going to really try to persuade listeners to react in a certain way, then, we need to appeal to their emotions while allowing them to bond with us as writers/narrators/characters, too.

Revisiting 'Yesterday' then, it's evident that *pathos* is present at the point in our analysis where we're listening only to the melody. In 'Yesterday', the appeal to emotion is present the moment we feel some kind of emotion from the melody. In my case, it's always a gentle melancholy, but it will, of course, vary from listener to listener. *Ethos* is present to an extent when we read the lyrics without biography (we believe McCartney has experienced some kind of loss, right?), but is heightened when we draw upon our research and the apparent origins of the song, where we *know* that he has experienced loss and is speaking from experience.

Aristotle goes on to posit that 'there are three divisions of oratory – deliberative, forensic, and epideictic. Deliberative speaking urges us to either do or not do something . . . Forensic speaking either attacks or defends somebody . . . [and] Epideictic oratory either praises or censures somebody'. 'These three kinds of rhetoric refer to three different kinds of time' (Roberts in 1995: 2159).

To expand this a little further:

Deliberative	attempts to make the future
Forensic	attempts to change what we see as truth about the past (attempts which may of course also affect the future)
Epideictic	attempts to reshape views of the present. An orator . . . can change the reality of how we value people and their creations. (Booth 2004: 17)

It is evident from looking at the lyrics to the *Telegraph's* '10 Best Protest Songs' (n.d.) that they almost exclusively use pathos to persuade the listener of their points. A lot of ethos in lyrics comes courtesy of the artist themselves, so where this is the case, it has been pointed out. It's also worth noting that all of the songs use at least one of the three divisions of oratory.

Song	Mode(s) of Persuasion Used (Pathos, Ethos, Logos)	Division(s) of Oratory Used (Deliberative, Forensic, Epideictic)
'Joe Hill' (1970)	Certainly not logos, as there is no real logical persuasive argument, here; ethos also absent as the narrator is admitting the whole story was a dream; pathos: a rallying call; a feeling that you're not alone; solidarity; and injustice. Definitely appeals to heart over head (especially now, a hundred years after Joe Hill's death, where a number of people won't have any immediate knowledge of the situation. *Any* emotional pull, therefore, comes from what we can glean *beyond* the Joe Hill story itself. Here, then, we have a man who was framed for murder, then shot, but who has metaphorically defied death by being in the hearts of working men who want to defend their rights. Pathos is still present, then, without proper context.	Forensic: Tries to show Joe Hill's conviction and execution as wrongful *Epideictic: attempts to show those striking as just (through the use of the wording 'defending', which shows them as fair rather than confrontational. Perhaps an attempt to change people's perspectives on Unions in general.*
'Strange Fruit' (1939)	Pathos: This is designed to instil horror and disgust in the listener, and it urges them to act. Particular words are used to achieve this effect. The third person narrative makes it *everyone's* story, and not just the singer's. Ethos: When sung by Billie Holiday, the sheer power and emotion in her voice make the listener believe the words coming out of her mouth.	*'Deliberative* – attempts to resolve the injustices toward black people and push for civil rights *Forensic* – attempts to show people the atrocities that have been carried out against black people in the past *Epideictic* – attempts to change people's complacency and acceptance of the abuse of black people (and, through the use of present tense in the song, show that these atrocities are still occurring).

(continued)

Song	Mode(s) of Persuasion Used (Pathos, Ethos, Logos)	Division(s) of Oratory Used (Deliberative, Forensic, Epideictic)
'This Land Is Your Land' (1945)	Ethos: There's enough detail in here for us to believe what the narrator is saying and that he has experienced hardship. Pathos: The 'you and me' lines make the listener directly involved, and forces them to walk the same path as the narrator. Positive words are used to create a picture of a beautiful world created by nature, then contrasted by negative world created by man's oppressions and inequalities.	*Deliberative* – attempts to make us think about social injustice and inequality and to question what role we may be playing in it. *Epideictic* – Makes people question whether America truly is 'the land of the free'.
'We Shall Overcome' (1963)	Pathos: Shows unity through the use of 'we', uses strong, rallying language. Gets an emotional response through offering hope.	Deliberative: The song urges us to believe in change (although it doesn't suggest how it can be brought about). It tries to change the future by making assertive statements in the present.
'Get Up Stand Up' (1973)	Pathos: Rallying call. The use of 'we' shows a unity with the people and that there is strength in this. Ethos: Marley is well known as an activist and advocate for the rights of black people, and someone who spoke up against poverty. We are likely to listen to him, therefore.	Deliberative – attempts to get people to reject the current status quo and stand up for themselves and their rights. Epideictic – attempts to make people question how religion is being taught to them (and how it is possibly oppressing them). Encourages people to live (and fight) for today rather than relying on salvation from external forces.

8

Accessibility, Cliché and Formula

What has been will be again,
what has been done will be done again;
there is nothing new under the sun.

Ecclesiastes 1: 9

In other art forms, particularly literature, when the personal pronoun *I* is used, a detachment from the author is formed, and it is assumed that the *I* is a fictional character, and, therefore, everything coming out of this person's mouth is fictional. In pop music, the opposite is true: for the most part we assume that the *I* directly relates to the writer and, more often than not, the singer (even if the song performed is not written by the singer).

One only has to look at the controversy surrounding the song 'Blurred Lines', in particular the line 'I know you want it' to see that the 'I' is not presumed to be the voice of the character, but of the artist. Why, then, does this kind of thing not happen to actors? Do we really believe, for example, that Larry David is truly playing himself in Curb Your Enthusiasm, rather than a grossly exaggerated version created for comedic purposes? Or that Sacha Baron Cohen is speaking his own beliefs when posing as Borat, Ali G, Bruno, or Admiral General Aladeen'?

(Fosbraey 2015: 21–22)

Look at the number of times Eminem and Marilyn Manson have had to justify their work as purely fictional when they have been vilified by the press or come under scrutiny in the courtroom. For example: 'A sex attack on a nine-year-old boy may have been inspired by the sordid lyrics of a song by the rap star Eminem, a court was told' (Bunyan 2002), or '[Marilyn Manson] blamed For 36 School Shootings' (*Larry King Now*, YouTube)

As Eminem himself said, 'It was hard enough to realize that I was famous enough that people gave a shit what I said, and even harder to believe that they'd take it all so fucking seriously' (Eminem 2008: 49).

Song lyrics have even been used by governments in their decision-making processes. When refusing Tyler the Creator entry to the United Kingdom in 2015, the letter from the UK government stated:

> Your albums *Bastard*, in 2009, and *Goblin*, in 2011, are based on the premise of your adopting a mentally unstable alter ego who describes violent physical abuse, rape and murder in graphic terms which appears to glamourise this behaviour.
>
> (Shepherd 2015)

This, in turn, forced Tyler, the Creator to defend himself, saying that 'these songs are written from the perspective of an alter ego – I wouldn't hurt a fly' (Shepherd 2015).

With all this in mind, and knowing the tendency to take lyrics as direct reflections of a writer's personality (and the potential dangers resulting from this), does it mean that artists are playing it safe with the subject matter they write about, knowing that anything they say in lyrical form may be linked back to them personally? Immediately this questions the amount of truth and/or creativity an artist can put into a song, especially those artists whose brand is vital to their success. For example, could we ever imagine Little Mix suddenly deciding to write lyrics in the first person where they took on the personas of serial killers? Or could we conceive of Justine Bieber inhabiting a character who condoned cruelty to animals? And does this mean the end of the big stars of the day talking about political issues? As Ed Sheeran says: 'Who the fuck wants me to sing about politics?' (Lynskey 2017: 29). Perhaps the answer to this is, as his rhetorical question implies, 'no one', but that's hardly the point: Ed Sheeran's biggest disincentive for talking about contentious issues is a fear of alienating fans by singing about anything that doesn't reflect the basic human condition (love, loss, desires, etc.) So, for now at least, that's what he and many others stick to – and with enormous success, to boot.

These may be examples, but it's certainly harder for lyricists to inhabit alternative perspectives to their own while writing in the first person, lest it be assumed it is they speaking, rather than a character. Unless, of course, what is being said is so over the top and so offensive it couldn't feasibly be attributed to a person.

A great example of this is Anti-Nowhere League's 'So What' (1983), where the narrator, either talking from the perspective of another character (a further separation from the author), the listener or himself, lists an increasingly revolting list of deeds he has carried out. These include, among other things, bestiality, abuse of the elderly, underage sex, sexually transmitted infections. As a listener, we assume fiction here, simply because we also assume someone would (i) never be so depraved and still at liberty, and (ii) admit to it even if they were. In this instance, then, we suspend disbelief as we would with literature or film, and separate singer/writer from narrator. The question is, then, whether we should do this for every song as a matter of course. Should we assume that the work is directly linked to a writer's personal life? This might be a bit of stretch, but it might be worthwhile for us to see lyrics as more fiction than fact (more on that later).

Can 'anything' and 'everything' be talked about in lyrics? And should 'anything' and 'everything' be discussed? It's an issue we return to later in Part II, but first of all, we need to look at that word *should* and who is voicing it. The 'duty' and 'responsibility' of the writer – is there any? Who decides what should be discussed? Music fulfils various roles in society: to bring pleasure, make people think, incite a reaction, make its artists money, inspire others to follow a similar path. Some artists may steer clear of controversy in order to sell more records (the more generic the subject matter, the better chance it has of selling big?) 'They're so scared to show intelligence, it might smear their lovely career' ('The World is Full of Crashing Bores', 2004b). Are there expectations surrounding what certain artists should write about? Are hip-hop artists expected to write about misogyny and violence? Are female artists whose physical appearance has been a major marketing tool expected to write about sex? And where does this expectation come from? Is it self-imposed? Is it from the record labels? The fans? And do certain artists rebel against this and make a name for themselves that way ('Do you know why Dre's record was so successful? He's rapping about big-screen TVs, blunts, 40s and bitches. You're rapping about homosexuals and Vicodin' (Eminem, 2000b). Although we discuss much of this in the 'genre' chapter, we look at generic subject matter here, considering what artists are currently singing about and what they have sung about in the past.

Although on a subjective level I can say that I dislike songs that are riddled with clichéd and hackneyed expressions and prefer lyrics which present well-worn subject matter in new and interesting ways, I can't say so objectively. Look at my previous sentence and note that I can only speak for myself when I define *cliché, hackneyed, well worn* or *interesting*. I might listen to a love song and pull faces as I get on my high horse and exclaim that I've 'heard it all before'. But I've heard thousands of songs in my lifetime, most of them pop, so that's bound to be the case. Can I say with any authority that 13-year-old me who *hadn't* heard thousands of songs before would say the same thing? Or would this love song seem new and interesting to me, and express sentiments I was myself just coming to terms with? And in a *new* way, because it was new to me? Straightaway we see that I can't even confidently determine cliché within my own listening experience, so how can I determine it on behalf of anyone else? Well, it's worth taking a look at.

In his book *Writing Better Lyrics*, Pat Pattison (2009) gives a list of clichéd phrases, rhymes and images, and we can see the point he is trying to make, even if he may well have been more accurate in titling the list 'most used' words and phrases. To make my point, it's evident by looking through the list that the majority of them are present in Beatles songs. So it seems in hindsight, then, that The Beatles look to have written 'clichéd' songs, when the reality is that, in a number of instances, they were among the first acts to use these 'clichéd' phrases – so, at the time, they weren't clichés! I'm aware that there is some hypocrisy to what I'm saying, because in my own writing I try to steer clear of cliché, but there have been many occasions where I have been trying so hard to avoid them that I've ended up writing something that seems forced and mechanical rather than free and honest; and I am sure the same has happened to you, too. Besides, who's to say that anyone else would see the 'clichés' from my original version as clichés anyway?

Having said all this, as a writer it's useful to be aware of what's been before, but, to quote an old songwriting friend of mine, 'we need to be self-aware, not self-conscious', meaning that if we want to be honest and upfront in our lyrics rather than working ambiguously via cloaked metaphors and symbolism, we should do so. Pattison makes a good point that clichés are prefabricated and use other people's emotions, not your own (Pattison 2009: 48), but his point that when generic language is used, listeners fall asleep (2009: 48) seems to ignore why a lot of music sells in large quantities: familiarity, accessibility and formula.

A good way of avoiding cliché is to put ourselves wholeheartedly into songs and write in an 'extreme realism' fashion, but this obviously won't appeal to some, and as we've seen in the chapter on biography, writers can never wholeheartedly give themselves up to a song and may not *want* to, even if it were possible.

> Regardless of how we define art or artistry, the very concept of writing a story seems to have implicit within it the notion of finding techniques of expression that will make the work accessible in the highest possible degree.
> (Booth 1961: 105)

On occasion, I listen to a song for the first time and am able to pretty much guess what the next line will be before I've even heard it. This might be due to the rhyme scheme or rhyme types being used, or the subject matter, or the storyline itself. Often it is a mixture of all three. And often, these are the songs that go on to become extremely popular and sell in vast quantities. Now, I'm not suggesting that songwriters *should* try to be clichéd or formulaic in their writing, but really popular songs do usually seem to have an element of the familiar to them, and we should consider this when we critically analyse lyrics.

> Listeners make associative links between musical elements that are present in any given piece, and at the same time make associations with similar or functionally equivalent elements or gestures in the wider repertoire of music with which they are familiar.
> (Dibben 2012: 346)

In its one-star review of the band Haim's album *Something to Tell You*, the I Newspaper says, 'The titles tell their own story: "Ready For You", "Right Now", "Walking Away", "I Want You Back" . . . it's like the song-writing equivalent of a child's colouring book' (Gill 2017: 37).

In literary theoretical terms, structuralist critics look for the various similarities between texts, going as far as to suggest that 'the nature of every element in any given situation has no significance by itself, and is in fact determined by its relationship to all the other elements involved in that situation' (Hawkes 1997: 17). Similarly, if we focus here upon the 'commonness' in pop music, where writers draw upon a variety of conventions or tropes in order to create a stability and uniformity of structure and subject matter, we will see that a great deal of pop music adheres to certain formula.

If we look at pop music over the last 60 years, we will see it is a medium that is built on a foundation of formula and repetition. Watch the Axis of Awesome's brilliantly entertaining *4 Chords* (2011) video, and we see how the same chord sequences are recycled endlessly, and the same goes for song lyrics. The *detail* within the songs will change over time, as technology changes and fads and fashions come and go, but the root themes stay largely the same.

> 'True Colours' was the work of Tom Kelly and Billy Steinberg, writers of Madonna's 'Like a Virgin'. Steinberg had intended it to be a song about his mother, but Kelly persuaded him to broaden its subject to universal sympathy.
>
> (Dimery 2013: 58)

Levitin notes that 'Safety plays a role for a lot of us in choosing music' (Levitin 2008: 242–43) and that music that involves too many chord changes, or unfamiliar structure, can lead many listeners straight to the nearest exit or to the 'Skip' button on their music players (Levitin 2008: 237). It might well be that safety plays a role in a lot of people *writing* music, too.

> BBC News recently ran a report on the amount of professional song-writers used to create certain hits, with some being experts in beats and grooves, some working on melodies, and some bringing the key moment, the hookline, written by specialists known as top-liners.
>
> (McAlpine 2010)

The music industry is now even using 'writing camps', 'where dozens of producers, musicians and "top-liners" (melody writers) create an endless array of songs, usually for a specific artist . . . [often giving briefs, like] . . . This song should be uptempo, sassy, girl-meets-guy' (Savage 2017). Will Hodgkinson also draws attention to the issue of songs by successful modern artists (he lists Ed Sheeran, Adele, Sam Smith and Emeli Sandé as examples) being written by 'teams of professionals' which 'may work as radio-friendly pop, but . . . won't reveal much about the human condition' (Hodgkinson n.d.).

Commercial success would suggest that lyricists need to keep their lyrics broad and accessible, writing about a theme almost everyone can identify with (particularly love, loss, sex, or dancing), use perfect end rhymes, have a defined verse/chorus structure and include at least an extra 'hook'.

When looking at the Top 40 best-selling singles of the twenty-first century (*Telegraph* n.d.), it is evident that most songs revolve around only a handful of different themes, with relationships (including love and break-ups) accounting for 24 songs.

The same is true when looking at any given singles chart (historically the determiner for what actually defines 'popular') from the last 50 years:

The most popular themes for songs in the UK Top 40 singles charts between 10 June 2016 and 16 June 2016 were as follows:

- Relationships (a major specific theme for 23 songs)
- Dancing (8)
- Sex (8)
- Money (7)

If we include 'sex' in the relationships category, then 78 per cent of the songs in this Top 40 revolved around this subject.

It is also worth noting that Sex, Money, Love and Dancing appear in a number of titles.

Top Forty of 9 June–15 June 1966:

- Relationships (including love and 'break-ups' – a major, specific theme for 25 songs)
- Regret (7)
- Sadness (4)
- Desperation (4)
- Longing (2)

The difference between this and 50 years ago? Mainly sex, money (usually boastful in 2016) and dancing. Relationships and break-ups have remained a constant popular theme.

Lastly, to compare 2016 and 1966, the Top Forty 9 June 1991–15 June 1991 shows that:

- Relationships (including love and break-ups) was a major theme for 20 songs, with sex a major theme for 7.

> Many of popular music's most memorable and emotional songs deal with the sexual, lustful side of love. 'As soon as music first emerges in cavemen and it has a rhythm', Rodney Crowell says, 'you have the sense of *sex* in it, because what is the most obvious human activity that has a rhythmic component?"
> (Levitin 2009: 277)

A selection of lyrics from the top 20 bestselling songs of the twenty-first century:

- 'I'm gonna give my heart away/And pray we'll stay together' – 'Evergreen' (Young 2002)
- 'I had hoped you'd see my face and that you'd be reminded/That for me it isn't over.' – 'Someone Like You' (Adele 2011)
- 'Oh, my, love, my darling I've hungered for your touch' – 'Unchained Melody' (Gates 2002)
- 'Gonna tell her that I'm sorry for the pain that I've caused' – 'It Wasn't Me' (Shaggy 2000)

- 'Nothing feels right, but when you're with me/I make you believe that I've got the key' –'Moves Like Jagger' (Maroon5 2011)
- 'Every night/Every day/Just to be there in your arms' – 'Can't Get You Out of My Head' (Minogue 2001)
- 'Her lips, her lips/I could kiss them all day if she'd let me' – 'Just the Way You Are (Amazing)' (Mars 2010)
- 'Turn away 'cause I need you more/Feel the heart beat in my mind' – 'We Found Love' (Rihanna 2011b)
- 'I won't tell you that I love you/Kiss or hug you' – 'Poker Face' (Lady Gaga 2008)
- 'I'm not here to let your love go/I'm not giving up oh no' – 'That's My Goal' (Ward 2005)
- 'When I'm with you I am filled with emotion/Can't you see that I'm giving you devotion' – 'Pure and Simple' (2001)
- 'And right now there's a steel knife, in my windpipe/I can't breathe, but I still fight, while I can fight – 'Love the Way You Lie' (Eminem 2010)
- 'I want you to love me' – 'Only Girl (In the World)' (Rihanna 2010)

All of these use different ways to express love (or the loss of love), and many contain awkward or forced rhymes, clichés and images that are so familiar to us we could recite them in our sleep. This reaffirms the notion that formula and popularity are connected, that cliché and the generic are often obligatory to making a simple connection with a listener, and that pop music discusses the same things over and over again, just in different ways and with different perspectives. For those of us who love song lyrics and admire the artistry of original turn of phrase, experimentation, idiosyncrasies and aesthetics, these may raise the blood pressure somewhat. But none can deny the statistical facts: these lyrics have underwritten songs that have sold in their millions.

Ultimate clichéd phrasing

Phrasing isn't exempt from the cliché idea, and we can look at this too:

'Forever as One' – Vengaboys (2000)

> 'And it cuts like a knife
> I'm going insane
> Wishing you would show me love once again

I'm losing my mind
But I have to carry on
We were meant to be together
Forever as one'

Pros: Instantly accessible as we've (likely) heard every phrase before. No
confusion.
Cons: As we've (likely) heard every phrase before, it may lose all meaning
and thus fail to impact upon us as a result.

Original ways to talk about love

Morrissey – 'First of the Gang to Die' (2004a):

'You have never been in love
Until you've seen the sunlight thrown
Over smashed human bone'

Arctic Monkeys – 'Suck It and See' (2011):

'You're rarer than a can of dandelion and burdock . . .'

REM, 'At My Most Beautiful' (1998):

'At my most beautiful/I count your eyelashes secretly.'
Pros: Phrases we won't (likely) have heard before, so it brings a freshness
to the subject matter.
Cons: These images may be so foreign to us that we don't make the connection between them and love, and they fail to impact on us as a result.

As Billy Bragg says, 'If you're angry about the world, you don't need to
learn how to play the guitar, or write songs . . . you can start a Facebook
page, write a blog or make a film on your phone; there are other ways that
people have to express anger' (Walsh 2017: 34–35).

Does this mean that our lyrics are naturally going to become more
'throwaway', and have less importance as the social media age continues?
Will pop stars save their political voice for the instant media of Twitter and

Facebook instead of taking stock, reformatting, and putting into song? The answers are not readily at hand and are probably the remit of another book. If we look at the lyrics of the above artists, we can see that they are generic enough for anyone to bond with yet, especially in the cases of Adele and Taylor Swift, give the impression that we are being presented with something personal, heartfelt and very individual. Breaking down some of the lyrics, though, it is evident that broad brushstrokes have been used to make them as accessible as possible to as many people as possible, thus alienating few and maximizing sales potential. By keeping the themes to extremely generic areas like break-ups, loss and regret, they are tapping into shared experiences which the majority of people have felt in some respect, even if not in the same way as the artists themselves. So, as it's non-specific in its actual content, Taylor Swift's 'Bad Blood' (reported to be a song 'about' a falling out with Katy Perry) can be applied to any falling out a listener has had, and 'We're Never Getting Back Together', can be applied to any break-up. The same goes for Adele's 'Someone Like You', 'Hello', 'Rolling in the Deep' and so on. Everything in these songs is designed to allow listeners to say, 'That's *so* right', then apply it to their own experiences and circumstances.

In 2009, Swift entered into a three-month relationship with US singer-songwriter John Mayer, which ended in February 2010. Later that year, Swift penned the track 'Dear John', which included the lyrics: 'Dear John, I see it all now that you're gone/Don't you think I was too young/To be messed with?' Mayer later said that the song "humiliated" him, and branded it "cheap songwriting" (Smith 2016).

Even though it actually included the supposed 'target's' name, the 'Dear John' letter itself (an idiom that points to the ending of a relationship) makes it generic, and the lines themselves reinforce this. Only the biographical material surrounding both artists brings the personal issue to the fore.

Let's take a moment to look at 'Bad Blood' (Swift 2014) as a specific example. In time-honoured tradition among the music press, its 'about-ness' is front and centre in any analysis, evidenced in two of the first articles to appear in a Google search: *Rolling Stone*'s 'The angriest song on *1989* is called "Bad Blood," and it's about another female artist Swift declines to name' (Eells 2014) or *The Mirror*'s 'Why Bad Blood Is REALLY about Katy Perry – The Complete Timeline' (Shenton and Wilson 2015).

If we look at the lyrics, however, rather than beyond (and into the surrounding material), there is nothing in them at all that can't be applied to any situation where there's been a falling out and/or animosity in a relationship (be it platonic or romantic). For example:

'Now we got problems/And I don't think we can solve them/You made a really deep cut' can be applied to any situation where pain has been caused.

'Did you have to ruin what was shiny? Now it's all rusted' can refer to any situation where something once good has turned bad.

'Did you think we'd be fine? Still got scars on my back from your knife' can be attached to any betrayal one has experienced (taking knife to be metaphorical and not literal, of course).

Let's take a look at the specific language and phrasing in two Green Day songs.

Firstly, 'Still Breathing' (2016) from the album Revolution Radio. Most of the phrases in this song are easy to understand, deliberately so, perhaps, as Armstrong is using similes to make the images so. They're not specific to him; they are collective images and phrases used to ensure everyone pictures (and, more importantly, feels) the same things.

If we isolate each one, we can get at the impact each line is supposed to have, but which uses simile instead of direct statement to either have more impact or be more aesthetically appealing within the song:

- 'I'm like a child looking off in the horizon'
  First line in the song, so it can get away with being a little ambiguous here. Unlike most of the phrases in the song, this line could mean a number of things, from 'being contemplative' to 'feeling isolated' to 'feeling calm'.
- 'I'm like an ambulance that's turning on the sirens'
  Way more direct here. Not many could argue that such phrasing would conjure up words such as danger *or* emergency. *But how does the simile work here when it compares a person (the singer/narrator) to an inanimate object? I am danger? I am in* danger? *I am struggling? I am someone who is beginning to struggle badly?*

- 'Oh, I'm still alive'
  The important word here is still. *Using* I am *instead would work from a syllabic perspective (separating* from *the contradiction gives us that extra syllable), but the word* still *really has an impact, suggesting that there is some kind of triumph over adversity, perhaps in spite of what's happened in the previous lines? If we look back now, then, the first line, which was ambiguous on first glance, almost* has *to take on a slightly negative meaning, if the narrator is 'still alive' in spite of what has happened. So . . . we would probably be drawn to a feeling of being isolated or lost, the next line then adding some kind of struggle.*
- 'I'm like a soldier coming home for the first time'
  Staying in context with what's been before, and, indeed, reading down to a repetition of the 'I'm still alive' line, we might well take this one as being another negative despite it being a potentially positive image. Our actual interpretation of this will depend heavily on our experience with soldiers, *ranging right from having actually been one to knowing only what we've read in the press or seen on TV. If we go with the vague understanding gained from the media, we might look toward a feeling of trauma or confusion.*
- 'I dodged a bullet and I walked across a landmine'
  Near misses. The first clause outright states this with the verb dodged *and the second implies it by the fact that the narrator has walked across a landmine and is 'still alive'. This is real stock imagery coming into play here, with 'dodged a bullet' being an extremely well-known phrase, and landmines linked with danger of serious injury. To have avoided* both *would mean that the narrator is very fortunate indeed. Perhaps we* are *moving into positive territory, now, with the narrator being thankful for surviving despite all that's happened.*

The pre-chorus section is also very heaving on stock imagery:

- 'Am I bleeding from the storm?'
  'Just shine a light into the wreckage'
  In this case, the storm *is simply a reference to some kind of struggle, and the* bleeding, *the impact it's had on our narrator. 'Shine a light' means to offer hope, and* wreckage *is the narrator's life.*

If we were to rewrite this first verse and pre-chorus to deliberately avoid simile and symbolism, we would have something like this:

> I am isolated I am distant
> I am struggling and now I am in danger
> Oh, I'm still alive
> I am confused and traumatized
> I have survived some near misses
> Oh, I'm still alive
>
> Am I damaged?
> Am I damaged from the struggles I have faced?
> Offer some hope to my ruined life
> So far away, away

The difference between the two? The original lyrics offer more chance for listeners to build a relationship with the song because they're actively participating in its meaning by both picturing the scenarios Armstrong has detailed and, probably in subsequent listens, trying to figure out what the similes are referring to. No words are foreign to us, so we aren't removed from the song in trying to figure them out, but they will potentially take on further meaning once our relationship with the song has formed and we have the freedom to explore the lyrics a bit more. The melody of this song is catchy, the backing pretty simple, and it's designed to be memorable very quickly (presumably why Green Day released it as the album's first single).

The (rewritten) direct lyrics speak to us about a very particular character (this will invariably be the narrator; see chapter about perspectives in song) so we are less likely to visualize ourselves, and there is no work to do in order to figure out meaning as the words are so direct.

So, in some cases, ambiguity can enhance a song, but it's always worth considering whether you are being *too* basic and obvious with your stock images. The pros are that with something like 'dodged a bullet' the listeners understand the reference instantly, allowing them to bond with the music rather than having to work on understanding the lyrics. The cons are that listeners will feel they've heard all this before and that it has nothing new to say to them. As with everything, it will all depend what a listener wants to get out of a song.

Our second example sees Green Day being more specific within their lyrics. If we consider the first verse (and refrain) of their song 'Wake Me Up When September Ends' (2004) from their album *American Idiot*, there are *some* phrases in this that we can immediately 'get' (we can all imagine summer coming to a close and moving toward autumn, for example), but other lines cut us adrift a little more:

> Like my father's come to pass
> Seven years has gone so fast
> Wake me up when September ends

None of this is generic phrasing. If we were to go searching for the context of the song (and it doesn't take long to discover Armstrong wrote it about the passing of his father) and then turn it into something with a 'mass meaning', we would have something like:

> My father died seven years ago
> It's gone so quickly, but still hurts
> Wake me up when I've had time to grieve

The meaning of the song was so ambiguous, in fact (especially when taken alongside its music video) that many interpreted it as a song detailing 9/11. Consider, if we had only *heard* the song, too, and not seen the lyrics, the apostrophe in *father's* would be impossible to detect, and the listener might hear *fathers*, making the song a collective loss, in spite of the personal pronoun *my*. So, although this song *seems* more specific on the surface, Armstrong has written it with enough ambiguity to allow multiple readings.

The use of pronoun could be important in comparing these songs, too ('a child'; 'an ambulance'; 'a soldier' – all unspecific – vs '*my* father'; 'wake *me* up'). We automatically refer personal pronouns back to the singer, too.

Stock phrases in songs will continue as long as the public are buying songs with stock phrases. Songwriters must make a conscious decision about what they want their lyrics to *do* – therefore, whether that is to be infectious and 'instant' (most easily achievable with recognizable syntax, stock images and perfect rhyme) – or to be more original in their writing but risk creating a distance between them and the listener. This doesn't mean, of course, that familiar imagery can't be new and exciting; that all depends on how the material is presented by the lyricist (note, I'm not really discussing the production here, which is the quickest and easiest way to make a song sound 'different').

Genre

In a question-and-answer interview with Bob Dylan for bobdylan.com, Bill Flannigan (2017) framed the following question:

> From the 20s into the early 50s, the line between blues and pop and country and jazz was very flexible. Robert Johnson, Jimmie Rodgers, Bing Crosby, Ray Charles, all tried their hand at everything. Why do fences come up between different styles of American music?

Dylan replied, 'Because of the pressure to conform.' This typically droll response actually says a great deal. Genre doesn't really have a huge amount to do with the art of songwriting. What it does have to do with is targeting songs for the audience who will listen to them and conforming to the audience's expectations. It is the pigeonhole songs are inserted into – blues, bottom left; hip-hop to the right; rock and roll, just over there; country, next to blues, but not on the jazz side. Some audiences like to take a tour – a bit here and a bit there; some like a mix, jazz-funk. 'Where will I put Jason and the Scorchers, boss?' By the rock-abilly, next to the bluegrass – no, the country; no, the punk . . . 'What about Prince, Seasick Steve, Tom Waits, Incubus, Los Lobos?' Well, as you can see genre becomes a little confusing. And yet if pushed, we could all give some rough answer if asked, 'What is your favourite music genre?' We have some ideas already what it or they are and who falls into those categories. But by now the categories, though blurred along the edges, are categorizable in some way.

This isn't meant to imply writers don't necessarily enjoy the genre they find themselves in, but actually it's harder to pigeonhole writers than particular songs. At the beginning of his career, Bob Dylan belongs firmly in the folk songwriting tradition that contained the likes of Woody Guthrie, Pete Seeger, Ramblin' Jack Elliott, Dave Van Ronk, Tom Paxton and Phil Ochs, but he soon (and famously) put that to the test as his career took off. Even if we might find it hard to fit certain artists neatly into certain genres, a lot of their songs can be categorized. It is an over-simplification to say it, but there are essentially two kinds of songwriter. There are those who write the songs, put them out there and then find their work categorized by their record label/management/media/fans after the event. Then there are others who are particularly targeting and even exploiting a specific genre itself (and this can be pop music, country, jazz or whatever). We will address both of these issues, but of course it's not an unambiguous, polar-opposites issue.

Looking back at the period Flannigan refers to in his article, 'the 20s into the early 50s,' his 'flexible' versus 'fences' idea is an apples-and-pears comparison because we are looking at a different world from the one we live in now. That was a world of radio and early television. Popular singers (and the emphasis has to be on popular because it's those we can reasonably track in this context) sang the songs they were given, or liked or chose without having to worry too much about crossing those lines. But let's not be coy: these radio and television stars did not fully represent the kind of songs being sung in blues bars, jazz clubs, night clubs, working men's clubs, country fairs, folk clubs, churches and the like. As both Dylan and Flannigan admit here, the lines did exist. As the fifties moved forward, jazz, blues, gospel, country, rock and roll, folk, pop and rock were all definable genre terms, and of course, as with all of these things, terms can then be subdivided 'Genre is a cultural practice . . . ,' said John Fiske (1987). '[It] attempts to structure some order into the wide range of texts and meanings that circulate in our culture for the convenience of both producers and audience.' We, all of us, who consume songs are pointed in a genre direction for our own convenience. We can hardly expect to walk into Ronnie Scott's Club in London and ask them to take jazz off the jukebox. Of course the rise of the singer-songwriter, like Dylan himself, coming out of the protest/folk Leadbelly, Woody Guthrie, Pete Seeger route, began to express through their own creative processes what those defining lines and markets were. But this still has its problems; the audience who like Patty Griffin or are looking for a new song by her, for example, will be pointed to the country section or perhaps the subgenre now labelled 'Americana', and internet searches will suggest a 'listeners also bought' list in the genre she has been placed, even if she doesn't present an authentic country voice. It isn't rocket science, though. Why would a fan spend time searching the jazz section for such a choice? But let's address the defining principles behind genre in relation to authentic songwriting and songwriting for a particular genre (which are not mutually exclusive).

It is easy to argue that the defining principles which frame high and low culture with all the value judgements that those terms express is a huge panoply of culture bookended by those terms. Using *opera* as a bookend and *bubblegum pop* as the other (and we are not being snobbish about this; it is just for the sake of an analogy), we get a common and understandable high-and-low-culture idea. However, for the purpose of this exercise, we would like to address it another way, which is one bookend being *original invention* and the other *organized convention*. At one end we have the innovative and unique, and at the other the manufactured or contrived formula, and it's useful for a songwriter to consider this. In the same way that cliché can come as a breath of fresh air to a reader or listener (to coin a cliché we usually avoid like the plague) the formulaically structured song can have a similar appeal. However, it is impossible not to consider this as a sliding scale rather than a brick wall of meaning – and few of us need reminding of the power of the verse, chorus, verse, chorus, bridge, verse, chorus and repeat formula. The difficulty with defining songs in this way is that although it pushes them into characteristic categories and genre boundaries, those boundaries are forever fluid and always shifting, until all we can really put forward is the idea that they are rubbing up close to each other.

When writing about film, Stephen Neale (1980: 6) states, 'Genres are not to be seen as forms of textual codifications, but as systems of orientations, expectations and conventions that circulate between industry, text and subject.' A similar thing can be said for songs, but it isn't quite as simple as this. Making films is a huge industry which requires the genre definition to be established even before filming starts – even raising the money demands it. Working in a songwriting genre, though, is much simpler, and indeed textual codifications are common. We could simply say we want to write songs like our heroes, Morrissey or Neil Young or whoever, but we can also see our songs coming out of the streets, locations or even ideas we were brought up in. For example, the 1960s Mersey sound (Liverpool) came from a specific location (hence the textual codification idea); or the original hip-hop was a subculture and art movement which developed in the Bronx in New York City during the late 1970s but soon spread across inner-city United States and into the United Kingdom. Therefore, as Fiske says, songs can also be inter-textual and even pre-textual – pre-textual in the sense that a songwriter can be immersed in the culture of the songwriting (such as the Mersey sound) or intend to address the genre when coming to write a new song. You don't have to live in the Bronx to engage with hip-hop culture. In my own youth, it was a case of a couple of us having acoustic guitars and enjoying that kind of music, so we gravitated to a mixture of traditional folk, singer-songwriters and what now passes for Americana (if that can actually be a description of anything, including a genre). But if I say, right now I am going to write a country song or a rap song or a cock-tail jazz number, then I have entered into a pre-textual contract with the genre. To this end then, song genre allows us to prioritize the familiar. It allows us to prioritize the similarities between one song and another in the chosen genre by working through the structural tropes and con-ventions an audience has come to expect. Indeed, this idea is explored in the marvellous Coen brothers' movie *Inside Llewyn Davis* (2013), which was partly inspired by the autobiography of folk singer Dave Van Ronk just at the point when the singer-songwriter, in the shape of Tom Paxton, Phil Ochs and Bob Dylan, began. And of course, in thinking about genre, Bob Dylan started his songwriting career as a fan of Woody Guthrie and the kind of genre he was working in.

Another thing that has to be considered is how genres have changed through the years, because this isn't static. Take rhythm and blues which originated in the United States, with its stylistic roots in blues and gospel, then incorporated soul music in the sixties via Sam and Dave, James Brown, Jackie Wilson, Otis Redding, Sam Cooke and Marvin Gaye, before morphing into R&B in the United Kingdom with the likes of the Rolling Stones and the Animals (for example), Writing today, the term *R&B* has now morphed beyond its simple meaning of 'rhythm and blues' into 'contemporary' R&B, which fuses (among other things) pop, soul and hip-hop, growing the extended family to gather with the likes of R Kelly, D'Angelo, Usher and Michael Jackson. And of course there are many easy ways to track this kind of progression. The easiest is in the influences you can trace through generations – Simon and Garfunkel after the Everly Brothers; The Beatles moving on from teenage skittle via Little Richard, Buddy Holly and Elvis Presley; the Rolling Stones with Muddy Waters, Chuck Berry and even Hank Williams as antecedents; and of course, 'even punk, despite all its posturing and claims of raw expression, found its roots in the same music as its predecessors' (Rachel 2013: XV). We could keep this family tree going through the generations until we get to the present day – and as we write, a *Guardian* newspaper headline asks, Is Harry Styles the new David Bowie (or not)? (Ellen 2017). In the song *Thank Me Someday*, Buddy Guy charts the progress of his own life from humble (read 'poor') roots, living in a little tent room shack on a cotton plantation in Louisiana, learning to play guitar on a two-stringed wood guitar, to becoming the successful songwriting performer he is today. The 70-year gap between the Buddy Guy of then and now (as we write) is palpable and quite unrecognizable, even though he is still working in his chosen genre of 'the blues'. What Buddy Guy shows is not only his longevity as a songwriter but also how he has ridden the changes as his chosen genre has transformed from then until now. And this is a crucial element, because he is still building on the old but bringing it up to date. In some way, then, it also says that being a genre songwriter can also ask you the question: 'So what are you bringing to the table that's new or are you just rehashing what is already there?' Even although you are engaged with the organized convention of the genre, is your song bringing its own original invention? But history and the progress of time isn't the only factor here.

Genres (and you can track this through films and other popular culture as well as songs) are also popular when they align themselves with the prevalent ideology of the time. For example, as we write this, Donald Trump is the president of the United States, and when he was running for election, he was doing so alongside the soundtrack which became the fastest-growing country subgenre, called 'bro-country'. Trump jumped on the blue-collar ideas of boots, alcohol, jeans, trucks, guns, girls and working hard, lining it up with the power chorus, the big punchline, usually with right-wing, nationalistic-style political leanings: 'Build a great a wall,' 'Make America great again', 'Drain the swamp.' And in this mix we can see how Bruce Springsteen's 'Born in the USA' (1984) is so inappropriately usurped, with people listening to the hook without realizing what the song actually means. 'Born in the USA', speaks of the harmful effects of the Vietnam War on American soldiers and also their treatment as veterans upon their return home. Indeed, it is so heavily laved with irony that the indifference and hostility with which Vietnam veterans were met is echoed in the song's subsequent misappropriation.

When we look to genre, then, we are also defining what kind of song-writer we are or want to be. Andrew Lloyd Webber is happy to cross genres with his various lyricists, Elton John and Damon Albarn have done the same. But if you are starting out as a songwriter, possibly even a singer-songwriter, you will be looking to enter a field that is already pop-ulated, but one that you want to be part of and whose music you like. So something you have to consider is the tropes that define that particu-lar field. And researching the tropes doesn't take a huge effort because you probably recognize them in the music you like. If you are a writer of love songs, for example, we have come a long way from 'moon in June' rhymes or starry-eyed clichés, but the romantic trope that is the 'moon' and 'stars' is timeless. Revisiting the assertion that, songwriters should be 'self-aware, but not self-conscious' in their lyrics means that although I may want to be open and honest in my songs, I might, for example, avoid writing about Satanism as a positive trait if I am an evangelical gospel songwriter, as my self-awareness shows that this isn't appropriate for the audience I am trying to reach.

So let's think about some tropes we could use – and of course play around with, and even distort. If you know what they are, you can break their rules, and this is a very good site to help you do that: http://tvtropes. org/pmwiki/pmwiki.php/Main/MusicTropes.

9

Impact: Subtlety versus Sledgehammer

Thinking versus feeling – should anything be avoided?

Some songs aim for pure impact to get a reaction, rather than making us *think* about what we're hearing. Where someone like Billy Bragg will write lyrics in order to raise awareness of certain issues, send a message and get people taking, others will go for the 'sledgehammer' approach; the assault on the senses which can't be ignored but makes us react rather than think.

Perhaps the most shocking song I've ever come across is 'Daddy' (1994) by Korn, which details the rape of a child by its father while the mother watches. What's the point of this song? Simply to shock? To raise awareness of child abuse? Just because we can write about anything, does it mean we have to?

Korn were clearly going for maximum impact with this song, evidenced by the musical backing, which starts as an a capella, gospel-like 'confession', with the son character using words absolutely full of pathetic language and imagery.

This section is followed by a few seconds of silence before we hear the instrumentation; first a very low, threatening bass line, then drums, wailing guitars, and a croaking, menacing vocal singing the lines 'Little child, looking so sweet/I rape your mind, and now your flesh I reap'. Again, lots of pathos, but whereas the introduction was attempting to elicit a feeling of sadness, these lines are intended to make the listener squirm, feel revolted, shocked or disgusted. Just the use of the words *child* and *rape* in the same sentence achieves this. For the chorus, the heaviness of the backing increases, and the singer switches to an angry, screaming style of vocal as he shouts the lines.

'Music is so powerful it can also work against a lyric's content, instead of with it. Generally, we expect words and music to be congruent, that is, pointing in the same direction' (Rooksby 2006: 96), but in this song, the lyrics rely on juxtaposition to achieve their shock value, contrasting innocence/purity with abuse/corruption.

- Innocence/purity: *love, sweet, pretty, play, innocent, child, daddy, mommy, mama, God, good boy*
- Abuse/corruption: *rape, dirty, fucked, scream, liar, hate, fucker, son of a bitch, ruined, pain, suffering*

The whole song, backing and lyrics, is an unsettling experience. Clocking in at 17 minutes 30 seconds overall, the last sung vocal line occurs at 5m 30s, after which is an extended four-minute outro section where the singer weeps, wails and shouts a number of expletives through his sobs as the guitarist scratches the strings, and the bass and drums continue. At one point, the instruments drop away, and we are left with the sobbing singer as a haunting female vocal joins, singing a lullaby (more juxtaposition, with it directly contrasting the violent music that has preceded it). At the end of this section is the sound of a creaking door, then four minutes of silence, followed by a three-minute 30-second conversation between an aggressive man and a scared woman apparently 'found in an abandoned house the album producer was cleaning' (Hidden Songs n.d.).

The juxtaposition in the music and lyrics, the discordance, the extended silence, the random conversation at the end: it's all working together to provide an experience, an experience which is confusing, uncomfortable and seemingly never-ending. Even when we think it's over and we're free from the nightmare (as it would be reasonable to suppose when silence follows a song), we're dragged back into it again. As a listener, I just wanted it to end, but that would be the point. We are trapped in this nightmare situation with the narrator. The whole song, therefore, could work as a metaphor for what the abused child is feeling, and the lyrics and backing are working together to achieve this.

This is a prime example of how lyrics are often reliant on the song's sound to achieve their overall goal. Put these lyrics to a different melody, with a different arrangement and different instruments, and limit it to a standard three-minute pop song, and a vast amount of its impact would be lost. Or it would at least be *changed*. Some reworkings and rearrangements of songs still have impact, but the overall feel is altered because of how the lyrics are working with the backing. For examples, listen to the Baseballs' doo-wop version of 'Bleeding Love' (2009), Ten Masked Men's Death Metal version of 'Baby One More Time' (1999) or any of William Shatner's spoken word covers.

Another very unsettling song is Lisa Germano's '… A Psychopath' (1994), and as with 'Daddy', much of the emotional connection with this occurs outside the lyrics, particularly via the recorded 911 call which plays throughout. The lyrics themselves would have some impact on listeners, as they have a foreboding feel to them, but they take on so much more significance when matched with the backing – both the 911 call, and the instruments themselves, which have a dreamlike quality to them. The vocal itself seems sedated, almost resigned; it doesn't have the fear in it of the woman on the 911 call, so is a different voice, a different perspective, but one which works alongside it to create an overall feeling. It brings sadness into the situation as well as fear, and the combination of the two is very effective.

Another song about abuse, Tori Amos's 'Me and a Gun' (1991), which tells the story of when she was raped at the age of 21, uses a different technique to have emotional impact on the listener. Amos sings the whole song a capella, and this forces us to listen to every single word and to note the emotion in her voice. There is nowhere for us to escape to as a listener, no guitar lines to analyse, no drums to tap along to, no countermelody or harmony. Just us and her voice, and it's a difficult listen because of this.

Getting us talking (and therefore reacting)

A songwriter that will forever be associated with his political activism is Billy Bragg, but he suggests that the songwriter's job may just be to start the discussion, to 'give people a different perspective of the world', and that 'if they want to change the world it's the audience's responsibility' not the artist's' (*Trailblazers* 2017).

I was lucky enough to be involved with songs for the album *This Changes Everything: 11 Songs about Climate Change*, but it was a challenge to write lyrics about this subject without sounding preachy. I decided early on that I'd take the approach where I would simply present and to think about the role of the songs within the world. As Joan Baez says, '[People] don't want to hear anything that they don't want to hear . . . You have to package it in a certain way so that it can break through the wall people put up' (Zollo 2003: 173), and this is fantastic advice from someone who has been singing protest songs for over five decades (check out her version of 'Joe Hill' I mentioned earlier – it is mesmerizing).

All of the songs I contributed were written in the first person, which meant that I was presenting a scenario, a character and an ethical dilemma and inviting the listener to form opinions accordingly, rather than going for the direct second-person *you*, which, I felt, would make the listener feel put upon, or guilty or lectured to. It was intended that the audience would participate in the song by passing judgement on the narrator and then looking inward when the points resonated. If I was using any technique of persuasion, it was via use of ethos, not because the listener needs to defer to the authority of the narrator, but because, through their eyes, they can identify with the emotion and confusion being put across. If listeners thus bond with the character because of their (often self-deprecating) honesty, they may think, 'Yeah, I'm like that' and then question whether they are happy with that or whether they want to consider change.

All songs use (or attempt to use) *deliberative* speaking in that they are urging us to think about how our current actions or inactions will impact upon our futures, and they are also *epideictic* in that they are trying to shape how we view our actions today by questioning our motives and moral judgements.

The song 'Lost' (Splendid Fred Records 2016b) explores how many of us are unsure how to act, or if we even want to at all. Specific pathos-strong words were used to elicit emotional responses (*nothing, devil, time apathy, moral, hell*):

> I stand at North Cape
> staring out of time
> into the nothing
> A rising feeling I'm
> Caught between the devil and my apathy
> Ozone moral hell

'Some Day' (Splendid Fred Records 2016c) looks at how we sometimes avoid the 'bigger picture' in order to give our loved ones a better lifestyle, regardless of how such actions may actually be ruining the world for future generations. Again, specific pathos-strong words have been used to make emotional impact (*arrogance, haste, deaths, blame, debt, rely on*):

> Our arrogance and haste may cause our deaths, but who's to blame?
> 'cause I'm in debt, pained to admit ethics are luxuries
> I can't commit to something that's so very far away
> And if I cared too much, I'd self-implode, my family rely on me . . .

The song 'Breed' (Splendid Fred Records 2016a) looks at perhaps the biggest issue of all: not just what world we'll be leaving for our children, but whether it's ethical for us to have them in the first place. Again – the first-person narrative sets this out as the narrator being the one who is open to having his or her decisions questioned, not the listener:

> I am gonna have kids, just to prove I existed
> I am gonna have kids irrespective of this mess

If there are gaps or provocative statements or things that we don't under-stand, it gets us talking. Take Rihanna's 2017 single 'Work' (2016), for example. On the face of it, it seems like an absolute throwaway lyric, where Rihanna is taking the 'any word will do', Will.I.am approach to songwriting. It may indeed be the case, but as Leila Noelliste points out in her article 'Unaware of Jamaican patois, critics blast Rihanna for speaking "gibberish" on her new single "Work"': 'Rihanna is not speaking gibberish, but Jamaican patois.' Noelliste goes on to give 'a loose translation in italics and parentheses' (Noelliste 2016):

> Work, work, work, work, work, work
> He said me haffi [He said I have to]
> Work, work, work, work, work, work!
> He see me do mi [He saw me do my]
> Dirt, dirt, dirt, dirt, dirt, dirt!
> So me put in [So I put in]
> Work, work, work, work, work, work [words in brackets from Noelliste]

Lisa Jansen comments, 'Whether she intends to actively highlight her ethnic background or uses Caribbean features as a stylistic device cannot be said for sure' (Gibsone 2016), but by using this technique, Rihanna is getting people talking about things they may previously have been ignorant of. And despite the actual lyrical content offering little substance, and still being relatively nonsensical despite this translation, it is still worthy of discussion, and this perhaps is its point. Lacing itself through this idea is diverse ethnicity and multiculturalism as a positive reflection of the modern world; and the more we are faced with what we don't understand, and learn from this experience, the more we begin to comprehend what an amazingly thing diversity is. It's all too easy to become embedded in our own cultural ghettos, and we have all seen too well how negative this can be. Look back at the musical influences and antecedents we have accepted from different cultures, and ask where we would be without them: jazz, blues, rock and roll, soul, reggae, country, folk, what has come to be known (in the West) as 'world music', bhangra – the list goes on and for the better.

Brevity

Something lyricists often strive for is the need to make their points as quickly as possible and to condense (as appropriate) storyline, character, political message into a short time frame. As Webb says: 'We must accomplish our aims and tell our entire story in a time frame of about three minutes' (Webb 1998: 37). Obviously, there are exceptions to this rule, perhaps evidenced most spectacularly through Genesis' 23-minute, 1,000-word epic, 'Supper's Ready' (1972), but for most writers, it's three minutes in and out, and even then, vocal time is shared with instrumental breaks, intros, outros and fade-outs, meaning we probably have, on average, a couple of minutes to say everything we want to say. Camp (2011: 96) suggests that 'good writers have a strong sense of how long their material will sustain the interest of their readers, and of how many words they need in order to tell a story as powerfully as possible'.

Anything that is said within a song, therefore, needs to be said with a real talent for succinct expression, and the ability to abridge lengthy, complicated narratives into their shortest possible incarnations. Will Self notes how Morrissey achieved this in the song 'Still Ill', where 'he is responsible – among other things – for encapsulating two hundred years of philosophical speculation in a single line: "Does the body rule the mind or does the mind rule the body, I dunno"' (Woods 2011: 165).

Breathing space

As songwriters, we have the option to create something like 'Subterranean Homesick Blues' (1965b), where there's barely time to draw breath (although Dylan does include the harmonica breaks to prevent the song from becoming too dense), or to create something like 'Echoes' (1971): a 20-minute song where there are lyrics for only two of those minutes. Sticking with Pink Floyd for a moment, look at the 'sung' periods in their albums *Wish You Were Here* (1975) or *Atom Heart Mother* (1970) versus *The Wall*. Floyd could write songs driven by music and songs driven by lyrics. But where lyrics are used, even sparingly like in 'Echoes' (1971) or 'Shine On You Crazy Diamond' (1975), these sections provide the climax or focus to the songs, almost as if (especially in the case of 'Echoes') the whole song is centred on these lyrical passages, even if they're fleeting. And writers can use this to their advantage, bringing in passages of lyric and moving away to instrumental breaks to create 'breathing space' for the songs.

Over the course of his career, Morrissey has used space and silences within his songs to build atmosphere. In the Smiths' 'Last Night I Dreamt That Somebody Loved Me' (The Smiths 1987), the introductory music continues for almost three minutes before the vocal comes crashing in. On first listen to it as a song, this may sound a little tedious and will undoubtedly have some people impatiently heading for the Fast Forward button, the impact of the sung section is arguably only so intense *because* of the experience of the instrumental section before it. In his solo career, he has used lengthy instrumental introductions on a number of occasions, in 'The Operation' (1995) (which includes a three-minute drum solo), 'Life Is a Pigsty' (2006) (three minutes) and 'I'm Not a Man' (2014) (one minute 30 seconds of background noise). On each occasion, especially with 'The Operation', the vocal comes as a relief and a release from the instrumental, and is a neat trick to immediately put us on the side of the singer for having 'rescued' us from the tedium that preceded their vocal section. Listen to these vocal segments in isolation, and they simply don't pack the same punch. Even Morrissey, who has used this technique more than many, knows that this isn't something to be done too often, though, and he will limit such a technique to one song per album (if employed at all). This says a lot about lyrical arrangement in the context of the song itself. Which is another important lesson to be isolated:

The lyric is a component of the whole song
and has to be seen in this context!

Some songs don't need a vast number of words either, and this 'sparing' approach can also be used in the lyric sections themselves. In Neil Young's song 'When the Morning Comes' (1970), he sings one line ('I'm gonna love you when the morning comes') over and over again, as the backing music changes around this refrain. If used once within an album of more conventionally structured lyrics, this really stands out and really works, but done too often, it will lose impact and mean a lyricist is unable to explore character or narrative. We can wonder, though, how much can be conveyed through a single line? This line of Young's is fairly generic, handling, as it does, the subjects of love and of night and day, but these 'condensed' lyrics can actually say a lot. Take 'The End' (1969a) by The Beatles.

McCartney had dabbled with extreme brevity on *The White Album* with the short tracks 'Why Don't We Do It in the Road?' (1968b), and 'Wild Honey Pie' (1968c), but with 'The End' (1969a) The Beatles employed the technique on a 'serious' song. Although not technically a one-line song because of McCartney's introduction ('Oh yeah/All right/Are you gonna be in my dreams tonight?'), all the impact of the song is realized within its final line, 'And in the end/The love you take/Is equal to the love you make'. Like Young's, this is a fairly generic observation concerning love, but given its place on the album, and listened to in hindsight, taking into account its place within the career of the band itself, its impact heightens dramatically, and it's famously become symbolic for providing a fitting bookend to the work of a group whose songs always focussed primarily on the subject of love. The fact that it's essentially a non-sequitur becomes largely irrelevant because its symbolism has outstripped the meaning of the words themselves.

The 'hot spice effect', for want of a better phase, is reliant on the music and instruments surrounding the lyrics, of course, and if a lyricist is a non-instrumentalist or non-producer, she is very much at the mercy of a collaborator in how successful such breaks will be. But being able to know when to give listeners time to reflect and when to bombard them with lyrics is something that can be used to very good effect. It can be limiting, yes, but it can also focus the mind of the lyricist, making him see the value of every syllable, and honing editing skills to the extreme. So, then, as songwriters, considering the gaps between the words and the verses/choruses/bridges can be almost as valuable as the words themselves, and a writer must always be looking at when to up the intensity and when to draw back from it to allow the listener 'thinking time'.

Exercise: Sum up the lyrical narrative of four songs in four words each.

Exercise: Look at these songs (or find some of your own) and analyse both lyrics and gaps, focussing on the relationship between the two and what impact this has on the listener:

'Breathe': The Prodigy (1997)
'Aneurism': Nirvana (1991)
'Around the World': Daft Punk (1997)

'Love in a Hopeless Place': Rihanna and Calvin Harris (2011a)
'Tubthumping': Chumbawanba (1997)

Exercise: Write a one-line song and play with the kind of impact you want it to have on the audience.

Exercise: Write down five things you would like to see change. These can be small and personal (e.g. 'I wish McDonald's Monopoly game for prizes went on longer), or bigger (e.g. immigration, hunger, climate change). From your list, expand each into a song, with each being a conversation where you try to persuade someone of your opinions.

Exercise: Write a set of lyrics that are knowingly controversial and inflammatory. Write in character if necessary, but deliberately try to upset people. Feel free to destroy the paper afterwards!

Part II

Speculations

Introduction

In a sister book to this, Amanda Boulter (2007: 105) discusses Frank Smith's three stages of writing:

- Pre-writing
- Writing
- Rewriting

It doesn't really matter what you are writing, this three-stage process is fairly similar in all cases, and in some ways this is the most important chart in the songwriter's book. The idea is obvious, but in paraphrasing Smith, Boulter says, 'Prewriting is the most mysterious, variable, and frustrating aspect of writing,' and 'rewriting is the writer's own response to what has been written.' However, writing, 'the slim and elusive filling in the sandwich', is the hardest thing to pin down. Think about how this affects you, because this section of the book addresses all three items, though not necessarily in any real order. That job can only be yours. What do you put in each category?

- Pre-writing – gathering ideas, notes, fragments of words, tunes, choruses, assorted rhymes you might like to adopt, assorted lines you have picked up along the way, thoughts on stories and metaphors and themes and subjects, and then making a coherent start.

- Writing – pencil to paper, voice to recorder, taking the first steps in pulling the fragments of your notes and so on (see above) into some kind of order and assembling the structured song, verse, chorus, bridge or so forth, thinking about the story, the images you want to convey, the effect you are trying to achieve.

- Rewriting – the best bit; it's the time when you sit with everything you have and hone the craft, polish the jewels and shine up the ideas, metaphors and punchy lines; trim the excess words, sharpen the chorus, tidy the bridge and so on; and then, finally, decide on the repetitions and individual characteristic that really bring out the essence of the song you are trying to capture and present in a public performance – whether it's 'Lovely Day' (Withers and Scarborough 1977) or Whitney Houston's version of 'I Will Always Love You' (Dolly Parton 1973)

Once you are clear about these points, the rest of this section will become obvious to you. In Part I of this book, we speculate on how the three stages of writing can work for the songwriter. We begin with pre-writing, but along the way we take tips from others who have been through this progression and have come through the other end. This process is designed to show how writing works, but also to remind you that if you just knock a song off, you get knock-off songs, and you are not really taking control of your art. And working on this idea of taking care of your art, although we don't subscribe to Gladwell's 10,000-hours rule (pretty well discredited),[1] we do consider practising your art to be a basic requirement.

Many of us begin as songwriters by copying, impersonating and even adapting the style of those we admire; there are obvious influences weaving through the song world, and it becomes clear that this is a part of learning the craft, honing the skills and beginning to branch out on your own. The Beatles did indeed have thousands of hours of playing and practising loads, but they were mostly playing other people's material

---

[1]http://www.businessinsider.com/new-study-destroys-malcolm-gladwells-10000-rule-2014-7?IR=T.

before they became the accomplished songwriters they went on to be. Similarly, Pablo Picasso didn't just turn up as an abstract or cubist or blue period painter; he put the hours in learning to draw, sketch, paint, sculpt and become an artist, who, like The Beatles, redefined the art itself.

Of course this is no guarantee anyone is going to like what you do. In today's (as I write) Guardian newspaper (UK), the highly respected songwriter Steve Earle is quoted as having said:

> Noel Gallagher is the most overrated songwriter in the whole history of pop music. They were perfect for the Brit press because they behaved badly and got all the attention. Blur were really great. That guy Damon Albarn is a real fuckin' songwriter. (2017)

Well, there are always going to be opinions – aesthetic choice insists on that, surely. All we can do is try to write the best song we can. And the first task is to address the inspiration which challenges us to write in the first place.

10

Inspiration and Ideas

I have often thought about these lines from T. S. Eliot's 'The Hollow Men': 'Between the idea/And the reality/Between the motion/And the act/Falls the Shadow.' (1925) There is something about the way they address the writer. We will talk about poetics later, but sometimes every songwriter might have an underlying idea of what these lines might mean to him or her. Jimmy Webb talks about them as being lines written by Eliot for other writers and asks the question, 'How do we get through Eliot's shadow zone and bring our songs to the light of day?' (1998: 5). How often have you had the perfect song in your head, the great idea, the big hit – you can hear it on the train or lying in bed or walking along Brighton sea front or driving the car – and Tom Waits tells a good story about being visited by the muse while driving (though I have taking it from someone else, and it may be apocryphal):

He was driving down the freeway one day . . . and he heard a little tiny trace of a beautiful melody, and he panicked because he didn't have his waterproof paper, and he didn't have his tape recorder, and he didn't have a pen, he didn't have a pencil – he had no way to get it . . . And he thought, 'How am I going to catch this song?' And he started to have all that old panic and anxiety that artists have about feeling like you're going to miss something, and then he just slowed down and he looked up at the sky, and he looked up and he said, 'Excuse me, can you not see that I'm driving? If you're serious about wanting to exist, come back and see me in the studio.

I spend six hours a day there, you know where to find me, at my piano. Otherwise, go bother somebody else. Go bother Leonard Cohen.'

(Gilbert 2011)

Of course, when Leonard Cohen was asked about inspiration he said, 'If I knew where the good songs came from, I would go there more often' (Appleford 2015). Well, it sounds like he should have sat at the bottom of Tom Wait's drive and watched as he took his car out, because, of course, Tom Waits was generous enough to give a good idea away when he had other things to do. Unfortunately, this isn't going to happen to you. There is no point in waiting outside the house of Paul McCartney, Mick Jagger, Elvis Costello, Randy Newman, Lucinda Williams or Steve Earle (you can write your own list); they are looking for the same thing as you and are not giving ideas away for free.

You know how it is, though: it's there, the tune, the chorus, the words – almost perfect, fully formed and dangling enticingly in front of you – but by the time you get down to working on it, it doesn't come out quite as you had hoped. Could that be the shadow Eliot refers to? The shadow which falls between the idea and the execution? Well, perhaps it's asking too much of a quotation out of context, but it does help as a metaphor when we are working on an idea we can hear in our own heads and still have the prospect of making happen as we hear it. That is what we are going to look at in this Part II of the book.

As referred to previously in Part I, Paul McCartney famously spoke about how 'Yesterday' came about, and it makes an interesting read because he had doubts about the song's veracity:

I woke up with a lovely tune in my head. I thought, 'That's great, I wonder what that is?' There was an upright piano next to me, to the right of the bed by the window. I got out of bed, sat at the piano, found G, found F sharp minor 7th – and that leads you through then to B to E minor, and finally back to E. It all leads forward logically.

(Miles 1998, p. 69)

Unfortunately, not all us are this lucky – or even dogged. As he also said:

For about a month I went round to people in the music business and asked them whether they had ever heard it before. Eventually it became like handing something in to the police. I thought if no one claimed it after a few weeks then I could have it. (Miles 1998, p. 69)

McCartney tells a similar story about dreaming a great song for the Rolling Stones and deciding it was probably one of theirs already, though he never found it. But you can see how even a top songwriter is riddled with doubt about the authenticity of his idea. This is even worse for the twenty-first century writer who can access new music instantly. In the case of 'Yesterday', the song hung around The Beatles camp for a long time and was known during the filming of the 1965 caper *Help*, as 'Scrambled Eggs' (which were the words before 'Yesterday' came about – both being three syllables when sung, namely scram-bld-eggs and yes-ter-day, and there is a lesson in the phonetics of songwriting here). McCartney worked out the sound he wanted, and then eventually the words came around. *Dum-dum-dum* or *lah-lah-lah* could become *scram-bld-eggs* and so on because he was thinking about how to fit words around the melody that asked for three syllables). It is a fairly common story, and even sharing it here almost seemed unnecessary. However, it reveals how, even at McCartney's creative peak, a song still needs to be nurtured. A lesser known example is McCartney's own description of writing 'Blackbird':

I developed the melody on guitar based on the Bach piece and took it somewhere else, took it to another level, then I just fitted the words into it. I had in mind a black woman, rather than a bird. Those were the days of the civil rights movement, which all of us cared about, so this was really a song from me to a black woman, experiencing these problems in the States: 'Let me encourage you to keep trying, to keep your faith, there is hope.'

(Miles 1998, p.153)

A 'black bird' could be (these days) a derogatory, colloquial term for a desirable/fanciable 'black woman', and I am almost embarrassed writing it here, except that this is an explanation. What can be taken from this is the process of gathering ideas, words and tune, and then getting them to all match up and still giving them meaning isn't easy, without encountering Eliot's shadow. It can be concluded that McCartney is a tunesmith and adapts or writes the words to fit, and these don't often come out of the kitchen tap. However, it also shows how he was able to move the colloquial (and certainly insulting term) into something 'other' and 'different' and much more interesting. But of course, other writers have different approaches, its all a matter of getting to where you want to be from whatever beginning you have.

When asked, 'Do you record yourself trying to find an idea?', the late Robin Gibb of the Bee Gees said, 'All the time. Barry and myself have a memo recorder on all the time because the simplest little melody here and there can sparkle, it can be a magical moment' (Rachel 2013: 33). Nick Cave's *The Sick Bag Song* (2015) gives a clue as to how highly he regards the idea and taking notes, written words and fragments down, even on an aeroplane, where literally anything to write on will do. Mark Knopfler described the writing of the song 'Money for Nothing,' (Dire Straits 1985) in a 1984 interview with critic Bill Flanagan. He talks of borrowing a piece of paper and starting to write the song down in a hardware store, using the words the appliance salesman (the central character in the song) was using while watching MTV on a bank of televisions so that he could keep it vital and of the moment; he wanted to use a lot of the language that the real guy actually used when he heard him. Indeed, the success of the song was very much linked with the 1980s rise as a consumer society, and the rise of MTV (the song launched MTV Europe), and MTV being mentioned in the song confirmed that consumerism idea. The fact is, he was able to write the idea down as it came, and at the time nothing else mattered. Circumstances dictate that you have to be open to the moment an idea comes to you, whether its watching some other guy talking about microwave ovens, refrigerators and colour TVs, or money for nothing and chicks for free. But Knopfler's adventure in a hardware store takes us to the reason we have the tools for recording the inspiration and ideas.

Were we to give the simplest and easiest advice before you start, it would be to make sure you have a notebook and pencil, a rhyming dictionary and a thesaurus close at hand. Using the notebook to sketch out, collect and collate ideas is as simple as it gets. 'When you have ideas how do you remember or capture them?' Rachel asked Ray Davies, who replied, 'It's a really good question. I literally do use serviettes in restaurants. I carry a bag around with me sometimes with various thick notepads. I've been a bit slack this year; I've only used two notepads up. There's always a few sheets of paper in my pocket' (Rachel 2013: 8). Of course in this, our present technological world, your smartphone can substitute because it is also your notebook, camera, tape recorder, internet access to a rhymes and thesaurus source (RhymeZone, http://www.rhymezone.com/, e.g.[1]) and can even record with drum patterns (Garageband, etc.) should you choose to access them. Most importantly, whether a piece of paper and a pencil or a handy electronic device, you should have a place where ideas and inspiration can be recorded. It is that simple, but don't just take our word for it – put it to use.

However, saying this is easy – and all books on writing song lyrics say something similar. Rickki Rooksby has a section in his book that offers '30 ways to find inspiration,' which is great. For example, no. 4 states, 'Try writing a lyric sketch in a public place. Bob Dylan is just one of those who would sit in a coffee-house for days at a time, looking at other customers, making up things about them and writing down whatever came into his head' (Rooksby 2006: 16). This is all very well, but What do we record? What do we write down? Then we come to that other great art question which songwriters are not exempt from; it's the question 'Where do you get your ideas from?' Well, all of us will have different answers. It's not always going to be the perfect rhyming couplet or literary metaphor, snappy title, great topic, teen dream stardust hook – or even the picture-perfect opportunity that has 'potential song' written all over it. It is literally the artistic switch that turns the light on with the word

---

[1] It's probably important to comment on the use of a rhyming dictionary here. Remember, it's just a tool and not the last word in rhyming (see below). Use it for ideas, but please don't fall into the trap of just accepting what is offered. Some of the best songs have been ruined because a forced perfect line, straight out of a dictionary, has been used. The cold, old moon in June is not necessarily the best way to go – but more about this later.

IDEA!

It's that moment when something comes out of nothing, the point where you have to write it down. For example, exactly what was going on when the words 'I am the walrus' came into being? Not 'I am the heartbreaker'; 'I am one of the broken-hearted'; 'I am the lonely guy in the heartache diner, hoping you'll be the right person to serve me coffee.' Let's begin by calling these the **fragments** that make the creative juices flow. Some may call them seeds; however, this suggests you can just pick them up, sow them and then watch them grow, but that's absurd, surely. We call them fragments because at this stage they are nothing else. Yes, they have to be nurtured and grown, but first of all they have to be recognized for what they are in the first place. So what we want to do is to get you to think around this, think laterally about what is taking place.

Fragments

Every artist, whether a painter, sculptor, novelist, poet. songwriter or some other creator, has been confronted by this question: 'Where do you get your ideas from?' This is often compounded by the viewer, listener or critic who says, 'I could do that!' The one we get is, 'I should write a book. I've got a good story to tell.' Here is the crucial point, though: if that person didn't do that, write that, make that, it's because he or she didn't have the idea in the first place. There is little point in saying, 'I'm going to write a 'Yesterday'-type song'; or 'I am going to write a song about boy meets girl, boy loses girl, then boy finds her again, and she is just head over heels in love with him' (happy ever after). These are not ideas; they are navel gazing, indolent musings, two guys chatting over beer-type cogitations and wishful thinking. It would be the guy quoted in the song, saying words like 'MTV and chicks for free,' then asking, 'What's so great about that? I could do that.' Ask an artist, especially a songwriter, to see her notebook, and you will see what fragments of ideas are. Our own notebooks for this book, let alone anything else we write, are full and even indecipherable to each other, far less others who might happen upon them. So let's think about some of these fragments that can bring about the start of an idea.

Fragment no. 1: Words

'Its only words,' wrote Barry, Robin and Maurice Gibb (The Bee Gees 1967). Words, the key constituent in any lyric – simple enough. We all know loads of them; there are many (maybe even too many) in this book, and for a songwriter it's just a question of getting the right ones in the right order. Well, we will discuss that a little later, because for now we are looking at 'words' as a source of inspiration, a starting point. But let's reiterate: writing words isn't about poetry, it is all about the song and the differences in the art forms. Even back in 1965, Bob Dylan was talking about this in a Q & A with Nora Ephron and Susan Edmiston:

Q: Do you consider yourself primarily a poet?
A: No. We have our ideas about poets. The word doesn't mean any more than the word 'house.' There are people who write _po_ems and people who write po_ems_. Other people write _poems_. Everybody who writes poems do you call them a poet? There's a certain kind of rhythm in some kind of way that's visible. You don't necessarily have to write to be a poet. Some people work in gas stations and they're poets. I don't call myself a poet because I don't like the word. I'm a trapeze artist. (Ephron and Edmiston 1965)

I like the trapeze artist idea very much, because that is what we all are, as we swing from subject to subject, thought to thought, looking for the elusive words that bring the song into being.

I write passing thoughts, overheard conversations, discovered quotations, advertising signs, mumbled threats, and words of kindness and endearment, on scraps of paper. Sometimes I mutter them into Dictaphones or record them on my answer-machine when there is not even an eyebrow pencil in hand to order to commit them to the page.
(Elvis Costello, cf. Rooksby 2006: 17)

Some tunes may get played and even described as songs, but I don't think there is such a thing as a song without words. Even Spike Milligan's 'The Ying Tong Song' (1953) had made-up ones, and indeed, *Sigur Rós was mentioned previously.*

Initially it can be a simple image, an idea or a couple of words. For example, you are riding the bus home when you see a poster, and a single word flashes out at you, or it just pops into your head while you are draining rice for dinner or flicking through a collection of Pablo Neruda's poems or queuing in the supermarket and someone mentions something had come to town; or you're just sitting in the corner, slumped over the guitar, piano, banjo, whatever, and it comes to you, the idea, the thought, the spark that lights the creative fire and says, 'There's a song here somewhere', so you reach out to grab it. You know how it goes; you can feel it beginning to bubble away, even though you're not quite sure what it is. Then again, what if it doesn't, and you are grasping around catching nothing but fresh air? Well, give it a push. Take a word that means something to you, something that you can build on, something you can develop. There are many easy and obvious ones: *love, joy, wonder, happy, sad, hope, misery, melancholy, dancing,* but think of something you can develop ideas around. I mean consider how many songs have rain as a central theme – the list goes on and on. It's not just about the weather, but a metaphor for many things life brings to our attention. There are many single words we can build ideas on; *rain* is an example, *summer* another; and how about *love, nature, mountains, lost, winter, silence, tale* and the single word *carnival* as an example:

Carnival: Just the one word. You are on the bus going into/home from town, and it catches your eye. So you remember it, write it down, type it into your tablet, speak it into your smartphone or whatever it is you do to record it. And then you spin it around, turn it upside down and inside out. *Carnival* – it's a decent word because it opens up much more than just eight letters grouped together. So ask yourself, what does it evoke, suggest, impress, put forward? What does it say? What does it endorse – that's a good way of thinking about it; does the image endorse ideas, behaviour and attitudes? What image does it conjure in your head? What images does it summon up for you? Well, map out some ideas. It has been suggested that Paul Klee said he began working by drawing a line and taking it for a walk. Try it out, sing over a chord, write the words down and then see where the association goes.

Verse or Version 1

Carnival ideas: cavalcade, parade, spectacle, pageant, pleasure, colour, fun, music, dancing, anticipation, excitement, celebration – add your own here.

What else? Go a little deeper, take a harder look at the idea:

Verse or version 2

Carnival –world upside-down, inside-out, topsy-turvy; no rules apply; desire, hedonism, decadence, chaos; excess of sex, drugs and alcohol – add your own here.

What else, well take it deeper still, keep digging and thinking about the direction you would like it to go in.

Verse or version 3

Carnival – half-empty glass, end of the day, everything comes to an end, broken promises, broken dreams, dashed hopes, betrayed boys, angry girls, heartache and rivers full of tears, Leonard Cohen's 'Famous Blue Raincoat' (1971) meets Hank Williams' 'Your Cheating Heart' (1953) in the bittersweet hall of pain as the happy celebration comes to an end and the reality of fickle love kicks in – add your own here.

or

Verse or Version 3

Carnival – half-full glass; a brand new start; lonely hearts meet; new love, cute boys, flirting girls; old friends reconcile, hearts full of tender thoughts and the moon hung low over the river never looked brighter; Charlie Chaplin telling you to 'smile' meets John Denver singing about sunshine on his shoulders where the world is a wonderful place to be, especially when love is in the air – add your own here.

It isn't so difficult to do this kind of sketch. But we can take this idea even further. If we think of the word *carnival* in a critical context, it is just a word and yet it becomes a suggestion where anything goes. Mikhail Bakhtin discusses the idea of *carnivalesque* and says, 'Carnival was the true feast of time, the feast of becoming, change and renewal' (Bakhtin 2008: 109). And he describes the carnival:

> as celebrating temporary liberation from the prevailing truth and established order, where everyone is considered equal. This temporary suspension, creates . . . a special type of communication not normally possible during everyday life. A 'world inside out' developed, with idiom filled the ideals of change and renewal.
>
> (Koning 2017)

And we can see how the songwriter can be part of the whole carnival idea, because songwriters engage with the prevailing culture of the day. Whether it be presidential politics or celebrating new year's day, the songwriter has something to say, so finding a topic to piggyback while saying it isn't really so hard.

Of course you can keep this whole 'carnival' thing going. Instead of settling for Verse 2, we could settle for the Version 2 of the ideas above and develop the lyrical context more; a lot of rock and roll has gone down this route. Sex and drugs and rock and roll, as Ian Dury sang, isn't all that original (although it's a great song from a great lyricist). We could even cut out the drugs and rock and roll – sex has a huge cache and in many guises. Through metaphor, for example, it was the squeaky clean popsters, The Carpenters who sang about space rockets in flight, surely an orgasm metaphor following afternoon delight (another metaphor), and we could take this through to the barely disguised metaphors in Led Zeppelin's 'The Lemon Song' (1969a), and of course we could move into James Brown and Barry White territory – or how about Lily Allen singing how her love life is just not fair? The crucial point here is that now you have the idea you can take it in many different directions and indeed use it with more than a single song. We have seen this done many times. The Irish singer, Mary Black, for example, has played around with the idea of 'The Holy Ground' (1993) in different ways (and in a different way from the Dubliners), and of course that title itself is slightly ironic and in keeping with the 'carnival' idea here because it has its roots in sailors and bawdy behaviour. The piece of ground in Cobh, County Cork, Ireland, known as the Holy Ground, was the town's red-light district in the nineteenth century. Then, it was known as Queenstown, and it was a major docking point for ships crossing the Atlantic, with the 'trade' that it would bring before and after a long sea journey.

Or we could take the single word further, on a more philosophical journey or a poetic or political one. What it takes is imagination in working the idea into something tangible and real which will appeal. Take *political*, for example. If you have seen the movie, *Selma*, you will know the civil rights marches are a kind of carnival event (using *carnival* in its broadest sense and in the way that Mikhail Bakhtin (1984), Allon White and Peter Stallybrass (1986) used it when thinking about *carnivalesque*). And once again we can try it:

> Verse or Version 4 – *Carnival* – forget the party, forget the fair, forget the circus over there, and think about the excluded, the woman, the gay, the black, the refugee, the kid who doesn't know it's okay to be queer, not one of us, not from around here.

Or even with laughter, as Bakhtin also wrote:

> It is one of the essential forms of the truth concerning the world as a whole, concerning history and man; it is a peculiar point of view relative to the world; the world is seen anew, no less (and perhaps more) profoundly than when seen from the serious standpoint. Therefore laughter is just as admissible in great literature, posing universal problems, as seriousness. Certain essential aspects of the world are accessible only to laughter.
> (Bakhtin 2008: 70)

There is no reason why humour can't be explored in this context. Or the cruelty of laughter, or the bittersweetness of it –and what about 'Send in the Clowns' (Sondheim 1973)? A carnival without clowns? To paraphrase, where are the clowns, there ought to be clowns . . . or even Tom Waits, with his narrator sitting in a bar with a beer (a carnivalesque idea) singing, 'I hope that I don't fall in love with you,' (1971) or indeed (and Bruce Springsteen after him) singing about taking his girl across the river to the carnival in 'Jersey Girl' (1981). But this is only one word, and already we have explored a myriad number of possibilities and ideas. Delving back to a distant past, The Seekers sang a number called 'The Carnival Is Over' (1965), which is actually a Russian folk song, adapted with English lyrics by Tom Springfield (brother of Dusty), circa 1965, and it basically addresses love and break-up – as in 'the carnival is over' – and indeed went on to become the 30th bestselling song ever. Not bad for a rewrite. But as Bob Dylan says, we are trapeze artists, we swing this way and that, grasping the air for anything that will stick and that we can use to wrap around a melody.

Fragment no. 2: Pictures

Once again, in this world of the smartphone and the ability to capture ideas instantly, I take photographs of anything I find interesting. I'm not really looking for the great photographic opportunity, but for something that contains the inkling of an idea. In the same interview as the one in which he called himself a trapeze artist, Dylan answered the following question:

Q: Burroughs keeps an album, a collection of photographs that illustrate his writing. Do you have anything similar to that?

A: I do that too. I have photographs of 'Gates of Eden' and 'It's All Over Now, Baby Blue.' I saw them after I wrote the songs. People send me a lot of things and a lot of the things are pictures, so other people must have that idea too. I gotta admit, maybe I wouldn't have chosen them, but I can see what it is about the pictures. (Cott 2006: 53)

Think of this as a pre-writing exercise – getting the picture to inspire the idea, not the other way around. I do a lot of walking and gathering (and visiting coffee shops, where I can listen to conversations, though I never tape them). But there is something wonderfully twenty-first century about being able to capture the image and having it instantly, without having to rely on the old Kodak Instamatic and wait to develop it or get it developed (with all the cost that entailed). We can see the image and capture it for later, load it onto Instagram or whatever and also, of course, plunder the internet images that already exist for ideas. I once did this with students by simply putting the word *Gothic* into Google, and – boom – we were offered more than 250 million results. But do your own research, and stay alert to things that interest you, at any time of the day.

(© Andrew Melrose 2017)

I woke up one morning in December, walked into my kitchen to make coffee and looked out of the window and saw this snow-covered chair which was sitting in my own garden. The image appealed to me, and as I snapped it I was flipping the story around in my head, mostly thinking about what it might say to a stranger.

It is just a table and chair after an overnight snowfall, and yet the story possibilities are immediately apparent,

- It's an 'empty chair', which conjures up all kinds of possibilities and possible metaphors. Why empty? Where are the people – the person who could sit here?

- It's only one chair at the table – loneliness, love lost perhaps?
- There is no one sitting on chair #1 – perhaps someone is missing, dead even, and there is heartache; and it's also a metaphor for the onset of a long winter ahead.
- There is no one sitting on chair # 2 – it's a metaphor of longing for the end of a long, cold winter when spring will return with fresh hope and optimism, and someone will return.

The chair ideas could go on and on. George Strait sings 'The Chair' (1985) as a country hit; Tears for Fears produced an album called *Songs from the Big Chair* (1985) Steve Winwood sang 'Vacant Chair' (1977), but go on – you know the list, and possibilities are endless, and the point is made. The chair itself is only a poke in the back that asks you to think about the ideas it holds.

These are two of my favourites in a series of pictures (I have a number of them) which I took during an arts festival in Arezzo, Italy. There was something surreal about the art installations themselves, but it was more than that. They seemed to say something about ordinary people being more extraordinary than their appearance suggested (see the note on tropes above). Once again what do these installations say about anything at all? In some ways, they remind me of René Magritte's *Golconda—Man*

(Both images © Andrew Melrose 2017)

Falling from the Sky (1898), but they do evoke thought and even humour, as well they might, because there was something funny about looking up and seeing them.

I could probably say immediately, 'Don't let the rain fall on me while I am falling from the sky', but they open up many ideas:

- 'Fly away Monday.'
- 'What else is there to do on a Tuesday but take to the sky?'
- 'Thank goodness it's Friday, and I can get out of here.'
- 'There's a hole in my shoe.'
- 'Flying is the only way to travel.'
- 'I can see you, but you can't see me.'
- 'I see you, but do you see me?'
- 'It's the only way to travel – Mary Poppins style.'
- 'Icarus, I know you were flying close to the sun, but I told you not to go out without your umbrella.'
- 'They thought I was just an ordinary Joe, bet they didn't see this coming.'
- 'Tom Petty sang 'Learning to Fly' (1991); Foo Fighters sang 'Learn to Fly' (1999); and Lenny Kravitz sang 'Fly Away' (1998).
- Guy Clark has a fantastic song on flying, called 'The Cape' (1995) (I especially like the version sung by Patty Griffin (2011), which you can find on YouTube) with the great lines:

All these years the people said
He's actin' like a kid
He did not know he could not fly
So he did.

The issue here is that it just needs a spark. Look for the unusual photo opportunity, and think about the image and the ideas it creates. That is what art is about; it is about reacting to life experience and twisting expectations, seeking out the intricacies that make us who we are. What was the spark that lit Clark's song – which begins with a boy tying a flour sack cape round his shoulders, climbing up onto the garage roof and jumping off? It may have been a true story from his own childhood or just an imagined idea of a boy who grew up to be a man. But when we read the lyric, it is actually more universal and about life as a leap of faith – though always trusting your cape does suggest there is an element of risk involved too:

> He's one of those who knows that life
> Is just a leap of faith
> Spread your arms and hold your breath
> Always trust your cape (Clark, Clark and Janosky 1995)

On a recent trip to the Guggenheim in Venice, Italy, I came across a neon installation. It was *Changing Place, Changing Time, Changing Thoughts, Changing Future* (2003) by Maurizio Nannucci, and the phrases of the title were lit up in neon lights. I'm not too struck by neon installations as a rule, although they can be like small poems in glass that light up, which has some appeal. I just liked the words and the immediacy of the word 'changing', which carries a new prospect with it, especially since we can adapt it to anything we like. Changing time – the times could be changing in a Bob Dylan kind of way; or me and you could have been heroes after ch-ch-changes and thinking about David Bowie.

- *Changing place* – By the time I get to Phoenix with Jimmy Webb (1967); I could have walked on the wild side with Lou Reed (1972); or in the ghetto with Elvis (1969b); could have been queen of the slipstream with Van the Man Morrison and then returned to a New England with Bill Bragg (1983).
- *Changing thoughts* – You were always on my mind (even though I messed you around); I used to think you were the queen of the prom, but not now; he was my hero back in '68; it's so funny we don't talk anymore (Tarney 1979), I don't love you anymore, the potential here is endless.
- *Changing future* – The things we do today will follow us into tomorrow, and songs do point in that direction, for example, 'Saltwater' (Julian Lennon 1991); 'I Need to Wake Up' (Etheridge 2005). Lots of political and protest songs these days are written about changing for

the future rather than lamenting the past or complaining about the present. This is a change in itself because we live in a much more aware world: we have access to information and understand global warming, the refugee crisis and so on with much more clarity than before. It isn't that writers are clairvoyant, but futures can be anticipated and change promoted.

Of course, the word *change* is open to more than this picture allows, and we don't have to spell out the possibilities and potential in great detail here, the idea is already presented. Put your own idea against 'changing':

- Changing partners
- Changing cities
- Changing

As an example or even a variation on the theme:

- New for old
- Her for her
- Him for him
- New directions
- Today I'm going to fly away

These are changes expressed in a different way,

This next picture is of John Lee Hooker's[2] guitar, hanging on the wall in Buddy Guy's Blues Bar in Chicago.

Now if that doesn't inspire something for the songwriter, well, I don't know. Straight off the cuff as I type here:

I remember
John Lee Hooker's guitar
hanging over the bar
on that cold winter's night in Chicago

---

[2] I had the handwriting confirmed by my colleague Dr Leighton Grist, University of Winchester, who knew John Lee Hooker and his handwriting.

(© Andrew Melrose 2017)

Well, sometimes you just have to give into it, and of course this small quartet of lines can be read in different ways: was it the guitar or the singer who was hanging over the bar? Did he see the guitar there, or hear it being played while standing at the bar? Bear in mind, when the song is sung, the picture above won't be getting handed around. It's one of the wonderful ways in which ambiguity can be explored with no explanation necessary because it is all down to the perception of the listener (or reader of the lyric in this case). No point in having me spoil the fun by telling the truth of it – but beer was involved.

This next picture is of a pier in the town where I live, Brighton, England, and it is full of ideas. Brighton has a famous episode in pop and cultural history, when the mods (like The Who) and the rockers (like Gene Vincent and the early Rolling Stones) descended on a bank holiday and gathered at the Palace Pier, chanting and jeering at each other, and threw stones when police tried to disperse them. For me, piers, especially this one with a fairground on it (and similarly the one in Santa Monica, California, to mention another I have seen) figure early in my recollection of songs. The fairground and rock and roll, roller coasters and Buddy Holly, the dodgems and the waltzer and sweet Gene Vincent, Johnny Kid and the Pirates, 'Shaking All Over' (1960), Bruce Springsteen and 'Tunnel of Love' (1987), or the Tom Waits song 'Jersey Girl' (1980) – all became emblems of pop culture because there is a place to dance at the end of the pier. Then again, it is down by the beach too, so it's the Beach Boys in teenage years on balmy Sunday afternoons that last all summer – and were those summers long and hot; of course they were, as we take the scene down to Santa Monica Pier, where I once heard a busker bashing out the Tom Petty and the Heartbreakers song, 'American Girl' (1976). The first time I heard the Monkees singing 'Daydream Believer' (1968) was at a fairground, and I find the whole idea of them magical and musical all at the same time. Take a moment to take yourself to one, and just absorb the music and the sea and the excitement, even on winter days (often the best in Brighton).

(© Andrew Melrose 2017)

This next picture is the ruined West Pier in Brighton, and for me it brings a more sombre frame of mind, less frivolous than the Palace Pier (as the Brighton Pier is now called again). It is often crowded with murmuring starlings, and it conjures up a different image of the place I now call my hometown. It once oozed Romanticism, and it had an old-fashioned

(© Andrew Melrose 2017)

Victorian ballroom where dance bands played in its heyday. It opened in 1866 and closed in 1975, and it offers history as well as jollity and memories. But even now, in its fading spleandour, it is still iconic and synonomous of the city.

I was sitting on my bike looking out over the water when I took this picture on my phone. I was just contemplating the light on the water and the silhouette of the wreckage as the sun began to drop, when a car pulled up alongside me, and I heard Van Morrison and the Chieftains leaking from the stereo. Van Morrison (1988) was singing:

> I would swim over the deepest ocean,
> the deepest ocean to be by your side.

I didn't do much with the idea at the time, but sitting here now, writing this, the whole memory, the image, the sunshine, the freedom of being out on my bike and 'Carrickfergus' (Van Morrison 1988) for a soundtrack not only reminded me of the scene, but the lyric brought something else to the table – and I am playing it again as I write. Now we could go back to the sentiment of that song quite easily. Or we could take it somewhere else:

- There is another life across the ocean; this small town doesn't have to be the end of the road.
- Standing at the edge of the world looking out for you, but that is a big ocean to cross.
- Still waters run deep.
- Keep the beacon burning; as soon as I can hire a boat I'll be over – returning home, or coming over to you, or looking for consciousness expansion ('Ain't Goin' to Goa', Alabama Three [1997]).
- We don't walk under the boardwalk anymore no. 1: (sigh, remember those long, hot summer nights, wake me up when September ends, or 'Sandy' (Travolta 1978)
- We don't walk under the boardwalk anymore no. 2: (but come the summer that's all going to change, Boogie Nights [Heatwave 1976])

Or even take the narrator right to the scene:

- Is the guy/girl sitting in the car behind me, listening to Van the Man, going to come over and say hi?
- I hope the guy/girl sitting in the car behind me, listening to Van the Man, doesn't end up being the next person to break my heart (well, you never know, do you?).
- A note to the guy/girl sitting in the car behind me, listening to Van the Man, or just doodling your own lines: 'I'm not free, but if I was, I could see us being you and me . . .' (Melrose 2018) (Note to partner: I'm thinking of moving to Nashville)

Taking this different view is something we will look at later, but I am reminded here that we can take this long or short view, the view from the scene or of the scene or in the scene or looking at the scene, but there are other ways of looking at this precept. For example, Billy Bragg said:

> Americans tend to write in cinemascope: wide-open spaces, mind-expanding poetry. The British tend to write with more characterisation and detail, more kitchen sink. Those aspects of British songwriting that I admire are looking at detail and examining it closely, drawing a conclusion from that rather than the sort of broad lyrics of 'This Land Is Your Land'.
>
> (Billy Bragg in Rachel 2013: 344)

I'm not sure I completely agree with this, although I can see how it can be summarized like this. Tom Petty sang about 'American Girl,' (1976) whereas, Elvis Costello sang about 'Alison' (1994a); nevertheless, Guy Clark, for example is an archetypal, very highly regarded American singer songwriter, and his song 'The Cape,' (1995) which I mentioned above, takes both a short and a long view. As does Jason Isbell in 'Speed Trap Town' (1971). We could draw a huge list showing these, and of course my list will be different from yours given that a list is incredibly subjective. What we can see, though, is that however we look at the world, the world itself is a hugely interesting and resourceful place – even on your own doorstep – and we haven't even looked at a 'Space Oddity' (Bowie 1969), sci fi and fantasy. As these pictures reveal, you don't have to live in sexily expressive towns like New York or Chicago to have a perfect day. It is all about taking the imagination for a walk— imagining situations, scenarios, circumstances, environments, locations, scenes, places, spaces and stories (which we will return to later when we look at subjects).

Fragment no. 3: Outside/Inside

I was thinking about the best place to discuss this idea, and the visual image section seems to be the most appropriate. Outside/inside is a fantastic lyrical idea to work with. It works on taking an outside item, for example something that can be visualized, and juxtaposing it with internal thought, and poets do it all the time. We mentioned lyrics not being poetry above, but this is definitely something we can learn from poets. Let me demonstrate how they do it, and then we can consider how to appropriate it (don't worry, T. S. Eliot would have approved). In Philip Gross's collection of poems, *Off Road to Everywhere* (2010), there is a fantastic example. 'Left Luggage from the Lost and Found' provides a playful exercise that prompts young people to write for themselves. Take a look at what Gross advises. We are to imagine an old crate being washed up on a shore. It's nothing special, described as a 'crate of raw planks/nailed together', and the narrator ponders on how it arrived there. Was it flotsam or jetsam?

Was it washed out to sea or tossed overboard? And then the narrator ruminates on what can be found inside, though the contents are a little more speculative than material, because inside we find a stillness and the reflection of a harbor light, even. We might even find laughter on the water captured inside.

The *outside* (the crate of raw planks and its journey to the narrator) followed by the *inside*, internalized response is simple enough to engineer and something we can all do. You can be driving, watching the road, looking at the trucks whizzing by (outside visual); listening to the tyres on the road (outside) and Elvis on the radio, singing 'Are You Lonesome Tonight' (1969a), and at the same time can be thinking about a 'baby' waiting in the booth just to the left of the door in the Last Stop Diner on Route 66 (inside); she left you feeling sad (inside), but you're going to win her back (inside) before she breaks your heart for good (inside). You can see what is meant. This doesn't have to be an 'outside' verse and an 'inside' verse in the way Phillip Gross suggests here. It can be mixed and matched quite easily within verses and even lines. 'I want a house with windows and a door, somewhere to sigh' – this line has both the inside and outside concepts in the same line, and it is easily recognized as being an outside visual (window and door) and an inside thought (somewhere to sigh) pertaining to what she wants to do inside a house which she is trying to visualize on the outside. It can be hugely effective. If you were going to do this, think about these ideas when you are writing – don't just take the easy route. Even write a list and then think about how you can make associations. But do remember, this isn't a definitive list, but just suggestions:

Outside	Inside
train leaving the station	heartbroken
that bottle of whiskey	lonesome
her red dress	love
ship on the ocean	wish I could just sail away
house on the hill	could we be happy
sunset over Chicago	I still have the blues
my lover	don't let me down
mother	misunderstanding

And it doesn't have to be a visual image:

Outside	Inside
driving my car	anticipation
listening to the sea	nostalgic for home
knocking on doors	lost
chicken soup	grief
taking the bus	excitement

Just a random list, but you can see how the song lyric allows the singer to work with more than just seeing, as outer and inner images are evoked, and external signifiers are combined with internal feelings and reactions to bring a combined image. The combination can also provide a huge personalized effect too, where the singer locates the song physically while giving that crucial piece of information we want about everyone we come across: what is he or she thinking? It allows the singer to take you into the person's thoughts, dreams, hope, fears and the whole panoply of human feeling.

Fragment no. 4: Found Objects

Carrying on the poetry theme, the expression *found poetry* is fairly well known to poets. It is a type of poetry created by taking the words, lines and even phrases and ideas – and indeed often entire segments – from other sources. These are then reassembled as another poem. Indeed, see *Three Regrets and a Hymn to Beauty* by Ian Wedde, who says:

> 'A Hymn to Beauty' recycles remembered and misremembered lines from many songs, by Emmylou Harris, Gram Parsons, Ryan Adams, Sneaky Feelings, John Lennon, Lou Reed, Johnny Cash, Jimmy Dorsey, Courtney Love, and several others. My thanks to the lyricists. There are remembered (and misremembered) fragments from philosophers and poets of the sublime, especially William Wordsworth and John Ruskin. Religious texts are also remembered, including the bible, the Tao-Te-Ching, Dhammapada, Pali canon and Tanakh. Like beauty, these fragments are imperfect.
>
> (Wedde 2005: 74)

Fragments – that word again. Found poetry is quite literally a poetic patchwork, comprised of original and other work cut and pasted together to produce something new – and actually not that uncommon. It is also a great lyric device, and there is a lot we can adopt from the process. John Lennon famously wrote about reading the news in 'A Day In the Life' (1967d), where he picks up a couple of stories which have been traced back to the source. One is the death of someone he knew in a car crash, and the other about 'holes [in the road] in Blackburn, Lancashire' – which he twisted very nicely into how many holes it took to fill Albert Hall, as a satirical jibe at the pop versus classical culture row. David Bowie was a famous exponent of the process, and he adopted the William Burroughs technique of 'cut-ups' where you take lines from other texts, such as poems, books, magazines, and so forth, and line them up in a lyrical collage. Now there is absolutely no reason why this can't be an important exercise. There is a whole host of ways it can be accessed, from poetry books to newspaper clippings – and indeed a combination of both. It is also a good way of getting over a lyrical block (say). Find a line, sing it, see how it shapes up, find a corresponding line, or even write a corresponding line, and off you go. As I write this, I have just read about an island where women are banned. I spotted it completely at random, and I would suggest that's a pretty good place to start. And okay, if you don't agree, there are plenty of others I haven't read – even just today.

But also, with 'found poetry' there is also *erasure*, once the name of a very popular band (some might recall). Erasure is also a form of found poetry or found art or lyric which is created by erasing words from an existing text, either in verse or prose style – it doesn't really matter. It is created by setting the words out on the page as a poem and calling it that. The results can be allowed to stand in situ, or they can be arranged into lines and or stanzas. We could do that with this paragraph, for example: read the highlighted bits:

> But also, with '**found** poetry' there is also *erasure*, once the name of a very popular band (some might recall). Erasure is also a form of found poetry or found art or **lyric** which is created by **erasing** words from **an existing** text, either in verse or prose **style** – it **doesn't really matter**. It is **created** by setting the **words** out **on the page** as a **poem** and calling it that. The

results can be allowed to stand in situ or they can be arranged into lines and or stanzas. We **could do that with this** paragraph, for example:

Then pull them out:

> found lyric erasing
> an existing style
> doesn't really matter.
> created words, on
> the page poem could do that with this.

Well, it's not William Carlos Williams, I grant you, but try it with a more lyrical text. Snatch the words, shift the tone, jumble them around, move them hither and thither.

Fragment no. 5: Conversation

Masters of the conversation lyric really started in the early 1970s with Joni Mitchell. Think of something like 'The Last Time I Saw Richard' (1971b); Tom Waits's 'Warm Beer and Cold Women' (Waits 1975), just to name a couple which you could check out, along with loads and loads of Randy Newman songs and Bruce Springsteen songs. These can take a number of shapes: a lone singer discussing an ex-lover in the case of Mitchell and Waits; an overheard discussion in the case of Randy Newman's 'Little Criminals' (1977); or someone delivering ironic advice, like Nick Cave's narrator (who could be your strangest cousin, twice removed, and the progeny of God-fearing parents, 'God Is in the House' (Cave 2003) or Bruce Springsteen's leaving-home song, 'Hungry Heart' (1980), where he tells you about how 'he' (he being the narrator) took a wrong turning and left his 'wife and kids in Baltimore, Jack.' Jason Isbell talks to us about a 'Speed Trap Town' (1971) and how he is trying to escape. The effect was radical in the seventies, and Isbell (among many, many others) reveals it has stayed with us. This is mostly because it takes us to everyday stories and stories we can recognize. Sometimes they are almost cinematic, like a short movie scene being given in a song – and of course the potential for the accompanying short MTV-style film is huge.

You can see how these can be researched without a huge amount of effort. Take yourself with a pencil and pad to the movies, a coffee shop, a pub, the top deck of the bus, a fairground queue, the corner shop, the foyer of a night club, the back seat of someone's car, along the aisle of a supermarket, to a place of worship, Berlin, Auchtermuchty, a Brighton LBGTQE karaoke bar on a Saturday night – indeed, anywhere you can catch people talking and listen to what they are saying. A lot of the time it's going to be nothing, but you have to be listening all the time because conversation songs are a great way to get your song rolling. Or even imagine yourself talking to someone, James Taylor sang, 'Hey mister, that's me up on the jukebox' (1971), which was also the title of the song. He's talking to the 'mister' in the song. Well, we could all do that, 'I'm looking for a little more than you're giving me now, but I like it better when you don't even try.' What is the 'me' narrator saying to the 'you' in conversation? Now this opens up lots of doors because the conversation you can have in a song need have no relation to the truth. 'Hey, Mr President of the United States, are you listening while I tell what is wrong and what is right?' Or even a letter: 'Dear Pope Francis, I'm a little concerned that you haven't bought my new record. Any chance we could talk it over?' A mock-up radio show: 'Good morning America, I'm talking you from KLM195'; or a tourist information centre: 'Welcome to Liverpool, home of the Fab Four.' And I am just riffing these – do your own.

Fragment no. 6: Subjects

This has been addressed before, and it is useful to do so again because it really is important. Before we move on with this topic, the first question we have to dispose with is this: is any subject barred from lyrics? Well, it's a foolishly wise question (there are lots of oxymorons in lyrics – *bittersweet* being well rehearsed). The comprehensive answer is of course not. However, there are issues to be considered in terms of public delivery. You can sing anything you like to yourself and your cat in your own kitchen. But songs for performance should preferably have some considerations. It's not our job to suggest censorship (I personally have nothing against some censorship – it's the self-appointed censors who worry me and of course some officially appointed ones too), but there are issues such as taste, decency, ethics, awareness of cultural appropriation, and then there are the ones that are all too often ignored. We cannot comment on your behalf, but personally we find racism, homophobia, gender inequality and so forth to be beyond the pale. And of course we don't have to listen to it, but it would be a shame if Elton John, Beyonce, Adele, Willie Nelson and the like couldn't sing your fantastic new lyrics in their song because you have a past steeped in something they don't approve of. I guess if you are playing in a self-proclaimed, fascistic, skinhead, redneck, right-wing, racist band you might be inclined to disagree. Just as long as you realize your audience reach will be narrower than most because you are catering for a minor audience demographic. But the fact remains, it is your band and your song. At the other end of this scale, similarly, for example, there is a huge modern Christian songwriting network, which can often be a bit circumspect in terms of lyrical quality. Nevertheless, political, religious and partisan songs are no less important, and if you are going to do them, let's make an effort to do them well. When Adrian Drover and Jimmy Webb wrote, 'Someone left the cake out in the rain/I don't think that I can take it/'Cause it took so long to bake it/And I'll never have that recipe again' for Richard Harris, 'MacArthur Park' (1968) they weren't thinking about baking, but about the metaphor, where the of object of the song is a one-off, and there is no recipe.

So from cakes to thinking about subjects, we can begin with the obvious and move on. The thing is, even from one word or a picture we can find loads of ideas and then consider the subject we are going to write about, because inside each idea there is a theme to be pursued.

We did *carnival* before, but take another single word – *love* for example – which is a great and timeless subject to write is about:

Love

Daniel Levitin, *The World in Six Songs*, wrote:

> There are love songs to reflect four stages of love: I want you, I got you, I miss you, and it's-over-and-I'm-heartbroken. Love songs reflect the

different kinds of love as well: the Romeo-and-Juliet love (I'd kill myself for this person); the more mature love of being together for decades and looking back; and the love of ideals, such as of country.'

(Levitin 2009: 274)

Actually, although the four stages of love are fine in and of themselves, as stated here, as a subject, he is right to say the 'different kinds of love' are a major issue, and that is what we mean by taking it further.

I want you – simple enough and easy to consider. A personal song from the singer to someone else and another conversation song (see above). And of course the millions of songs we could refer you to here are not really necessary but do think about different ways of saying what you want to say, because it doesn't have to be that simple 'I want you' idea. Bruce Springsteen, for example, takes us down 'Thunder Road' (1975), where the hero arrives at Mary's front door; when she comes to the door, Roy Orbison can be heard singing 'Only the Lonely' (1961) on the radio), and the hero says, 'That's me and I want you only' before pleading not to be turned away because he doesn't want to be alone again. The 'I just can't face being alone again' is the same 'I want you' idea turned on its head. 'Every Breath You Take' (1983), by The Police, sounds like an 'I want you' kind of song until you realize the words are a sinister tale about a selfish, obsessive ex-lover who wants to control a former partner in a relationship that is already over. In fact, the song is more about jealousy than love, though it seems to be wrapped up as a love song – a bittersweet oxymoron (we have seen that word before). The simple 'I want you' becomes 'I'm watching you, and if I can't have you' – well, I will let you work out the threat. As Sting suggests, the song is actually quite sinister and ugly, but disguised as a gentle little love song, when, of course, it's quite the opposite.

'I Got You Babe' – probably one of the best pop duets ever written, Sonny and Cher (1965), designed to melt even the hardest heart when they sing, 'I got you babe.' Who else could sing, 'When I'm sad, you're a clown' and get away it (see *carnival* above). Another duet is 'Don't Go Breaking My Heart,' (John and Dee 1976). Indeed the 'I got you' song is timeless because it can be written in so many different ways. And of course we are talking conversation songs again (once you start to recognize them, they pop up everywhere). Sung in appreciation is the commonest interpretation, but when there is a common trope, there is also the counter case. It reminds me of the movie *On the Waterfront* (Kazan 1954), with Terry Malone (Marlon Brando) telling his brother, Charley (Rod Steiger) that but for him, 'I coulda been a contender. I coulda been somebody, instead of a bum, which is what I am.' In other words, with all the brothers in the world, I got you. It's a great sentiment that can be run through songs that are another take on love, friendship, siblings and so on, where the 'I got you' isn't necessarily that good a deal. Indeed, in writing this I seem to recall a Supertramp song from way back called 'Breakfast in America' (1978), where the lyric reflects this idea: 'Take a look at my girlfriend/She's the only one I got/Not much of a girlfriend/Never seem to get a lot.' Charming huh? Then again it also has the lines, 'Ba-ba-ba-dow, ba-bow-dum-doo-de-dow-de-dow, de Ba-ba-ba-dow, ba-bow-dum-de-doo-de-dow Na na na, nana na na na na.'

I miss you – I was a young man when I first heard Janis Ian's heart-rending song 'Jesse' (1974). 'There's a hole in the bed where we slept,' a sentiment which was trampled over by the aforesaid Sting who also wrote the much less subtle song about a bed being too big. At the time I didn't know I was recognizing a universal theme of loss and love lost and longing, which I confess affects us more as we get older. Bruce Springsteen and his stark song 'You're Missing' (2002) take the starkness of the 'I miss you' theme to a different level. Lori McKenna, Hillary Lindsey and Liz Rose wrote 'Girl Crush' for Little Big Town (2014), and it isn't until the last line of the first verse and the second verse that you realize it's not a woman-on-woman crush, but a female narrator saying, 'I want to taste her lips' because she tastes of her ex-lover, whom she wants back. It sounds a little trite writing it like this, but its amazingly effective way of writing the 'I miss you' story (https://www.youtube.com/watch?v=PdO5V x2RU5I). Storytelling in the 'I miss you' refrain can be really interesting. Bob Dylan's 'If You See Her, Say Hello' (1974) is supposed to be about the break-up of his marriage (though, in typical Dylan style, he doesn't confirm this and suggests its more about Chekov's writing; also, the song is very anonymous, and we would have to assume much to be sure he was writing about himself – once again, and typically, he will never confirm it). Either way, the song takes a solitary look at a relationship break-up with some nice twists.

If you see her, say hello, she might be in Tangier
She left here last early Spring, is living there, I hear.

But this 'I miss you' is also another sentiment that can be taken many ways. It's not a song (though it could be), but didn't Hannibal Lecter miss Clarice? I don't make this point to be flippant, but to explore the idea that we are all capable of missing someone. The African philosophy of the self, *ubuntu*, is the idea that can be loosely translated as 'a person is a person to other persons'. Indeed, Springsteen also captures this very well in his song 'If I Should Fall Behind' (1992), and it speaks of the human condition and the fact that we are sociable beings, and loneliness is a human emotion ripe for plucking from the songwriters' fruit tree (and on the word *plucking*, it may be apocryphal, but when Bob Dylan was asked how come he was so prolific, didn't he say he just reached up and plucked the songs out of the sky?). The thing to consider carefully, though, is how biographical these songs lyrics seem to be – and you must take that as 'seem to be' because songwriters are storytellers and not necessarily biographers. And the way to develop this is to step back and write as a narrator for a character. For example, imagine you are writing for Michael Corleone in *The Godfather* or Demi Moore in *Ghost*, when she is missing Patrick Swayze, or something Adele might sing, or for Willie Nelson or Rod Stewart or Tom Jones or whomsoever to sing. There is a whole tradition of writing 'I miss you' songs for other people who don't write themselves or who like to do cover versions of songs as well as their own. Bruce Springsteen almost made Tom Waits's song 'Jersey Girl' his own.

It's over – from Maggie May's lover having to go back to school (Stewart 1971) to 'I'm loving angels instead' (Williams 1997) or even 'I will always love you' (Parton 1973), the 'it's over, lost love, why did you leave me, I've left you' song is a staple in the songwriter's diet. So consider how you can take the simple idea of it and turn it around into being different from everyone else's: Taylor Swift's 'All Too Well' (2012a) through to Jim Steinman's melodramatic, 'Total Eclipse of the Heart' for Bonnie Tyler (1983). 'Tracks of My Tears', by Smokey Robinson (1969) gave us a new take on this old subject, but at the same time almost redefined the soul genre as a classic Motown sound. And if it had been sung by the Supremes or any other such female band, it would have still sounded great. But Smokey Robinson and the Miracles did a good job of toning down the masculinity, and as a result the gender of the song can be completely neutral – which was unusual for soul music. It's a hugely simple and yet massively effective lyric.

So the love song lyric can take on many shapes and sizes, subjects and approaches. We could also think about:

Love of my country – 'New England', Billy Bragg (1983)
Love of my home – 'Sweet Home Alabama', Lynrd Skynrd (1974)
Love of my dog – 'I Love My Dog', Cat Stevens (1967)
'Lester', Crowded House (1999)

Love of my anything you like it to be; me to be; how you would like to be seems to be in order.

And then of course, as with change (above), we can address it in different ways if we like. Tom Robinson's 'War Baby' (1984) plays with all kinds of ambiguities and yet is essentially a love song. 'Life's Been Good' (1978) by Joe Walsh is about the fact that he loves his life as a guitar-playing, songwriting rock star, and what's not to like?

And of course, where love exists, sex has always been close by and surprisingly well accepted, even on the most conservative of radio stations:

Many of popular music's most memorable and emotional songs deal with the sexual, lustful side of love. 'As soon as music first emerges in cavemen and it has a rhythm,' Rodney Crowell says, 'you have the sense of sex in it, because what is the most obvious human activity that has a rhythmic component?'

(Levitin 2009: 277)

We will look at rhythm later, but still, on the subject of words, we can begin to look further and at the combinations. In the next chapter, we look at the issue of 'to rhyme or not to rhyme,' but there are many other things to consider in getting started with ideas around love as a subject. We can move around many territories here: *'Je t'aime . . . moi non plus'*, by Serge Gainsbourg and Jane Birkin (1967), is famous for its (faked) passionate delivery, and it's hard to listen to Prince without knowing he had a lot to say on the subject. But I say more on this later.

Hopefully, then, you get the picture. If you take this Subjects idea on, you can draw up your own list or chart or way of working. Love is a fine subject, but tie it in to other things, or even consider moving on to other subjects, like poverty and freedom and stop the war and refugees and mother earth and save the whale and save the planet and – well, you get the picture; the whole tapestry of life as we know it can be tied into the lyric. In 'The Sacred Wood,' T. S. Eliot famously said, 'Immature poets imitate; mature poets steal; bad poets deface what they take, and good poets make it into something better, or at least something different.' Well, it's the same for songwriters. Take ideas and work them into serious thinking; watch the news on TV and steal the ideas; read the newspaper, there is always something to sing about around those stories – 'I read the news today oh boy' – something interesting occurred in China or Brighton, or about a refugee who crossed the Mediterranean in a boat only to wind up in a towering inferno in London (a hugely but sad story that unfolded as I was writing this chapter).

Books, literature, poetry (I have a particular fondness for Pablo Neruda) should also be in the songwriter's field of vision. You are dealing with language, the power of words, so seek out others who write, from William Boroughs to Jack Kerouac, Allen Ginsberg to Tom Ford. And listen to well-known wordsmith songwriters – Bob Dylan, famously, but Steve Earle, Morrissey, Randy Newman, Joni Mitchell, Thom Yorke, Eddie Holland, Woody Guthrie, John Prine, Eminem, Sam Cooke, Bjork, Lucinda Williams, Billy Bragg, Michael Stipe, Patty Smith, John Lennon, Chrissie Hynde, Joe Strummer, Madonna, Tom Waits, and Bernie Taupin are all worth looking out for. But I'm just plucking names out of the air; go on and make your own list and think about the links they are making too. Mark Knopfler wrote 'Romeo and Juliet' for Dire Straits (1980); so did William Shakespeare (1597). Read them alongside their influences. Didn't John Lennon mention Edgar Allen Poe once? Tim Rice must have read the Bible before writing *Jesus Christ Superstar*, surely? What is clear is that even looking at a sample of names, their influences are clearly greater than just listening to the radio/jukebox/iTunes/Spotify or wherever they do their listening. In his recent Nobel Prize speech, Dylan (2017) mentioned Buddy Holly, Leadbelly, John Donne, Shakespeare, Sonny Terry and Brownie McGhee, Charlie Poole, the New Lost City Ramblers, Jean

Ritchie, *Don Quixote, Ivanhoe, Robinson Crusoe, Gulliver's Travels, Tale of Two Cities, Moby Dick, All Quiet on the Western Front* and Homer's *The Odyssey*. Now he was accepting the prize for his contribution to literature and might be just showing off a little, but then again, why would he? You don't have to show anyone the list and pretend to be someone you are not; you are writing this for yourself. No one will care if your influences are Aristotle or Harry Styles if you are looking for the right line (and I wonder if that's the last time I ever mention both of them in the same sentence?). It's just another exercise so you can start to bring ideas together. But it's a little more than that. It allows you to develop ideas you might not have considered before.

What about Daniel Defoe's *Robinson Crusoe*? How could we address the idea of Man Friday in the twenty-first century? It could be a decent political song idea, antiracist perhaps, or equal opportunities for all or even just a love song: 'I don't need you to be my Man Friday, I want you on a Monday too.' It could be a decent country song line. I am just riffing on a vague idea plucked out of the air, but it already has potential. And I confess, as I am writing this, my iTunes has shuffled to Patty Griffin singing 'Making Pies' (2002). Do check it out – lyrically it is very interesting and has a Randy Newman quality. What it seems to deal with is the ordinariness of a working and domestic life, but then it opens up to a huge statement on loneliness, loss and eventually an antiwar link. For years I had dismissed it as just a song I like (her singing has a haunting edge), but closer inspection revealed more than I had anticipated: https://www.youtube.com/watch?v=2HC7KABegj0. And it really does show much more depth than the chorus, 'I'm making pies', reveals. And as I write this, I was reminded of the wonderful John Prine song 'Hello in There' (1971) which takes a similar line in that it's a domestic tale with a huge underlying story. Now I would doubt if Patty Griffin hadn't heard John Prine since they are working in a similar genre, but I wonder if there is any influence there? Of course both songs question Billy Bragg's claim that Americans write cinemascope songs compared to the British tendency for a more kitchen-sink approach. What is clear, though, is that the idea is everything, and yet much easier to capture than it appears – you just have to start looking.

11

Storytelling

The word *lyric* derives from the Latin *lyricus* via the Greek λυρικός (*lyrikós*), the adjectival form of lyre, a musical instrument which was a bit like a handheld harp— and I guess a forerunner of the guitar for the minstrel. The Greeks spoke of lyrics as *ta mele*, which are poems to be sung. In his Nobel Prize speech, Bob Dylan wrote:

> Our songs are alive in the land of the living. But songs are unlike literature. They're meant to be sung, not read. The words in Shakespeare's plays were meant to be acted on the stage. Just as lyrics in songs are meant to be sung, not read on a page. And I hope some of you get the chance to listen to these lyrics the way they were intended to be heard: in concert or on record or however people are listening to songs these days. I return once again to Homer, who says, "Sing in me, oh Muse, and through me tell the story." (2017)

And we can see how the centuries in the history of the song are long in length but divided by little, because little has changed. It was not until the European Renaissance that writers regularly began to write their lyrics for readers, rather than composing them solely for musical performance and passing them on orally (which has its own problems with accuracy). I remember my own daughter, age three, asking for the 'Butter Song'. I had no idea what she was asking for until she sat on the floor, bade me do the same then took my hands to sing the child's nursery rhyme:

Row, row, row your boat,
gently down the stream,
merrily, merrily, merrily, merrily,
life is but a dream.

She thought it was, 'Life is butter dream,' and how often have we done something like that in our lives, misheard and let the mishearing stay with us, even when it doesn't make sense. I'll bet it happens in kara-okes all over the world – and indeed Peter Kay has made a great show out of it: https://www.youtube.com/watch?v=UMYorpYNMKc, Money for nothing and chips for free? Sweet dreams are made of cheese? All the lonely Starbucks lovers? I once sang, 'Sitting in a sneezy snack bar,' instead of sleazy. And writing this reminds me of the live version of John Prine's song 'That's the Way That the World Goes Round', where, before the end chorus, he mentions the time he was asked for the 'happy enchilada' song. When he said he'd never written a song about any kind of enchi-lada, far less a happy one, she said, 'Yes, you wrote a song about a happy enchilada. So he asked her how it goes, and she said, 'It's a happy enchi-lada and you think you're gonna drown.' Now if you do get a chance to hear the live version, you will see why. What he actually sings is, 'It's half an inch of water and you think you're gonna drown.' But I have to admit she has a point, the vocal pronunciation does blur the real words and the sense of the song. What does this say about the real lyric or intention? Well, it was pointed out earlier, the lyric relies on the listener's sensitiv-ity to the meaning. And that meaning can come through many different experiences. Meaning and experience are often intertwined, and once a song has taken on a significance for us, it is hard to shake off that initial impression. Nevertheless, that shouldn't stop us from progressing with the idea of storytelling.

When we think of it, singers, especially the singer-songwriters, haven't come far from the travelling minstrel idea, which is still strong with us today. And this perception was increased when including song lyrics with albums became commonplace. Of course, with the new system of buying songs by download (without that lyric luxury), a thriving online industry of lyric reproduction is rife. Few reading this book will not have heard of websites such as Metrolyrics or AZLyrics, and very useful they are too. Historically, the musical lyric form of a Dowland or Bird co-existed with the dramatic and poetical forms of Shakespeare, Sydney, Spenser and all, at a time when the full implications of Caxton's fifteenth-century introduction of the printing press to England were beginning to be realized. From there, it was a sense of inevitability that the written and sung words would develop hand in hand, but differently when they could be reproduced so quickly. And it is crucial we emphasize *differently* here. What both poetry and song lyrics share is their ability to tell a story differently from other art forms because of the way we and they (the lyrics) use words – and of course the song lyric, as we have already said, is a different kind of storytelling again.

Storytelling is a foundation stone in the art of songwriting. I grant you, often it has been so simplified into a candy-coated pop song that it is hardly worth telling, but it's something that we should be taking seriously, both for the history of songwriting, through the early ballads, to the present-day potential. The ability to tell a story, to engage with the world around us is one of the most important parts of being human. *Homo fabula*, we are the storytellers, and it is what enlightens us, civilizes us and makes us human. It isn't quite as instant as a photograph, but the immediacy of the song lyric, the way it can capture a moment almost as it's happening, makes it an incredibly potent art form. Walter Benjamin refers to this as a *Dialektik im Stillstand* – 'dialectics at a standstill'. He writes in *The Arcades Project* that art 'prefigures' the arresting of thought and action; historical time becomes encapsulated so that the crystallised effect of this dialectics at a standstill is to render time as present rather than as a flow of past/present/future, in the imagistic configuration of the now – in the immediacy of the actual event as the bubble unfolds and then pops. In other words, the immediate output of the performance moment throws:

> 'a pointed light' on what has been. Welcomed into a present moment that seems to be waiting just for it – 'actualized', as Benjamin likes to say – the moment from the past comes alive as never before. In this way, the 'now' is itself experienced as preformed in the 'then', as its distillation.
>
> (Translators' Foreword to *The Arcades Project* 1999: xii)

An image lingers as we begin to form it into words and music, turning the lyrics around to fit the tune and then reforming it as a snapshot of a memory. The photographs in the previous section, as representations of the moments captured, do little justice to the moments themselves and only really invoke part of my memory of them. To some extent, the poetry of the situation could be captured and enhanced through further representation – in an accompanying poem or a painting or a song lyric, as an ekphrastic intervention which would open up a dialogue, though often refracted through *différance* (to paraphrase Jacques Derrida's much abused idea), which is the only way it can be, surely? As Jen Webb and I once wrote:

> Jacques Derrida has written, the 'future, this beyond, is not another time, a day after history. It is *present* at the heart of experience. Present not as a total presence but as a *trace* . . .' (Derrida 1978: 95). And this could be rephrased as 'the future story': an as-yet unread, unheard narrative, which is not situated in another time, a day after history, but is present at the heart of experience. Present not as a total presence but as a trace. The intimacies of such temporal and ontological connections, working in ancient and retold stories, can shed light on present contexts as they absorb the past and open up to the future.
>
> (Webb and Melrose 2011)

That is what art does. In the world, work is what we do, but art is who we are. Art, like the song lyric, is the civilizing force that defines us and records our progress as the human race, as we absorb the past, in the present, for the future. Songwriters write about contemporary life and what W. H. Auden called the 'human position'. It is the ongoing discourse we call art; or what Benjamin might have called the 'pointing light' of art – a powerful example of its protean, innovative, creative and critical reflections and engagements with contemporary life.

So let's look closer at the idea of storytelling in the lyric. Essentially, a simple difference between song lyrics and poetry is the difference between two different art forms, in which sibling words can perform in different ways. In some ways (and as a simplified assessment which I have borrowed from Katherine Coles), the poem is small on the outside, but big on the inside. That is to say, it is an economical collation of words formed into meaning, which moves away from the familiar and the expected to take readers into an experience where they have to reason and think it through. In the main, a song can do these things too, and of course lyrical poetry stalks the line between speaking and singing. But a song is there to capture what the poem cannot, which is another experience, a listening experience wound around melody and rhythm and hearing, and is presented as a completely different art form. The poet, Edward Hirsch (2006) recalls:

> I remember once walking through a museum in Athens and coming across a tall-stemmed cup from ancient Greece that has Sappho saying, 'Mere air, these words, but delicious to hear'. The phrase inscribed into the cup, translated onto a museum label, stopped me cold. I paused for a long time to drink in the strange truth that all the sublimity of poetry comes down in the end to mere air and nothing more, to the sound of these words and no others, which are nonetheless delicious and enchanting to hear. Sappho's lines (or the lines attributed to her) also have a lapidary quality. The phrase has an elegance suitable for writing, for inscription on a cup or in stone. Writing fixes the evanescence of sound. It holds it against death.

Here, I am reminded of Pope's 'echo to the sense', which is also an echo of the Sapphic 'Mere air, these words, but delicious to hear' mentioned in this quotation. The song lyric, like so much early poetry. is written down from 'mere air', but the lyric differs by being accompanied by a musical score to supplement the 'mere air'. This 'mere air' becomes wrapped in music that can be tabbed as notes on paper, but ultimately played on instruments where the words and music marry into a single piece, and thereafter recorded on recording devices to accompany words that tell the story being signified in the art form. Wallace Steven said, 'In poetry you must love the words, the ideas and images and rhythms with all your capacity to love anything at all' ('Adagia'). The song is no different but it just addresses these in a different way by adding the special ingredient called music. Music allows the lyric to be approached in a different way because it also approaches the audience differently; it appeals to different senses.

But what does this mean for the songwriter? It means that like all art forms, it is a force to be reckoned with and one of the founding pillars of the human condition. Practically speaking, an important thing we have to realize is that a song is a limiting art form. It works in a very limited time frame. You have a finite amount of space in which to tell your listeners something which they should know. Even the longer ramblings of Bob Dylan in his early days are restricted by the space on a long-playing record – and some may remember the old 45 rpm single from those days (Dylan's own 'Like a Rolling Stone' (1965a) broke the mould by being longer than the average three-minute song released on a 45rpm vinyl record – coming back into fashion in a record shop near you). In the main, every word in a song matters because you have a finite amount of space in which to deliver it; you are not writing a Shakespearian soliloquy. For example, 'Long May You Run' (1976), by the Stills-Young band, is only 104 words long. In this short space of time, and in most cases, you are going to tell a three- to four-minute story. So every word has to be carefully drafted and crafted to fit. We don't have the luxury of novelists, with their winding plots and meandering prose taking us along country roads where we can take in the view while nurturing heartache and the possibility of love in the future (while a subplot reveals our long-lost cousin has left us more money than a horse has hairs – to paraphrase an old Shel Silverstein lyric). Neither do we have the luxury of the poet who expects us to read and absorb the tenure of the poem as though we are holding a Ming Dynasty vase. What we have is the same economy of the poet who writes short poems, but with a need for lyrical dexterity that can be delivered in a three-minute (for the sake of getting a number) sound bite. With a hook and chorus (often as not) that brings us back to it time and time again, stops us in our tracks as we are walking into town, catches us unawares in the gym with our iPod on shuffle, hits us in the car with a force so potent that we sing along – my children and I love singing (and car dancing) along to 'Human' [2008], by The Killers, and 'Hungry Heart' [1980], by Bruce Springsteen. As Dylan wrote, quoting Homer, 'Our songs are alive in the land of the living . . . Sing in me, oh Muse, and through me tell the story" (Dylan 2017). So that is where we will go next.

Storytelling is a very traditional craft in the songwriter's armoury, mostly because it is the origin of songwriting itself. Minstrel and balladeer songs have always been a way of recording and transmitting stories which deal with the human condition. We have moved away from praising the great Homeric-style battles, and even the Biblical themes of struggle, but we have much in common with that historical tradition. For example, such as in the Song of Songs in the Old Testament. Traditionally Jewish and recited in a celebrating of the coming harvest while commemorating Moses' escape from Egypt, they are also distinctive in their celebration of sexual love, another huge part of the human condition. They give the expressions of two lovers praising each other and longing for each other, and there is little in the history of the world, recorded in the world's art, more universal than that simple story; timeless and almost without parallel, where would we be without it – Margaret Atwood tells that story in *The Handmaid's Tale* (1985), but the story itself is timeless and universal.

- **The universal story** – a universal theme is something that applies to us all, regardless of cultural, religious or geographical differences and are the ways in which we connect over common leitmotifs such as love, death, time, nature, faith, religion, desire, enmity, happiness, sadness, honesty, dishonesty, innocence, experience, greed, generosity, survival, parenting, friendship and kinship: all mutual themes the world over, and it is not too difficult to see how many of them figure in the songwriting canon. And it is important to say here too that a combination of more than one of anything isn't unusual. Love and death are often paired, and we could bring in sadness, experience and desire in too, just for good measure. A word of caution on the universal theme is to remember not to be too didactic, especially when you tread on someone else's thoughts and beliefs. Each to his own is a good measure of tolerance, but if you can't, try to stick to choosing your own cause (although see 'Protest' later). Better Shiva loves me than hating someone else's religion because you love Shiva (for example – or whomever; remember, this is just an example and not a prescription).
- **The me, myself and I story** – often told in the first person as a personal reflection, or an individual engagement on love, death, time, nature, faith, religion, and to which we could add loneliness, nostalgia, hope, fear and frustration; woe is me; I'm never going back, take me down country roads; I'm coming home after doing my time. Patty Griffin (2002) has a great song called 'Making Pies' in the first-person reflective mode, and indeed it can be anything from climbing the tallest mountain to blowing bubbles. Once again, though, as Griffin

reveals, the subject doesn't have to be simple. Guy Garvey is a master of this: try 'Jesus is a Rochdale Girl' or 'Grounds for Divorce', to name just two. Or Damian Rice with 'Colour Me In,' which has an inimitable take on the lyric. It would never occur to me to try to squeeze the words 'like a dogless bone' into a song, but it works, and uniquely so. But the chorus begins, 'So come let me love you', and this leads us nicely to the next paragraph because the two – I and You, Me and You – are almost impossible to separate at times, as you will see.

- **The you, you and me, me and you story** – also often told in the first person (as in me to you); all of the above, but speaking about 'you' as in another person: do you know how much I love you, do you care, do you think, have you seen, is there nothing you won't do just to make me feel blue? And of course the 'I' and the 'you' lyrics are interchangeable and often tied together – and great for duets. Steve Earle loves to write a duet: 'I Remember You' (2002), 'I'm Still in Love with You' (1999), 'You're Still Standing There' (1996), 'Poison Lovers' (1997), 'Goodbye' (1995) or even 'Days Are Never Long Enough' (2007), to name a few. Once again it's easy to take the easy way out, and I could go back to Guy Garvie, as before, with 'Starlings'; or Damian Rice with 'Amie' – 'I saw a spaceship fly by your window'. There are many ways to tell a good story, and you can really open these up to lots of treatments, from historical or literary musings like Romeo and Julie to Hans Solo, Princess Leia and beyond; Neil Young chose Pocahontas (1979) once. And of course the race, gender and sexual preferred specifics are entirely up to you.

- **The protest story** – anti-war; anti and pro-political figures; anti- and pro-political ideas; anti- and pro-agendas such as the environment, or more specifically environmental issues: save the whale, ban the bomb, don't frack with my future. At the start of this section, I mentioned Bruce Springsteen's 'Born in the USA' (1984). I could add 'Shipbuilding', by Elvis Costello (1983), both excellent songs which make you think about the cause they are putting on display. It doesn't have to be the less subtle. 'I Feel Like I'm Fixin' to Die Rag,' (Country Joe McDonald 1991), which is recorded forever in the Woodstock movie (1991). 'Be the first family on your block to have your boy come home in a box' is famous for its ironic take on the Vietnam war and actually giving the narrator of the song a great tongue-in-cheek lyric. I confess to a fondness for that song from my own teenage years, and indeed protest songs as a convention. The Specials 'Free Nelson Mandela' (Dammers 1984) spoke to a whole generation, as did 'Biko', by Peter Gabriel, to the same generation, which was about the death of Steve Biko during the apartheid regime in South Africa before Nelson Mandela was released. And of course there is the famous 'Do They Know Its Christmas', which has a habit of making a comeback every now and then. But from 'Strange Fruit' (Holiday 1939) on anti-racism (and the lynching of African Americans in the United States); Sam Cooke's 'A Change is Gonna Come; and the likes of Tom Robinson's 'Glad to be Gay', on gay rights, as we would expect, we can see how the protest song has a lot of mileage to be unrolled. Some songwriters, like Phil Ochs, go down that road deliberately, and some, like Country Joe McDonald, get pitched into the protest songwriter category because of a one-off coincidence, which his Woodstock performance was. Up until the point he sang 'I Feel Like I'm Fixin' to Die Rag,' there was no 'Country Joe' in his name, and it was coined by the announcer after he sang the song (which he had previously written for The Fish).

- **The acquiesce story** – ideas like 'I agree with you'; 'we're all in this together'; 'don't let me be misunderstood'; 'when you return you will find me, Penelope-like, knitting and waiting'; 'I knew you would come back to me'; 'I'm going nowhere' are often an acceptance of your lot, a 'shut up and put up with it' lyric. The most famous must be the country standard by Tammy Wynette and Billy Sherrill (1968), 'Stand By Your Man', which is a huge country music staple idea, although Dolly Parton turned that song on its head with 'To Daddy' (most famously recorded by Emmylou Harris). But the best are penitent songs. Penitent lovers; penitent men not going back to jail; penitent, 'I'm sorry, I never meant to make you cry'; Sorry I lied to you, mistrusted you, left you, thought nothing better of you' – you get the picture. The amazing Huddie 'Lead Belly' Ledbetter wrote wonderfully new and vital songs which have remained timeless. A song like 'Goodnight Irene' (1933) – can we believe that date? – which has been recorded by the likes of The Weavers, Frank Sinatra, Ry Cooder and Eric Clapton, is essentially about a man who is talking about accepting his lot– quit ramblin', quit gamblin' and staying out late at night – and telling himself to say goodnight to his sweetheart, Irene, and to go back to his wife.

- **The contemplating story** – ideas like 'if I had only'; 'maybe we should have'; 'maybe if you thought about it'; 'do they know it's Christmastime at all', 'send in the clowns', 'the snakes in the well', 'what if the sun never shone again', 'did you see that perigee moon last night, a romantic light on a cold dark night', 'if I had a boat all come to the thinking'. The thing about contemplation is it is also observational and something we all do as daily routine while we go about our everyday business, walking down the street, making the bed, cooking the dinner – all those chores that need little thought allow us to contemplate. So get into the habit of taking in the ideas; writing the interesting ones down; listening to things that interest you, like radio programmes – all it takes is a line, a word, an image to act as a catalyst to push the idea forward. Sometimes the best lines simply come out of fresh air just like this. Also, remember, not everyone can contemplate the world from the top of Mt Everest, but we can read, view, imagine a way of relating vicarious experience. No one involved in the movie *Titanic* actually sailed on it, but the story still got told. A good way to think about this too is to read writers who contemplate. Remember lyrics are word games, and poets write words too. Think about contemplative poets.
- **The 'walking in another's shoes' story** – I wonder what it's like to be you? I am a poor refugee trying to get over to your land. Fiction writers do this all the time: *Grapes of Wrath* isn't about John Steinbeck, but about walking in the shoes of Tom Joad. And of course, didn't Bruce Springsteen (that great storyteller) (1995) write 'The Ghost of Tom Joad' (1995), among other songs like 'Stolen Car' (1980)? The great thing with this theme is being able to get away with having to be personal while still telling stories that mean something to you. Walking in another person's shoes is a validation of ideas that concern you but happen to others. In many ways it's a vicarious experience idea; the story is mediated by an 'other', or someone who is 'other' – such as a refugee for example. We can't essentially tell the refugee or Tom Joad story, but we can pass on a second-hand experience of it.

A good example is the Emmylou Harris song 'My Name is Emmett Till' (2011). The story is told in Emmett Till's first-person voice. Now obviously Emmylou Harris is not the fourteen-year-old boy who was murdered in Mississippi because he was seen flirting with a white woman, 21-year-old Carolyn Bryant. Of course Emmylou isn't the first person to use Emmitt Till's story; Bob Dylan did so in 1962 (and he confessed he stole his tune from Len Chandler (http://chalktalkbooks.blogspot.com/2015/12/the-death-of-emmett-till-song-1955-by.html). Just because someone else has used the idea before doesn't mean you cannot. We, all of us, see things in different ways. If we were all asked to create a song by taking a single suggested lyric (in a workshop, say – and we have done this), then you can bet everyone will come up with something different. Even when we are dealing with universal ideas on common issues, we come at them from different directions. Its human nature to be similar but different.

- **The experience story** – yesterday; I remember when; when I was a young boy, girl, farmer; war is no joyride; stuck on a Texas highway with no credit on my phone or gas in the car; a boy named Sue – the experience story is an interesting one. I once worked with a singer who wrote a song, in the third person, about a fisherman who left home every Monday and returned with his catch on a Thursday (always a Thursday because the community was Catholic and ate fish on Fridays). In the meantime, his wife slept in 'cold linen'. Once he sang it in a fishermen's pub in small port just south of Edinburgh. The fishermen who had just collected their wages bought him a drink and said he must have experienced their life. He didn't, he merely had the information as a vicarious experience, that is he had been listening to the men on and off and collated their thoughts on their life. So the experience song can essentially be imagined or real. Then there is the song that deals with life experience, 'Stolen Car' by Springsteen (1980), for example, have that cinematic-style experience of girls and cars to pass on – a bit like hearing *The Last Picture Show* (Bogdanovich 1971) being enacted through your headphones.
- **The big idea story** – the musicals *Paradise Lost, Jesus Christ Superstar* and *Evita* – you can see where we are going with this. But this doesn't just have to be a musical. It can be individual songs that deal with big

ideas, and big issues are not hard to look out for. Anti-war, green issues, global warming, the refugee crisis, building a wall across the United States' southern border, a pro or anti-gun stance have all been a good storyline for many country songs. 'In The Ghetto' made famous by Elvis Presley, was a big idea for its time, and unless we are dealing with universal themes, the big idea does tend to be of the moment. The songwriter writing about 'cruise missiles' being stored in the United Kingdom a few years back might be writing about 'fracking' now. But the subjects of being anti-nuclear and anti-fracking have different generations and agendas. 'All You Need Is Love' (Beatles 1967) is a big idea; so too John Lennon's 'Imagine'.

- **The celebration story** – happy birthday (great song by Stevie Wonder), happy new year, Easter always being on a Sunday, the clichéd but money-spinning Christmas hit, once a huge tradition in the United Kingdom, with John Lennon, Paul McCartney, Roy Wood, Elton John and Noddy Holder and Jim Lea all contributing to popular hits. These can be personalized; obviously 'Master Blaster', by Stevie Wonder (1980), about peace coming to Zimbabwe and a time of hope for the third world, was more optimistic than prophetic, but it's a great celebration song. '1999', by Prince (1982), is an anthem for the *fin de siècle* (literally 'end of century'); though mostly used for the end of the nineteenth century, we are wordsmiths and can use it as we wish. Kool and the Gang have a great 'Celebration' (1980); Freddy Mercury wrote 'We Are the Champions' (1977). Of course, there is the antithesis: dare we mention 'The Final Countdown'? There – done it; now move on while I go and catch some fresh air (nothing personal, just can't stand that song).

- **The lament story** – oh, how we love these. 'Oh Lonesome Me' (Gibson 1958) takes the story straight to the personal breakdown of a relationship (see love above), but this can go so much further. A lament or lamentation is a passionate statement of heartache, grief, sorrow and often soaked in melancholy, and the human race has a history of lament stories through poetry, prose, music and song across cultures, countries, gender and other so-called boundaries. I'm Scottish and pìobaireachd music (any pipe music) has a strong lament tradition, as do many of the lyrical songs of Robert Burns. It is a tradition that goes back centuries. And we can see the traditions of the lament being characterized all over the world. The great American folk singer Tom Paxton tells the September 9/11 story in his lament entitled 'The Bravest' (2002), a song for the firemen who attended the destruction of the Twin Towers, World Trade Centre in New York, many of whom died saving others on that fateful day.

Christopher Booker's *The Seven Basic Plots: Why We Tell Stories* has seven plots:

- Overcoming the monster
- Rags to riches
- The quest
- Voyage and return
- Comedy
- Tragedy
- Rebirth

And we could see how these pan out for the songwriter; rags to riches, for example, is a fairly common one; Dolly Parton's 'Coat of Many Colours' (1971) but there are masses of them. And think of the variations: 'A Fairy Tale in New York' (Finer and McGowan 1987) takes a rags-to-more-rags approach. A great 'you and me' conversation, a duet piece sung by Shane McGowan and Kirsty MacColl, it tells a fine story in just over four minutes – and who can resist a song which has the immortal lines 'You scumbag/you maggot/you cheap lousy faggot.'

Storytelling, though, is universal and all around us. Everyone knows or has heard an interesting story. Only the other day I caught the video where Bob Dylan (1962) admitted to stealing the tune for 'The Death of Emmett Till' from Len Chandler. That's a story all to itself in the song-writer's almanac, surely – wouldn't you agree? But it is not hard to find a number of such stories about Bob Dylan, and we might return to the T. S. Eliot idea: 'Immature poets imitate; mature poets steal; bad poets deface what they take, and good poets make it into something better, or at least something different.' As Morrissey (1994) has shown in 'Now My Heart Is Full'. Here we have the songwriter growing into his own skin, and its biographical leaning is an obvious accumulation of thoughts on his own life. In 1995, he said:

> This song was the definitive expression of my change to adulthood, of my maturity. And, to be honest, I was very happy to be able to sing this text, to have reached this state. After this song I could perfectly retire: I've come full circle.

Coming a full circle is fully explained in the lines 'Now My Heart Is Full'. Sitting in a corner and writing or saying, 'I think I might write a song about my contentment' isn't the idea; that is the result of the ideas he pulled together, the fragments of ideas that have followed him around finally coming to rest. And surely the title describes something we all aspire to in our lives.

Having mentioned influences, though, 'Now My Heart Is Full' uses and refers to Graham Greene's (1938) *Brighton Rock* characters as a support cast to the narrator, who he identifies as the singer by keeping the song in first person.

> Tell all of my friends
> I don't have too many
> Just some rain-coated lovers' puny brothers
> Dallow, Spicer, Pinkie, Cubitt

Ask yourself why he might be using this cast of 'rain-coated lover's puny brother'? And even the real actor, Patric Doonan. Research why that might be. Is it an idea you can use?

And then sometimes too you just have to get on with it.

> I don't give a hoot what the writing's like, I write any sort of rubbish which will cover the main outlines of the story, then I can begin to see it.
>   (Frank O'Connor, 'The Arts of Fiction No 19', *The Paris Review*)

Frank O'Connor isn't talking about songwriting here, but we know what he means. Indeed, we need only go back to McCartney's 'scrambled eggs' for a clue. Wherever you choose to write, you should do so with a set rule, which should say something like.

Don't worry! Just write!

Go on, make up your own slogan, but when you do make sure the subtext says: there is no points system which penalizes you for bad lines, wrong words, scored-out doodles, dodgy rhymes (like 'moon in June'), duff similes, gobbledygook, gibberish, pretentiousness, affectation, Americanisms if you are not American, a Liverpool accent if you are not from Liverpool, substituting a French word because its sounds sexier . . . the thing is, writing is not the performance; it is the creative process which leads to a song that will be performed at a later date. And that later date will have seen the song go through many changes, edits and rewrites to get it right. Even in collaboration, there should be rules that say anything goes, no idea is too small and we don't chuck anything away until we are sure, because you never know what it will end up producing.

12

The great song title

One of the great things in songs is capturing a really good idea. We all know one of them and have moments when we think: I have a great idea for a great song here. For example, I am going to ask the listeners to imagine if things in the world were different. Well, that's a thought, a wondering out loud – but it's not really an idea. But then sitting with your notebook (virtual or not) and coming up with a really simple piano riff and a first line with *imagine* in it, and then writing down a title called 'Imagine,' followed by appropriate lyrics about how a world could be different if we did indeed imagine, and the title after the lyric begins to take shape – that's an idea. Surely we would all put up with scraps of paper, random lines, scorings out, rough words being assembled into some kind of order to come out with the well-organized song they became. Think these through for yourself: What song title really comes to mind? Then ask yourself whether your collection of bits is set up to really tell a story. Taking some title at random here, without actually analysing the lyrics themselves, we can see the ideas taking shape. Sometimes I see a title after I write the song, but other times the title is the song, and without it the song couldn't have taken shape. So write your own to work through. Scroll through a personal jukebox for some song titles and think about why you like them, what appeals, what comes to your attention, and then write them down. It's not a list of favourite songs, but a list of great or interesting titles which shows how ideas can be built up into something interesting. Sometimes I have worked with songwriters who have a title and an idea, but little else, and they have asked me to help develop the idea. Nothing wrong with that at all – New York is indeed a wonderful town; so too Chicago, and do I hear London calling? By taking fragments of ideas and then taking the ideas into a song, we begin to see how it's 'built'. If you get a good song title, write it down.

And this brings out a good idea for an exercise too. Pick your favourite song, and do something else with it – even rewrite it. This is an exercise we have both used when teaching songwriting. Indeed, if you are a non-instrumentalist, although you will need to forge links at some point in order to achieve the musical side of the song, in the meantime you can practice your craft by rewriting the lyrics to existing songs. Here's a good way of doing it:

Rewriting an existing song

- Decide upon a 'feel' for your song. Uplifting? Thought-provoking? Disturbing? Sorrowful? Annoyingly catchy?
- Expand upon this. What content/images/descriptions/characters will you use to achieve this?
- Write your idea as prose first, so you have content to work from. When you're done, highlight the phrases or words that achieve the 'feel' of your song.
- Select the song you're going to rewrite. Consider whether you want it to reflect the mood of your lyrics (e.g. sad lyrics, sad-sounding music) or juxtapose (e.g. sad lyrics, happy sounding music).
- Look at the structure of your chosen song. Identify what it's doing with regard to verses, choruses and so on. Identify the rhyme scheme and types.
- For example, take 'All My Loving' by The Beatles (1963b).

Structure: Verse 1, verse 2, chorus, solo, verse 3, chorus 2, outro.

Rhyme scheme: Verse 1: AAACCA; Verse 2: AABCCB; Chorus: AA rhyme types: identical or perfect

– Now copy the line structure onto a blank sheet of paper:

Verse 1: six lines; Verse 2: six lines; Chorus: two lines; Verse 3: six lines; Chorus 2: two lines (or four including outro).

– Start to populate the empty lines by moving the highlighted phrases across from your prose. Don't pay any attention to syllabic count, rhyme scheme or type at the moment. Keep doing this until you have the skeleton of the story you want to tell, in the required amount of lines. If rhymes occur naturally, allow this to happen, but don't hunt for them.

– Now start editing. We first need to look for a 'fit': making the words fit into their respective lines without having to stretch syllables or run them together. Refrain still further from looking at rhyme at this point. Check regularly that you're 'being true' to your original 'feel' or story during your edits. If it's turning out you're sacrificing these in order to get the words to fit, take a step back and consider how you may do both. When you've done this, start to look at rhyme.

– First, an important question: do you *need* rhyme? If you feel you do, consider why you think so. Is it for rhythm? Is it to make the song more memorable? Is it because you feel there *should* be rhyme? If it's the last, ignore the urge! But if you think rhyme is genuinely necessary for the good of the song, start to work some in.

Just remember that the story should dictate the rhyme, not the other way round.

– At this point, you may wish to revisit the rhyme scheme of the original. You might have naturally done this when writing anyway. *Or* you may wish to change the scheme. One thing I would advise against, though, is following the rhyme *types* of the original. It's likely this will lead to very forced writing where you're searching for particular words for the sake of rhyme, not because they're the *right* words.

13

Collaboration

I hadn't intended to write on collaboration, but then again, as this book is a collaboration, I thought, 'Why not?' Because actually it's a really good opportunity to move songs forward. As I wrote elsewhere in collaboration:

> The story of the solitary genius reached its apogee during the Romantic period and has remained attractive; but in fact writers are not solitary at all. They are attached to each other by skeins of influence and patterns of friendship, critique and review. They are attached, too, to the industry that is the field of literary production—agents, editors, publishers, designers, printers, distributors, reviewers, booksellers, and readers. And they are attached to society more broadly, having been made human beings within their particular culture and time, and with their tastes, knowledges, and predilections established by their personal and communal history.
>
> (Webb and Melrose 2011: 107)

Pat Pattison recounts a story about the time he collaborated with Stan Webb (no relation to Jimmy or Jen Webb):

> The best advice I ever got on co-writing was from Stan Webb . . . The door opened . . . He came in and then he did something curious. He shut the door again, re-opened it, shut it again, and then pushed it hard to make sure it was closed . . . [then said] you can probably tell by looking at me that I'm gonna say some of the dumbest things you've ever heard . . . But, as long as that door is closed, nobody needs to know.

Then he said:

> Say everything that comes into your head. Say it out loud, no matter how dumb it is. Don't censor anything. If you say something really dumb, you might give me an idea that's not quite as dumb . . . If you'd never said the dumb one, we would never get to the great one.
>
> (Pattison 2009: 290)

What Stan Webb was basically saying was, behind the closed door anything goes, Pattison called it a 'no' free zone, where the word *no* was never said, and you just keep going until a yes is said. It's a good system because isn't that actually what we do in private? We can actually write any old rubbish down until the nuggets begin to appear. It's a standard working practice before we start to distil the lyric, separating the grainy clichés and other mulch, much like extracting a fine whiskey from everything that goes into making it.

There are a couple of different ways to think about collaboration, though. There is the Elton John, Bernie Taupin way, where one is the musician and the other the lyricist; similarly, Holland, Dozier, Holland, where Eddie Holland was the lyricist; similarly, Morrissey and Marr, when they were The Smiths; Lennon and McCartney, before they started writing on their own, were a real collaborative team, both of them chipping in lyrics and tunes, and indeed McCartney did it again with Elvis Costello. What it does is maximize on ideas: you might come up with a line or a thought that your partner can relate to or take elsewhere, help you out of the cul-de-sac you have found yourself in, and of course vice versa. There is a good YouTube clip with Lori McKenna talking about 'Girl Crush' as part of the CMA Songwriters Series (https://www.youtube.com/watch?v=KcaYcwsC47s), which won song of the year. Working in collaboration can be hugely satisfying in what can be a lonely life. Indeed, Red Hot Chili Peppers' and U2's songs are usually credited to all the members of the band.

There isn't a huge amount to add to this process, mostly because collaboration is something everybody in a band or who works with others understands. It's something useful to consider, especially if you are a lyricist and not a musician, because the musicality of the lyrics is really important to the end result.

14

To rhyme, or not to rhyme: that is the question

We have already stated that lyrics are not poetry, though we agree with Jimmy Webb when he says, 'Not all great poetry is lyrical but all great lyrics are poetic . . . Which is to say all great lyrics use the devices of poetry – *metaphor, simile, imagery, alliteration* and *meter*, among others' (1998: 12). And while rhyme is often associated with poetry (though less so these days, where there is more freedom), it is fair to say that rhyme is first and foremost a musical device (and I maintain this even in the face of up-in-arms poets). Musically, it pleasures that basic of senses, the one we first react to as babies, hearing itself. It's a mnemonic exercise in recognition, combining music with words to delight us, especially in popular songs, ballads and the like. And combined with a distinctive voice, they develop our memories – and rhyming has a huge part to play in this. Poetry attracts the senses through our reading and sometimes through the recitation, but the song lyric is like no other, because in a perfect situation it comes straight to us through the sense of hearing; and what a delight it is to be able to 'listen', especially to something that can bring such enormous pleasure, and even more to someone who brings joy in the delivery.

Of course, as we have also said already, although there is a very close relationship between song lyrics and poetry, there is a distinction to be made between the two. As Jen Webb (2017) (no relation to Jimmy) has written in an article about Bob Dylan receiving the Nobel Prize for Literature in 2017:

> The first poems were almost certainly sung – but centuries ago, the two creative modes parted company. They operate now according to a different logic, depend on different traditions, and are located within very different ecosystems. This is not a question of relative quality; it is a question of categories.

Jen Webb's point acknowledges this, but the difference in categories is marked. Nick Cave (Lewis 2015) says the same with regard to the aforementioned *The Sick Bag Song*:

> There was certainly a point where I had to let go of the idea that it was just a really long song. Then I had to get over the particular hurdle of writing something that would open myself up to a certain amount of criticism, possibly. Because I'm stepping outside what I normally do, which is song writing, into something that there's a whole different critical approach to, which is poetry. I've always stayed away from poetry. Maybe I *should* stay away from poetry!

And let's leave the last word with the aforementioned Bob Dylan (2017), from his Nobel Prize–winning speech:

> Our songs are alive in the land of the living. But songs are unlike literature. They're meant to be sung, not read. The words in Shakespeare's plays were meant to be acted on the stage. Just as lyrics in songs are meant to be sung, not read on a page. And I hope some of you get the chance to listen to these lyrics the way they were intended to be heard: in concert or on record or however people are listening to songs these days. I return once again to Homer, who says, 'Sing in me, oh Muse, and through me tell the story.'

Nevertheless, understanding poetics, where lyrical shape, rhythm, rhyme, scan is all down to wordplay, is an important aspect of writing. And like poetry, we can begin to categorize the topic, subject matter, type of lyric, and for this we will take Dylan's Homer 'and through me tell the story' and ask you to think about *story*.

Rhyme is the repetition of the same end sound or sounds – moon/ June, tall/fall, mole/hole, orange . . . well, you get the idea. It can be one of the most satisfying and disastrous characteristics of songwriting – there goes the oxymoron again. A good rhyme will carry your song long into the night, its mnemonic qualities lingering in the heads of the listeners for a long, long time. As Citron (1990: 109) writes:

> No matter how new or daring your concept, how outlandish and original your harmony, most listeners feel more comfortable with rhymed lyrics because:
> 1. rhyme gives weight to our thoughts
> 2. rhyme follows the natural contours of the melody
> 3. rhyme creates a musical effect with words that have similar sounds
> 4. rhyme jogs our memory and helps us remember the song
> 5. rhyme helps the listener guess and understand our message

Then again, a bad rhyme, a forced rhyme, a clumsy compromise for the sake of a rhyme can kill a song stone dead. We have all heard them, the clumsy forcing rhyme for the sake of it. Though of course this is subjective, in some cases it's amazing what you can get away with. Remember the Grammy-nominated 'Horse With No Name', by America (Bunnell 1971)? 'I've been to the desert on a horse with no name/It felt good to be out of the rain/In the desert you can't remember your name/'Cos there ain't no one for to give you no pain.' I cringe writing it down, and yet it was a huge hit. So definitely one with mnemonic charm, though don't ask me if I admire that last line. To be fair, in the sleeve notes to the *Highway: Thirty Years of America* (2000), Dewey Bunnell did comment on the language he used on the song:

> I have taken a lot of poetic license in my use of grammar, and I always cringe a little bit at my use of 'aint's,' like 'ain't no one for to give you no pain' in 'Horse'. I've never actually spoken that way, but I think it conveys a certain honesty when you're not picking and choosing your words, and you use that kind of colloquialism.

Actually, for me, the entire line 'ain't no one for to give you no pain' is in my top 10 of worst lyrics ever. It's such a clumsy line – why is there a 'for to' there? And of course it's a double, double negative because written like this, it means there *is* someone to give you pain – or does it? – because no one ever said songs had to have literal sense. A song is a song, not an example of literal language – another thing we can share with the poetics of poetry.

In this chapter we look at rhyme and its potential and whether we need it or not. We also look at 'perfect rhyme' and 'imperfect rhyme', to give them de-gendered designations (we would like to say, they are often referred to as 'masculine' and 'feminine' rhymes because they refer to so-called strong and so-called weak rhymes, and we only mention this in case you have come across the terms before).

Let's begin with the most obvious thing to say about writing a lyric. It is not necessary to rhyme. Paul Simon's (1968) 'America' doesn't have a single rhyme, except a small imperfect coupling, 'seems like a dream'. But even as they are coupled here, the song doesn't actually depend on it rhyming, and if we had never heard the 'seems' and 'dream' coupling, I'm not sure we would have ever missed it – the song being such a brilliant 'story' (see above) which we concentrate on more as a dextrous lyrical accomplishment. We talk more about internal rhymes further down this chapter.

Other examples of none or sparing rhymes for popular songs for you to check out are (famously) 'Moonlight in Vermont' 'Annie's Song'; and my own favourite, 'The First Time Ever I Saw Your Face'. There is a *skies* and *eyes* in 'The First Time Ever I Saw Your Face', but by the time we get to the *skies*, the strength of the rhyme has virtually gone. The same goes for *hand* and *command* – they fit well and rhyme well and indeed look great on the page (Do any of you do that – write things that look symmetrical on the page?), but the song doesn't rely on the rhyme and could live with replacements quite easily. Then again, just because we can write songs without rhyme, it doesn't make our struggle to find them any less reasonable, because there is no question that they can and do add something special to our hearing and even to our lives. There is a great deal of joy in a good rhyme in a good song. It may only be an aesthetic enjoyment. but when was *jouissance* in anything but the physical or intellectual pleasure, delight or ecstasy which reminds us we are alive?

Rhyme comes to us early in childhood in the songs we hear as children, and of course the name *nursery rhymes* gives the game away. Earlier I mentioned:

> Row, row, row your boat,
> Gently down the stream,
> Merrily, merrily, merrily, merrily,
> Life is but a dream.

The perfect rhyme in *stream* and *dream* hold this little melody together very well. and it's not hard to see how songs move around like this for children:

> Simple Simon met a pieman
> Going to the fair.
> Says Simple Simon to the pieman
> Let me taste your ware!

Rhyming *Simon* with *pieman* in the same line is a mild nudge onto the imperfect rhyme, but *fair* and *ware* come to the rescue well enough, and it doesn't stray far from the perfect nursery rhyme. One of my favourites plays around a lot more:

> Rub-a-dub-dub, we sail in a tub,
> And where do you think we'll go?
> An island I see with bananas in trees,
> Coconuts swaying merrily.
> Let's step ashore; there's so much more.
> Oh, what a beautiful scene!

There are internal rhymes (contained within the line) *dub* and *tub; ashore* and *more*, and even though its theoretically a little more sophisticated than straight line end rhymes, its hardly difficult to understand why it works. As I said above too, the rhyme in the nursery rhyme is mnemonic and is intrinsic to our early recognition patterns – words and the speakers. And it is probably worth saying something about that here. Later we talk about rhythm too, and it is intrinsic to the rhyming patterns here that the rhythm sits perfectly, rhyming on the beat. Clap along while reciting or even singing these, and you will see how and why they work so well.

But consider how important this rhyming is in child development before considering your own means of developing it. In his chapter 'Writing and Education: The Value of Reconciling Teaching and Research', Paul Munden (2016) wrote:

> Ken Robinson, in his keynote talk at the Confident Creativity conference in Glasgow, March 2005, presented a chart he referred to as 'The decline of genius', depicting our diminishing capacity for analogous, lateral or metaphorical thinking as we 'progress'.

Age	Capability
3–5	98%
8–10	32%
13–15	10%
25+	2%

This is an interesting set of ideas, especially because most reading this will be over the age of 15. What it tells us is that the early mnemonic device of lyrical rhyming for children, especially when it is associated with the happy, clappy sound of singing (such as in a nursery rhyme) has a profound effect on their development at this early age of maximum capability. Being aware of this is useful because we can see why it stays with us throughout our lives. Tapping our feet in time, clapping in time and feeling the rhyme sitting on the beat is an intrinsic part of human development. In fact, it is so intrinsic that we almost take it for granted. Though should we worry about this? I think not. Because what actually happens is, in taking it for granted, we turn to more advanced ideas; for example, our concept of metaphor changes too. As Munden also reminds us, Aristotle says:

> The greatest thing by far is to be a master of metaphor. It is the one thing that cannot be learnt from others; and it is also a sign of genius, since a good metaphor implies an intuitive perception of the similarity in dissimilars.

And as we have discussed previously, our development of the basic rhyme in songwriting, in storytelling, for example, coupled with our intrinsic desire for metaphor and a more thoughtful approach, comes about as we mature as thinkers and writers. The rhyme may have been with us from childhood, but the development of it as a metaphorical and emblematic song lyric comes much later. Nevertheless, no matter how metaphorical you hope to be, the rhyme works in a song because it resonates with the musical pattern and punctuates the thoughts being assembled while allowing the listener to anticipate what is about to be said – promoting familiarity with the subject. Let's turn to rhyme itself, then, by asking, what makes a rhyme rhyme?

What makes a rhyme rhyme?

Simply put, a perfect rhyme is comprised of words which have matching vowel sounds with not too dissimilar consonants sounds. For example, *host* and *post, past* and *fast*. It's not a hard and fast rule, for example *frost* and *post* works, as do *flack* and *park* if a little pushed; *crashed* and *past* work too, for obvious reasons, though they are not strictly perfect. And we could see how 'he *crashed past* the *host* waiting for the *post* to arrive, despite the morning *frost*' picks up rhyming along the way. The fact is most of this information can be had from the rhyming dictionary or its equivalent (https://www. rhymezone.com/ and http://www.rhymer.com/ are free to access, among many others), which all songwriters should have in their armoury. I'm not going to insult you here by suggesting good and bad *rhymes*; like good and bad *times*, they are all in the province of what *rhymes* best for *you* and *who* else you are trying to *best impress*. What's probably more important, having discussed *why* we use them, now we can discuss *how* we use them.

What kind of rhymes are there

Perfect rhyme

Often, the worst kind of mistake a lyricist can make is to write a perfect iambic pentameter, metrical rhyme (or something similar) which looks pretty on the page, and then expect someone (including yourself) to put a tune to it. And if you haven't gathered, the simplest is an **AA BB** or **AB AB** rhyme, with each line ending with a rhyme, such as:

AA BB
A – crow
A – know
B – fly
B – die

AB AB
A – crow
B – die
A – know
B – fly

They look fine written down on paper, and it might be okay as a song; certainly I have seen it done, but it loses room for spontaneity and generally sounds a little stiff in the delivery. So move it around a bit – the variations aren't hard to suggest:

AB CB
A – crow
B – die
C – cried
B – fly

A BB A
A – crow
B – die
B – fly
A – know

AA BCC B
A – crow
A – know
B – die
C – cried
C – tried
B – fly

ABC ABC DC
A – crow
B – die
C – cried
A – know
B – fly
C – tried
D – hope
C – died

Indeed, some of the best songs miss the line and let it lie fallow, as in

ABC ABC DC
A – crow
B – die
C – cried
A – know
B –
C – tried
D – tender
C – died

And of course the missing B line could be any of the lines as the music and delivery dictates, because nobody says you have to fill every line – quite often leaving breathing space or space for emphasis works well.

ABC ABC DBCDE
A – crow
B – die
C – cried
A – know
B – X
C – tried
D – tender
B – sigh
C – X
D – remember
E – crying

You can work your own way through permutations like these now that there is some understanding about what rhyming essentially means; and we will talk about internal *rhymes* in *lines* – like this *one* I have just *done* – next, however imperfect the *rhyme might* be – like *tender* and *remember* (with a double and a triple syllable thrown in for good measure). Let's, then, consider some alternatives to the perfect rhyme.

Imperfect rhyme

Also called half *rhyme*, near *rhyme*, oblique *rhyme* or off *rhyme, it is* a *rhyme* in which the vowels and/or the consonants of the predominant or stressed syllables are identical. an example being:

> time/crime
> breeze/leave
> soul/old
> eyes/light
> yours/tears
> fine/time

Or even words that look as they should on paper but need 'nursing' in a song, such as these:

> love/move

It's not difficult to see how these could be brought into a verse when we are looking for a more intimate way of addressing the listener. A perfect rhyme can be too exact and a little stiff, which makes it a little unrealistic. These days singers tend to go for a more intimate contact with the audience, and the more informal imperfect rhyme lends itself to this because it leans closer to real conversation.

Internal rhyme

I mentioned this above, the internal rhyme in a song is a wonderful way of accenting the line. Previously, I mentioned 'America', by Paul Simon, and the only rhyme in the entire song is an internal, where he sings,

'Michigan *seems* like a *dream* to me now.' We can see the rhyme sitting safely in the middle of the line, but it is wonderfully effective. Often it's used to emphasize or accentuate the line, as in the case of 'America', but it brings a nice rhythmic sense to the storytelling. Work some of them out on paper just to see how they work:

* How does the *crow know* what you are thinking?
* *Excuses* are *useless* without good intentions.
* Can you *remind* us how to *find* love on the other *side* of the track?

It works well as an alliteration too:

* The tractor move<u>s</u> <u>s</u>o <u>s</u>low down the dirt road track.

And of course there are the combinations:

* <u>kiss</u>ing me soft*ly*, <u>miss</u>ing me bad*ly*

Identical rhyme

Rhyming a word with itself, is usually done as a homonym, where each of two or more words have the same spelling or pronunciation, but different meanings and origins. It's a great way to use a word which can have more than one meaning. One of my favourite examples of this is actually in a Patty Griffin song, 'Nobody Crying' (2002a), where she pulls together:

wish you well/wishing well

And we can do this easily, if we think it through:

call to arms/lift your arms
the chair [person] is in the chair [seat]
check out the check on her dress
leaves fall in the fall
nothing to see but sea
Jack Daniels drank only Jack Daniels 'til he was full to the gills on gills

Family rhyme

Family rhyme is a perfect rhyme substitute. Close, almost married to, imperfect rhyme, in the family the rhyming syllables have the same vowel sounds and the consonant sounds after the vowel are phonetically related, but the rhyming syllables begin differently – so you can see the family connections. Examples are actually quite familiar:

    cut/stuck
    kiss/wish
    run/funk

Additive Rhymes have identical vowel sounds, and the consonants after the vowel add a little sound to resolve and stabilize the line:

    free/speed
    glow/stove
    fit/grits
    fine/resigned
    cry/smile

It is also used where we use more than one word to emphasize the lyric; it's a 'fine line'; she was a 'child bride'; his Elvis pelvis thrust – well, you get it.

Subtractive Rhymes have identical vowel sounds, but the consonants after the vowel subtract a little sound to slightly destabilize the line:

    speed/free
    stove/glow
    resigned/fine
    smile/cry

Assonance rhymes occur where the identical vowel sounds and ending consonants belong to different phonetic families:

    life/tide
    blood/rush
    fool/rude
    fire/smile

Consonance rhymes are where different vowel sounds and ending consonants are Identical:

friend/wind
defence/innocence
one/gone
one/alone
scars/fears
filled/crawled

No rhyme

The no rhyme song isn't such a novelty, especially these days, and I have already mentioned examples. This doesn't have to be a problem for the writer; indeed, it can be a great deal of fun and is often very effective. But it's worth bearing in mind why a good rhyme appeals to us.

Accents rhyme

There is the issue of accents and the way we pronounce the rhyme. *Pies* and *lies* may sit nicely on a line, but we have all heard *tricks* and route *sixty-six*, which we accept without much thought (imperfect as it is). And there's even the way Bob Dylan manipulates the rhymes in 'Oxford Town', but this can be taken so much further. There is nothing to say we have to be completely literal and without accent to play with the rhyme. 'We have got to get out of this hell of a mess' might be a decent, literal line but why can't it be 'We *gotta* get *outa* this *helluva* mess'. And of course the vocables which singers so love are equally at home as a rhyme. We aren't going to say, 'I am so blue' when the song demands '*Ooh who ooh*, I'm feeling so *blue hoo hoo* for *you hoo hoo/Doncha ha ha* have me up all *na na* night singing those *boo hoo hoo blues.*' Okay a little over the top, overworked and comic (perhaps), but you get the meaning. The fact is, a song takes on a life of its own where rhyme is concerned. It is not Homer, Shakespeare, a perfect Don DeLillo sentence or an article in the *New York Review of Books*; it's the line of a 'saw-haw-hong' (song) – which may look ridiculous written down like this but sounds just fine.

One of the best things about rhyming, though, is getting the really nice ones to work. Don't force them: look for alternatives, and look at the lyrics of those who do it well. Morrissey, for example, is a master rhyming wordsmith; so too, Glen Tilbrook and Chris Difford (1979) (listen to 'Up the Junction'), Bob Dylan, Fifty Cent, Adele, Steve Earle, Elvis Costello, Joni Mitchell (1971b) (who managed to rhyme *figure skater* with *coffee percolator* in 'The Last Time I Saw Richard'), Randy Newman and Nick Cave. But the truth is, you will have your own ideas. Check them out and then check out the rhymes used. There are very few words that will not rhyme in some way. *Orange* famously doesn't have a perfect rhyme, but don't let that stop you from using it – after all not everything has to rhyme. Also, better to find a good half rhyme than a cheap solid rhyme which does half a job. Your listeners will forgive a half rhyme before they forgive something forced, like 'collagen' and 'apologizin' from Kanye West (for example). And once again, get your own – you know you have heard lines that just make you wince. And I will close this section in time for tea and a *scone*, which rhymes with *anon* or *bone*, depending on how your accent delivers the vowel. Confusing? Not really. The cake is yours to bake – just don't leave it out in the rain (name that tune and songwriter – 'MacArthur Park', by Richard Harris [1968a]).

15

The marriage between words and music

Every song is made up of lyrics and accompanying music – that's a fact. But the 'to read or not to read' music is a question that will never go away, especially between those who do and those who don't. Jimmy Webb can, John Lennon couldn't and I don't need to go further with this idea. The fact is, some people can hear melody and play it, and some can hear melody and write it down, but ultimately there is no right and wrong – though some might add it's a good job Andrew Lloyd Webber could transcribe the music for Tim Rice's lyrics. I once heard them 'sing' an early song composition on UK television (the Michael Parkinson show, I think): Tim Rice is no Elaine Paige.

The thing is the music is the means of delivery; it's the art form that takes the lyric from eyes on the page to the ears, and it can be as basic as a single chord. The idea of a one-chord song isn't such a new one. John Lee Hooker (1968) was quite famous for single-chord tunes in his time: check out 'Wednesday Evening Blues' or even Robert Wilkins's 'Rolling Stone'. It also might come as no surprise that the Beatles worked at one-chord songs, particularly with 'Tomorrow Never Knows' (The Beatles 1966b), though if you listen, it's really not quite a single-chord song; same, too, with 'Norwegian Wood'. Basically the melody in 'Tomorrow Never Knows' is sung over a single sounding chord, but the dissonance that creates is part of the charm and technique – especially using the sitar sympathetic strings as a drone string effect. The drone strings keep a constant sound, and the melody is overlaid. This can be heard most famously in bagpipe music, where the pipe drones hold the melody. 'Helen Wheels' (Linda and Paul McCartney 1973) is almost the Beach Boys meets Suzie Quatro as a song, but it's a great exercise in moving the lyric around a single-chord melody, showing the dexterity of rock and roll, as inherited from the likes of John Lee Hooker. Indeed, its perfect boy band fare, and though Def Leppard did a fine version, I am surprised it's not been purloined by a boy band already. Indeed, there is a nice story behind it. In the book *Paul McCartney in His Own Words* (1976: 80), McCartney said:

> Helen Wheels is our Land Rover. It's a name we gave to our Land Rover, which is a trusted vehicle that gets us around Scotland. It takes us up to the Shetland Islands and down to London. The song starts off in Glasgow, and it goes past Carlisle, goes to Kendal, Liverpool, Birmingham and London. It's the route coming down from our Scottish farm to London, so it's really the story of the trip down. Little images along the way. Liverpool is on the West coast of England, so that is all that means.

And I add this just to continue the storytelling and ideas line addressed previously – see, ideas really are all around.

The point is, being a songwriter is not necessarily about being Mozart, Schubert, Marvin Hamlisch, Leonard Bernstein or even Andrew Lloyd Weber. Musicality is something we all possess: we like what we hear and we can learn to play what we like, even if it's just one chord. We would like to be able to say, 'Here is the "music well" of you – go and draw from it, and we wish you well in the effort.' But it's not like that. What it comes down to is the magic of music, the music we hear in our own head that just seems to get there. Of course its influenced by what we hear, what came before, and by the anticipation of something we are trying to get close to, but I am so glad this book is about lyrics and not music, which is so much harder to explain. However, there are places we can go to when thinking about sequences and the marriage between music and lyrics.

I mentioned *iambic pentameter* before – literally, it is a common meter in poetry consisting of an unrhymed line with five feet, or accents, each foot containing an unaccented syllable and an accented syllable. Well, in real terms, in some ways it's the perfect pop or rock song meter because that definition translates as da-*dum*, da-*dum*, da-*dum*, da-*dum*, da-*dum*. Think about it: whether you speed it up or slow it down, it coincides with the common heartbeat. Tap your chest while saying out loud, '*Shall I compare thee to a summer's day.*' It works perfectly on the beat. Now instead of five accents, think of eight played in straight 4/4 time, da-*dum*, da-*dum*, da-*dum*, da-*dum*, da-*dum*, da-*dum*, da-*dum*, da-*dum* – just like most rock and pop songs, and I guess the idea of perfect beats is a good way to start thinking about how you line your lines and rhymes up. Indeed, replicate the da-*dum* effect against 'Helen Wheels', and you will see what I mean. But there are ways, as McCartney shows, how you can change the musicality of the straight da-*dum* by the way the lyrics are phrased, pulled off the beat, sung under the beat and through the beat, and by and lengthening the line over the beat, because the back beat is there to hold the rhythm while the music takes the lyrics for a walk (or a run in the case of rock and roll).

What we are talking about is the musicality and the structure of the delivery, as opposed to the music itself, which is a whole new thing altogether. As Jimmy Webb wrote:

> The one thing that I find myself unable to explain after decades of contemplation is why a composer will or should choose one note over another. In my practice it is an entirely subjective response that – I almost regret to say – seems to originate in the source of my emotions, wherever that is. In an objective sense, the composer is able to read the words and to attempt making the music mirror or intensify the meaning of them . . . But at the end of the day – as the British like to say – the soul makes the hard decisions utilizing its emotional ears. Only one postscript might be added: If the composer has heard a sad song and been moved by it, his criteria for expressing 'sadness' may in some way be molded by this experience. (1998: 260)

Turning the lyric into a song comes in many guises as the lyrics are woven round a tune and vice versa, and composers can only go with their own gut reaction, experience and the tune they hear in their head. This is isn't a book on musicality, though lyrics do possess this, or even whether to think about major or minor keys or even a combination of these, but a book on how to put lyrics to chords and tunes you are already doodling with. This is where genre becomes useful again. If you want to write a sub-country song like Jason Isbell or an English pop tune like Guy Garvey, your experience and immersion in that music will tilt you in that direction. The same goes for moods and subjects. If there is sadness to be written about, and you are listening to a lot of sad songs, they become bound up in your experience and will have an effect – even if you choose to write the opposite for the cathartic effect. And this will be aligned to other factors like your musicianship or that of your collaborators. A lack of music playing ability didn't do the punk generation any harm at all, and indeed a three- or four-chord country player or blues player or rock and roll player can get by. But there are some crucial things to look out for, which I list here:

Have I heard that tune before? When I heard 'Speed Trap Town' (2015) https://www.youtube.com/watch?v=0ghXad3cWnY by Jason Isbell, I thought there was something vaguely familiar about the phrasing and snatches of the tune. It nagged at me for a bit because the phrasing is quite precise. And then I remembered 'Girl in the War', by Josh Ritter (2006), https://www.youtube.com/watch?v=kqLssKusGzM. Check them both out side by side. Both are very different songs – but hang on: there is something quite eerily similar in the musical phrasing. I'm not suggesting plagiarism, but more of what Webb calls the 'subconscious – that silent collaborator' (1998: 260), drawing parallels. Though sometimes it's hard to decide. And to be honest, I am sure we have all written and sung something we really like without actually realizing we might just have heard it before. Indeed, a Los Angeles jury determined that Robin Thicke and Pharrell Williams's (2013) 'Blurred Lines' was essentially a steal from Marvin Gaye's (1977) hit song, 'Got to Give It Up', and it cost them a cool $7.2 million (US). It seems pointless to say it, but if you claim to be channelling the spirit or feeling of another's work, you just might find yourself closer to the truth of it than you think. Then again, Neil Young confessed he had taken 'Borrowed Tune' from the Rolling Stones because he was too wasted to write his own.

What has this to do with writing song lyrics? Well, not a lot except when we are making a song out of the lyrics and the chords sequences, and the marriage between words and music is an important part of the art form. We hear the tune we are trying to write to support the lyric, but our subconscious is bombarded with melodies on a daily basis (as we say in the Introduction). It's hard to live in the twenty-first century without being exposed to music and musical motifs around which songs are or can be constructed. Not to mention our own influences. You only have to google 'Led Zeppelin influences' to see what can and has been done in the past. Furthermore, in choosing to write in key C major, say, there are a finite number of notes to be played around with, even though the order in which they are played has huge variations.

16

Structure and Rhythm

One of the simplest things to say about life is that we human beings are used to structure. We get how it works: normally, we sleep through the night, eat breakfast in the morning, lunch in the middle of the day and then dinner before the day ends. That is to say, *normally*, and songs are the same: normally, there is structure to them. Pat Pattison (2009: 180) calls it the 'Five Elements of Structure,' putting it this way, and it is hugely cogent:

> Every section of every lyric you write uses five elements – and always the same five elements – of structure. These elements conspire to act like a film score and, in and of themselves, create motion. And motion always creates emotion, completely independent of what is being said. Ideally structure should create prosody – support what is being said – strengthening the message, making it more powerful.

The five element of structure are listed here:

1. Number of lines
2. Length of lines
3. Rhythm of lines
4. Rhyme scheme
5. Rhyme type

Number of lines: Did you know a Shakespearean sonnet has 14 lines? The first 12 lines are divided into three quatrains with four lines each.

In the three quatrains, the poet establishes a theme or problem and then resolves it in the final two lines, called the couplet. Once again, songs are not poetry, but this idea of structure is important. It says a great deal about prosody: the patterns of rhythm and sound or the patterns of stress and intonation in the lyrics forming the line in a song. It also helps you to understand the idea of how a song's structure helps with its delivery. Taking a look at the lyrics sheet of your favourite songs, you will probably see a different structure (which is not to say a Shakespearian sonnet cannot be put to music; I have tried it – it can), but one quite structured nevertheless. And if we think in straight 4/4 timing, for example, a very easy structure could be a simple 24-line song, viz:

- **Verse :** four lines
- **Chorus:** four lines
- **Verse: :** four lines
- **Chorus :** four lines
- **Bridge:** four lines
- **Chorus:** four lines

Taking the basic rules that even something like the Shakespearian sonnet offers:

Verse 1: introduces the topic, situation, problem etc.
Chorus: emphasizes the hook

Verse 2: takes the theme forward
Chorus: [re] emphasizes and repeats the hook

Bridge: accentuates the topic, situation, problem and so forth, and allows for space to pause and reflect on the earlier portions of the song or to prepare for the climax or concluding chorus

Chorus: [re] emphasizes the hook

Simple and to the point – and the point is that you have the opportunity to structure your song in a way that suits the story you are about to tell. Let's look at it another way – because you might even find writing the structure useful when pulling the lyrical content together:

Musical Intro	Verse 1 (words here)	Chorus (words here)	Verse 2 (words here)	Chorus (repeat)	Bridge (words here)	Chorus (repeat)	Musical Outro

But play around with it:

Chorus 1	Verse 1	Chorus 1	Verse 2	Chorus 2 (no need for just one)	Bridge	Chorus 1 and 2	Guitar break	Chorus 1 and 2	Chorus I and 2 repeat and fade

Or take a famous song to work out, like 'All You Need is Love' (The Beatles 1967a). Have a listen to it while looking at the following chart. It is an interesting structure – made all the more so because it essentially has two choruses, one of which plays as a musical refrain throughout. Now, I am pretty certain it wasn't originally written with this 'love, love, love,' refrain playing almost throughout (though it might have been), and we can see how the production and performance enhanced the song itself. Lyrically and structurally, though, it's actually not all that unconventional.

Intro & Chorus 1	Verse 1 & chorus 1 backing	Chorus 1	Verse 2 & chorus 1 backing	Chorus 2	Chorus 1 & Guitar break backing	Chorus 2	Verse 3 & chorus 1 backing	Chorus 2 repeat ad lib	Outro

This could go on ad infinitum with such an example, as you already know. These permutations are all up to you and how well you feel the song hangs together. However, it is a great exercise. In my experience the fledgling songwriter tends to try to push too much into the song and often needs a good edit – not just for clarity but for musicality and all the other prosodic tensions you are trying to create. This is not just common in songwriting. How many times have you read a potentially good book that has just gone on too long, or seen a great movie idea go wrong because structurally its just not hanging together well enough?

Sometimes I want to say, 'Why don't they learn how to do all the good bits and then concentrate on it like that?' It's mostly because the creative process takes over, and often the 'structure' suffers. At least in your early songs, stick to a plan that works; then stick to your plan. Eventually you will be able to improvise and develop, but to do this you need to know the basics. Sometimes there is nothing worse than a writer who has a great verse and great chorus with a great hook but ruins it with overkill until its begins to trip its own self up – and once again check out your favourite songs and see how it works out for them.

Length of Lines: Even if you don't read music or understand how music is split into bars, beats in the bar and so on, you will hear a song line by line, and you will also hear how those lyrical lines correspond with the musical ones (to give them a non-musical description). As Pattison says (2009), though, 'the length of a line is not determined by the number of syllables, but by the number of *stressed* syllables [my italics].' It is the stressed syllables which help 'determine the musical bars'. And adding to this, we could look at an example. Three lines in succession, with four stress lines, is an ideal start, and then the verse is rounded off with a three stress. Take these lines of different lengths:

> 　　1　　　　2　　　3　　　4
> Her **eyes** are a **midnight blue**
> 　　　　　　1　　2　　　3　　　4
> And give no **clue** that **she** even **likes you**
> 　　　　　1　　　2　　　3　　　4
> Just one **look** in the **cold light** of **day**
> 　　1　　　　2　　　3
> Could **stop** a **truck** in its **tracks**

The four-stressed lines give the leading information on the story, and the three-stressed fourth line opens up the intrigue, or 'instability' as Pattison calls it. What the three regular lines do is feed us ideas, but the payoff tells us she is not a woman to be messed with – and the three stressed syllables help with this delivery, where the missing fourth stress is a pause that lets the singer linger and the listener ponder. You might have hear some clichéd singers end a line like this in the following way:

1   2   3   4
Could **stop** a **truck** in its **tracks** – yes she **can**
1   2   3   4
Could **stop** a **truck** in its **tracks** – oh **man**
1   2   3   4
Could **stop** a **truck** in its **tracks** – hell **yeah**

Oh dear, says I, I'm only guessing here but I never knew a songwriter/
lyricist who would write this kind of cliché, which some singers tend to
ad lib. But actually leaving it hanging adds to the intrigue a little more
(well, I think so).

Rhythm

This is a tricky one. If you are a music teacher who is explaining
musical rhythm and notes and stressed words hitting beats, it is perfectly obvious. If you have ever tried to write – or even rewrite – a
verse in a hymn, you will see what I mean. Traditional hymns are
very precise, mostly because congregation members are all following a fixed musical score. There isn't space to improvise on how the
lyric is delivered when the rest of the congregation are singing along.
Similarly, football/rugby crowds, if you have ever hear a Twickenham
(English rugby stadium) crowd sing 'Swing Low Sweet Chariot', you
will hear what I mean. The rhythm of the delivery depends on the
precision of everyone trying to hit the same pacing, and you will not
get the improvisation of Ladysmith Black Mambazo, for example.
However, interpretation of rhythm is an essential part of a good
delivery, and even singers who interpret the same song do so differently. Aretha Franklin sings a different version of Carole King's '(You
Make Me Feel) Like a Natural Woman'; Glenn Campbell (who died
while I am writing this) sings 'Wichita Lineman' (Webb 1968) differently from James Taylor. So regular rhythms are the way we write
songs on paper, but writing around an instrument, drum pattern or
some such allows us to play with the rhythm of the lines a little. And
this is so crucial to performance.

Rhyme scheme rhyme type I look at this extensively above. We all like a good rhyme, and with rhythm rhymes can be a little subjective. To use a motoring analogy, though, they should be road signs in the song, not speed bumps. They are there to supplement the song and enhance the remembering in the listener. Look back at the chapter on schemes and types, with this proviso: don't get wedded to a rhyme for the sake of it; a bad one can kill a good song.

What we are looking for in structure is a way to move the story of the song through to its conclusion in the best possible way. Every story has a beginning, a middle, and an ending, though not necessarily in that order; every day, week, month, year is the same; school terms, university semesters, football matches, slow dances in a roadhouse on a Saturday night are the same. We live structured lives, and at its simplest a song fits into that idea, even when it stops us in our tracks so we can say, 'Wow!' A song is another story in the story of our lives.

Conclusion: Unveiling the critically creative writer

Writing Song Lyrics has had a series of aims:

- To explore the importance of song lyrics as an academic subject in their own right
- To understand the importance of author biography, and how it can be manipulated
- To analyse how we listen to music, and how this can influence our writing
- To discover how different lyricists persuade, influence, and elicit emotional reactions in us
- To discuss the role of cliché and formula in lyrics
- To discuss the importance of rhyme, rhythm, and structure
- To find inspiration for our own lyrics
- To explore storytelling techniques
- To be creative and critical at the same time, and how the two can be mutually beneficial to us as songwriters

Throughout, it has been our intention to make this book both interesting and through-provoking; both challenging and accessible; both serious and fun. The initial idea for writing this was to right the wrong that in academia, song lyrics are somehow seen as a 'poor relation' to the mega-powers of poetry and literature, when they are so influential in our everyday lives. By fusing the critical with the creative, the academic with the informal, we have aimed to show that thinking deeply about the lyrics we listen to can help develop our own lyrics, just as how studying the language and symbolism of a poem may improve our poetic voice. We have also attempted to demonstrate that although there are patterns throughout the history of popular music lyrics, we can be original whist still adhering to the tried and tested formulae of 'catchiness', 'repetition', or even 'cliché'.

Lyrics can be simplistic and monosyllabic; they can be sprawling and epic; they can be odes to loved ones, rants at hated ones, rallying calls for the oppressed and victimised; they can be a much-needed friend during dark times; they can make us feel happy, make us feel sad, make us thoughtful, make us angry; as we have already said, 'a song is another story in the story of our lives.' As writers, they present us with opportunities to tell our own stories, and to impact others with our words. And if we combine the power of these words with the power of music, it leads us to a combination that brings meaning, hope, passion, enlightenment, wonder, joy, comfort and humour to millions of people every year. If this books helps you to realise this then, great. If it makes you think about being a better songwriter, then also, great. But along the way, don't forget to enjoy yourselves. After all, in the words of Paul McCartney: 'We don't work music, we play it' (McCartney, 2013).

References

Adele. (2011). 'Someone Like You'. In *21* [CD]. XL; Columbia.

Alabama Three. (1997). 'Ain't Going to Goa'. In *Exile on Coldharbour Lane* [CD]. Geffin Records.

Allen, G. (2000). *Intertextuality*. London: Routledge.

Amos, Tori. (1991). 'Me and a Gun'. In *Little Earthquakes* [CD]. Atlantic; EastWest.

Anti-Nowhere League. (1983). 'So What'. In *Complete Singles Collection* [CD]. Cherry Red.

Appleford, Steve. (2015). http://www.rollingstone.com/music/live-reviews/leonard-cohen-offers-rare-peek-into-his-process-at-popular-problems-preview-20140911, accessed 1 July 2017.

Arctic Monkeys. (2011). 'Suck It and See'. In *Suck It and See* [CD]. Domino.

The Axis of Awesome. (2011). *4 Chords*. https://www.youtube.com/watch?v=oOlDewpCfZQ, accessed 3 July 2017.

Baez, Joan. (1970). 'Joe Hill'. In *Woodstock* [CD] Rhino.

Bakhtin, M.M. (1984, 2008). *Rabelais and His World*, new edn. Transl. by Helen Iswolsky. Indiana: Indiana University Press.

Barthes, R. (1977). *Image, Music, Text*. London: Fontana Press.

Batchelor, T. (2015). 'Albarn Slams Pop's 'Selfie Generation'. *i*. 20 April, p. 23.

The Baseballs. (2009). 'Bleeding Love'. In *Strike* [CD]. Rhino.

The Beatles. (1963a). 'All I've Got to Do'. In *With the Beatles* [CD]. Parlophone.

The Beatles. (1963b). 'All My Loving'. In *With the Beatles* [CD]. Parlophone.

The Beatles. (1963c). 'Hold Me Tight'. In *With the Beatles* [CD]. Parlophone.

The Beatles. (1963d). 'It Won't Be Long'. In *With the Beatles* [CD]. Parlophone.
The Beatles. (1963e). 'Not a Second Time'. In *With the Beatles* [CD]. Parlophone.
The Beatles. (1964). 'She Loves You' [Vinyl 7" single]. R5055. Parlophone.
The Beatles. (1965a). 'Norwegian Wood'. In *Rubber Soul* [CD]. Parlophone.
The Beatles. (1965b). 'Yesterday'. In *Help* [CD]. Parlophone.
The Beatles. (1966a). 'Here, There and Everywhere'. In *Revolver* [CD]. Parlophone.
The Beatles. (1966b). 'Tomorrow Never Knows'. In *Revolver* [CD]. Parlophone.
The Beatles. (1967a). 'All You Need Is Love' [Vinyl single]. Parlophone.
The Beatles. (1967b). 'Lovely Rita'. In *Sgt. Pepper's Lonely Hearts Club Band* [CD]. Parlophone.
The Beatles. (1967c). 'She's Leaving Home'. In *Sgt. Pepper's Lonely Hearts Club Band* [Vinyl]. Parlophone.
The Beatles. (1967d). 'A Day in the Life'. In *Sgt. Pepper's Lonely Hearts Club Band* [Vinyl]. Parlophone.
The Beatles. (1968a). 'Martha My Dear'. In *The Beatles* [CD]. Apple Records.
The Beatles. (1968b). 'Why Don't We Do It In The Road. In *The White Album* [Vinyl]. Parlophone.
The Beatles. (1968c). 'Wild Honey Pie'. In *The White Album* [Vinyl]. Parlophone.
The Beatles. (1969a). 'The End'. In *Abbey Road* [CD]. Apple.
The Beatles. (1969b). 'Something'. In *Abbey Road* [CD]. Apple Records.
The Beatles. (1995). 'Free as a Bird' [CD single]. Apple Records.
The Beatles Anthology. (1995) [DVD] UK: EMI Records.
The Bee Gees. (1967). 'Words'. [7" single]. Polydor.
Benjamin, Walter. (1999). *The Arcades Project* (transl. Howard Eiland and Kevin McLaughlin). Cambridge, MA, and London: Harvard University Press.
Berger, John. (2016). *Confabulations*. London: Faber.
Beyonce. (2016). 'Sorry'. In *Lemonade* [CD]. Columbia: Parkwood.
Birkett, J. (1998). *Word Power: A Guide to Creative Writing*, 3rd edn. London: A. & C. Black.
Black, Mary. (1993). 'The Holy Ground'. In *The Holy Ground* [CD]. The Grapevine Label.
The Black Eyed Peas. (2003). 'Hey Mama'. In *Elephunk* [CD]. A&M; will.i.am; Interscope.
Blur. (1997). 'Essex Dogs'. In *Blur* [CD]. EMI.
Blur. (1999). 'Tender'. In *13* [CD]. Food; Parlophone.
Booth, W.C. (1961). *The Rhetoric of Fiction*. London: The University of Chicago Press.

Booth, W.C. (2004). *The Rhetoric of RHETORIC*. Oxford: Blackwell.

Börjars, K. and Burridge, K. (2010). *Introducing English Grammar*, 2nd edn. London: Hodder Education.

Boulter, A. (2007). *Writing Fiction: Creative and Critical Approaches*. Basingstoke: Palgrave.

Bowie, David. (1969). 'Space Oddity'. In *David Bowie* [CD]. Mercury Records.

Bowie, David. (1979). 'Repetition'. In *Lodger* [CD]. RCA.

Bragg, Billy. (1983). 'New England. In *Life's a Riot with Spy vs Spy* [CD]. Polydor Records.

Braxton, Toni. (1996). 'Un-break My Heart' [CD]. LaFace.

Brecht, Bertolt. (1977). 'Against György Lukács'. In T. Adorno, W. Benjamin, E. Bloch, B. Brecht, and G. Lukács (eds), *Aesthetics and Politics: The Key Texts of the Classic Debate within German Marxism* (transl. R. Taylor; Afterward F. Jameson). London: Verso.

Buford, B. (1992). *Among The Thugs*. London: Arrow.

Bunnell, Dewey. (1971). 'A Horse with No Name'. America. http://www.access-backstage.com/america/song/song005.htm, accessed 1 July 2017.

Bunyan, N. (2002). 'Eminem Lyrics Are Blamed for Sex Attack'. The Telegraph. http://www.telegraph.co.uk/news/uknews/1405669/Eminem-lyrics-are-blamed-for-sex-attack.html, accessed 3 July 2017.

Burroway, J. (2007). *Imaginative Writing: The Elements of Craft*, 2nd edn. New York: Pearson/Longman.

Bush, Kate. (1978). 'Wuthering Heights'. In *The Kick Inside* [CD]. EMI; Harvest.

Byrne, D. (2012). *How Music Works*. Edinburgh: Canongate.

Camp, L. (2011). *Can I Change Your Mind?* London: Bloomsbury.

Capital FM. (2015). '*Tissues at the Ready! The 11 Most Emotional Sad Songs GUARANTEED to Make You Cry*'. 95–106. http://www.capitalfm.com/music-news/sad-songs-playlist/, accessed 22 December 2016.

Campbell, Glen. (1968). 'Wichita Lineman' [Vinyl Single]. Capitol.

Carless, D. and Douglas, K. (2011). 'What's in a Song? How Songs Contribute to the Communication of Scientific Research'. *British Journal of Guidance & Counselling* 39, no. 5: 439–54. https://doi.org/10.1080/03069885.2011.62 1522.

Cash, Johnny. (2002). 'Hurt'. In *American iv: The Man Comes Around* [CD]. American Recordings, Universal.

Cave, Nick. (2015). *The Sick Bag Song*. London: Canongate.

Cave, P. (2009). *Can a Robot Be Human?* Oxford: Oneworld Publications.

Charles, Ray. (1958). *I Got a Woman*. https://www.youtube.com/watch?v=Mrd14PxaUco, accessed 10 July 2017.

The Chemical Brothers. (2005). 'Galvanize'. In *Push the Button* [CD]. Virgin; Freestyle Dust; EMI.

Childs, P. (2008). *The Essential Guide to English Studies*. London: Continuum.

Chumbawanba. (1997). 'Tubthumping. In *Tubthumper* [CD]. Republic Records.

Citron, Stephen. (1990). *Songwriting: A Complete Guide to the Craft*. New York: Limelight Editions.

Clark, Guy, Clark, Susanna and Janosky, Jim. (1995). 'The Cape'. Susanna's Sanctuary. https://secondhandsongs.com/work/22271/all, accessed 22 July 2018.

Cobain, K. (2003). *Journals*. London: Penguin.

Cocker, J. (2012). *Mother, Brother, Lover: Selected Lyrics*. London: Faber & Faber; Main Edition.

Cohen, Leonard. (1971). 'Famous Blue Raincoat'. In *Songs of Love and Hate* [CD].Columbia.

Collins, Phil. (1988). 'A Groovy Kind of Love'. In *Buster: The Original Motion Picture Soundtrack* [CD]. Virgin.

Common People. (1995). In sources: Pulp. (1995). 'Common People'. In *Different Class* [CD]. Island.

The Corrs. (1998). 'So Young'. In *Talk on Corners – Special Edition* [CD]. Atlantic.

Costello, Elvis. (1983). 'Shipbuilding. In *Punch the Clock* [CD]. FBeat, RCA.

Costello, Elvis. (1994a). 'Alison'. In *My Aim is True* [CD]. Columbia Records.

Costello, Elvis. (1994b). 'Kinder Murder'. In *Brutal Youth* [CD]. Warner Bros.

Cott, J. (2006). *Bob Dylan: The Essential Interviews*. New York: Wenner Books.

Cross, C.R. (2002). *Heavier Than Heaven*. London: Hodder and Stoughton.

Crowded House. (1986). 'Don't Dream It's Over'. In *Crowded House* [CD]. Capitol/EMI.

Crowded House. (1999). 'Lester'. https://www.youtube.com/watch?v=Cr3u-qBNrCE.

Curtis, D. and Savage, J. (eds). (2014). *So This Is Permanence: Ian Curtis*. London: Faber and Faber.

Daft Punk. (1997). 'Around the World'. In *Homework* [CD]. Parlephone France.

Dann, T. (2006). *Darker Than the Deepest Sea: The Search for Nick Drake*. London: Portrait.

Denora, T. (2006). 'Music and Self Identity'. In A. Bennett, B. Shank and J. Toynbee (eds), *The Popular Music Studies Reader*. London: Routledge.

Destiny's Child. (2001). 'Happy Face'. In *Survivor* [CD]. Columbia.

Devereux, E., Dillane, A. and Power, M.J. (eds). (2011). *Morrissey – Fandom, Representations and Identities*. Bristol: Intellect.

Dibben, N. (2012). 'Musical Materials, Perception, and Listening'. In M. Clayton, T. Herbert and Middleton, R. (eds), *The Cultural Study of Music: A Critical Introduction*, 2nd edn. New York: Routledge.

Dimery, R. (ed.). (2013). *1001 Songs You Must Hear Before You Die*. London: Quintessence.

Dire Straits. (1980). 'Romeo and Juliet'. In *Making Movies* [CD]. Vertigo; Warner Bros.: Mercury.

Dire Straits. (1985). 'Money For Nothing' In *Brothers in Arms* [CD]. Vertigo; Warner Bros.; Mercury.

The Divine Comedy. (2001). 'Eye of the Needle.' In *Regeneration* [CD]. Parlophone.

Dixie Chicks. (2002). 'Long Time Gone'. In *Home*. Sony.

Doane, R. (2014). *Stealing All Transmissions: A Secret History of the Clash*. Oakland: PM Press.

Drake. (2013). 'Started from the Bottom'. In *Nothing Was the Same* [CD]. OVO; Aspire; Young Money; Cash Money; Republic.

Dylan, Bob. (1961). 'Death Of Emmett Till. In *Bob Dylan* [CD]. Columbia.

Dylan, Bob. (1965a). 'Like a Rolling Stone'. In *Highway 61 Revisited* [CD]. Columbia.

Dylan, Bob. (1965b). 'Subterranean Homesick Blues. In *Bringing It All Back Home* [CD]. Capital.

Dylan, Bob. (1975). 'If You See Her, Say Hello'. In *Blood on the Tracks* [CD]. Columbia.

Dylan, Bob. (2017). 'Bob Dylan – Nobel Lecture'. Nobelprize.org. Nobel Media AB 2014. 8 June 2017. https://www.nobelprize.org/prizes/literature/2016/dylan/lecture/, accessed 1 July 2017.

Ecclesiastes 1:9, Holy Bible: New International Version.

Eckstein, L. (2010). *Reading Song Lyrics*. Amsterdam: Rodopi.

Eells, J. (2014). 'The Reinvention of Taylor Swift'. Rolling Stone, September 8. http://www.rollingstone.com/music/features/taylor-swift-1989-cover-story-20140908, accessed 11 June 2017.

Eels. (2005a). 'Check-out Blues'. In *Blinking Lights and Other Revelations* [CD]. Vagrant.x

Eels. (2005b). 'The Stars Shine in the Sky Tonight'. In *Blinking Lights and Other Revelations* [CD]. Vagrant.

Eels. (2005c). 'Suicide Life'. In *Blinking Lights and Other Revelations* [CD]. Vagrant.

Eels. (2005d). 'Things the Grandchildren Should Know'. In *Blinking Lights and Other Revelations* [CD]. Vagrant.

Eliot, T.S. (1925). 'The Hollow Men. In *Eliot's Poems: 1909–1925*, Faber.

Ellen, Barbara. (2017). 'Harry Styles Is the New Bowie? That's Not What I'm Hearing'. The Guardian, April 8. https://www.theguardian.com/comment-isfree/2017/apr/08/harry-styles-the-new-bowie-thats-not-what-im-hearing, accessed 1 September 2017.

Elton John and Kiki Dee. (1976). 'Don't Go Breaking My Heart'. [7" single]. MCA.

Eminem. (1999a). '97 Bonnie and Clyde'. In *The Slim Shady LP* [CD]. Interscope: Aftermath.

Eminem. (1999b). 'Kim'. In *The Marshal Mathers LP* [CD]. Aftermath; Interscope: Shady.

Eminem. (1999c). 'Role Model'. In *The Slim Shady LP* [CD]. Interscope: Aftermath.

Eminem. (2000). 'Stan'. In *The Marshall Mathers LP* [CD]. Aftermath; Shady; Interscope.

Eminem. (2000a). 'Criminal'. In *The Marshal Mathers LP* [CD]. Aftermath; Interscope; Shady.

Eminem. (2000c). 'Steve Berman (Skit)'. In *The Marshall Mathers LP* [CD]. Aftermath; Shady; Interscope.

Eminem. (2002a). 'Hailey's Song'. In *The Eminem Show* [CD]. Aftermath; Interscope; Shady.

Eminem. (2002b). 'Sing for the Moment'. In *The Eminem Show* [CD]. Aftermath; Interscope; Shady.

Eminem. (2002c). 'Cleaning Out My Closet'. In *The Marshall Mathers LP2* [CD]. Aftermath; Interscope; Shady.

Eminem. (2004). 'Evil Deeds'. In *Encore* [CD]. Aftermath; Shady; Interscope; Goliath.

Eminem. (2013). 'Headlights'. In *The Marshall Mathers LP2* [CD]. Aftermath.

Eminem (with Jenkins, S.). (2008). *The Way I Am*. London: Orion.

Eminem, featuring Rihanna. (2010). 'Love the Way You Lie'. In *Recovery* [CD]. Aftermath; Shady; Interscope.

Ephron, Nora and Edmiston, Susan. (1965). 'Bob Dylan Interview'. Interferenza. http://www.interferenza.com/bcs/interw/65-aug.htm, accessed 1 July 2017.

Etheridge, Melissa. (2005). 'I Need to Wake Up'. [CD single]. The Island Def Jam Music Group.

Europe. (1986). 'The Final Countdown'. In *The Final Countdown* [CD]. Epic.

Everett, M.O. (1998a). 'Dead of Winter'. In *Electro Shock Blues* [CD]. DreamWorks Records.

Everett, M.O. (1998b). 'Elizabeth on the Bathroom Floor. In *Electro Shock Blues* [CD]. DreamWorks Records.

Everett, M.O. (1998c). 'Going to Your Funeral Part 2'. In *Electro Shock Blues* [CD]. DreamWorks Records.

Everett, M.O. (2008). *Things the Grandchildren Should Know*. London: Little, Brown.

Finer, Jem and Shane McGowan. (1987). 'A Fairy Tale in New York'. In *If I Should Fall From Grace With God* [CD] Pogue Mahone.

Finn, N. (2017). 'The Origin of 'Nails in My Feet'. http://neilfinn.com/2017/03/the-origin-of-nails-in-my-feet/, accessed 2 June 2017.

Fish, S. (1994). *Is There a Text in this Class?* Cambridge: Harvard University Press.

Fiske, John. (1987). From Ch 8, p. 24.

Fitzgerald, F. Scott. *Tender Is the Night*. (1934). New York: Charles Scribner's Sons.

Flannigan, Bill. (2017). "Bob Dylan: Q&A with Bill Flannigan'. Bob Dylan Newsletter, March 22. http://bobdylan.com/news/qa-with-bill-flanagan/, accessed 1 July 2017.

Foo Fighters. (1999). 'Learn to Fly'. In *There Is Nothing Left to Lose* [CD]. RCA.

Fosbraey, G. (2015). 'Disrupting Status Quo: Analysis and Play in Songwriting'. *Creative Academic*, no. 2A (June 2015) 'Exploring Play in Higher Education' http://www.creativeacademic.uk.

Fosbraey, G. (2017). 'I'm (Not) Your Man: Reading Leonard Cohen's Lyrics without Leonard Cohen'. In P. Billingham (ed.), *Spirituality and Desire in Leonard Cohen's Songs and Poems: Visions from the Tower of Song*. Newcastle upon Tyne: Cambridge Scholars.

Franklin, Aretha. (1967). '(You Make Me Feel) Like a Natural Woman' [7" vinyl single]. Atlantic.

Frisicks-Warren, B. (2006). *I'll Take You There: Pop Music and the Urge for Transcendence*. London: Continuum.

Gainsbourg, Serge and Jane Birkin. (1967). 'Je t'aime … moi non plus'. [7" single]. Fontana.

Gale, L. (2012). 'The Pitch List'. http://www.gq-magazine.co.uk/gallery/gq-sport-best-football-club-ground-game-anthems-songs, accessed 22 December 2016.

Gambaccinni, Paul. (1976). Paul McCartney in His Own Words Putnam Pub Group; Reissue edition.

Gates, Gareth. (2002). 'Unchained Melody'. In *What My Heart Wants to Say* [CD]. BMG; S Records.

Gaye, Marvin. (1977). 'Got to Give It Up'. In *Live at the London Palladium* [CD]. Tamla.

Genesis. (1972). 'Supper's Ready' (1965). In *Foxtrot* [CD]. Charisma Records.

Germano, Lisa. (1994). '… A Psychopath'. In *Geek the Girl* [CD]. 4AD.

Gibson. (1958). 'Oh Lonesome Me'. RCA Victor.

Gibsone, H. (2016). 'Talking Tactics: Rihanna and the Pop Stars Who Change Accent'. *The Guardian* (February 12). https://www.theguardian.com/music/2016/feb/04/talk-that-talk-rihanna-the-cunning-linguist.

Gilbert, Elizabeth. (2011). 'Elizabeth Gilbert in conversation with Paul Holdengraber, May 5, 2011' https://www.nypl.org/audiovideo/elizabeth-gilbert-conversation-paul-holdengraber-0, accessed July 1 2017.

Gill, A. (2017). 'Album Reviews: Haim – Something To Tell You'. *i*. 7 July 2017, p. 37.

Girls Aloud. (2008). 'Fix Me Up'. In *Out of Control* [CD]. Fascination.

Gorillaz. (2005). 'Fire Coming Out of the Monkey's Head'. In *Demon Days* [CD]. Parlophone.

Gottlieb, R. and Kimbal, R. (eds). (2000). *Reading Lyrics*. New York: Pantheon Books.

Gottschall, J. (2013). *The Storytelling Animal*. New York: Marriner Books.

Gracyk, T. (2001). *I Wanna Be Me: Rock Music and the Politics of Identity*. Philadelphia: Temple University Press.

The Great Albums podcast. (2017). *'Nirvana – In Utero (w/ guest Tyler Plazio)*. https://thegreat-albums.libsyn.com/nirvana-in-utero-w-guest-tyler-plazio, accessed 9 March 2017.

Greenblatt, S. (1995). 'Culture'. In L. Lentricchia and T. McLaughlin (eds), *Critical Terms for Literary Study*, 2nd edn. Chicago: University of Chicago Press.

Green Day. (2004). 'Wake Me Up When September Ends'. In *American Idiot* [CD]. Reprise.

Green Day. (2016). 'Still Breathing'. In *Revolution Radio* [CD]. Reprise.

Greene, G. (2019). *Brighton Rock*. London: Vintage.

Griffin, Patty. (2002). 'Making Pies'. *1000 Kisses* [CD] ATO Records.

Griffin, Patty. (2002a). 'Nobody's Crying'. In *1000 Kisses* [CD]. ATO Records.

Griffith, Patty. (2011). 'This One's for Him - A Tribute to Guy Clark.' In Jerry Jeff Walker (ed.), *This One's for Him: A Tribute to Guy Clark* [CD]. Ice House Music.

Gross, Phillip. (2010). *Off Road to Everywhere*. Cromer, Norfolk: Salt.

Guetta, David, featuring Flo Rida and Nicki Minaj. (2011a). 'Where Them Girls At?' In *Nothing but the Beat* [CD]. Virgin; EMI; Astralwerks.

Guetta, David, featuring Nicki Minaj. (2011b). 'Turn Me On'. In *Nothing but the Beat* [CD]. Virgin; EMI; Astralwerks.

Guns 'N Roses. (1988). 'One in a Million'. In *Lies* [CD]. Geffen.

Guthrie, Woody. (1945). 'This Land Is Your Land'. In Woodie Guthrie: *The Ultimate Collection* [CD]. Not Now Music.

Hamilton, P. (1996). *Historicism*. London: Routledge.

Hammer, M.C. (1990). 'U Can't Touch This'. In *Please Hammer, Don't Hurt 'Em* [CD]. Capital Records.

Hardcastle, Paul. (1985). '19' [Vinyl Single]. Chrysalis.

Harris, Richard. 'MacArthur Park'. (1968). [Vinyl Single]. Dunhill Records.

Hawkes, D. (1996). *Ideology*. London: Routledge.

Hawkes, T. (1997). *Structuralism and Semiotics*. London: Routledge.

Hayden, E. (2014). *Sigur Ró*. New York: Bloomsbury.

Hear'say. (2001). 'Pure and Simple'. In *Popstars* [CD]. Polydor.

Heatwave. (1976). 'Boogie Nights'. In *Too Hot To Handle* [CD]. Epic Records.

Hidden Songs. (n.d.). 'Korn: "Michael & Geri" from Korn'. http://hidden-songs.com/korn-korn, accessed 29 July 2017.

Hirsch, Edward. (2006). 'Mere Air, These Words, but Delicious to Hear'. Poetry Foundation (January 23). http://www.poetryfoundation.org/learning/article/177210.

Hodgkinson, W. (n.d.). 'Ed Sheeran Is Killing Music'. Little Atoms. http://little atoms.com/film-music/ed-sheeran-killing-music, accessed May 17 2017.

Holder, R.W. (1995). *Euphemisms*. Oxford: Oxford University Press.

Holiday, Billie. (1939). 'Strange Fruit'. In *Gold – 100th Anniversary Edition (1915–2015)* [CD]. Not Now Music.

Hooker, John Lee. (1968). 'Wednesday Evening Blues'. In *Blues Before* Sunrise [CD] Bulldog Records.

Hooton, C. (2015). 'The Story behind Johnny Cash's 'Hurt'. Still the Saddest Music Video of All Time'. http://www.independent.co.uk/arts-entertain-ment/music/features/the-story-behind-johnny-cash-s-hurt-still-the-saddest-music-video-of-all-time-a6683371.html.

Hopps, G. (2009). *The Pageant of His Bleeding Heart*. London: Continuum.

Hornby, Nick. (2014). *31 Songs*. London: Penguin (re-issue edn).

Ian, Janis. (1974). 'Jesse'. In *Stars* [CD]. Columbia.

Isbell, Jason. (2015). 'Speed Trap Town'. In *Something More Than Free* [CD]. Digipak.

Jay-Z. (1998). 'Hard Knock Life (Ghetto Anthem). In *Vol.2 … Hard Knock Life* [CD]. Roc-A-Fella Records.

Jessie J., featuring B.o.B. (2011). 'Price Tag'. In *Who You Are* [CD]. Lava; Island.

Johnny Kid and The Pirates. (1960). 'Shaking All Over'. [7" single]. HMV.

Jones, Jack. (1964). 'Wives and Lovers'. https://www.youtube.com/watch?v=mZbusN-n8rE, accessed 10 July 2017.

Jones, O. (2012). *Chavs: The Demonization of the Working Class*. New York: Verso.

Jowett, G.S. and O'Donnell, V. (2012). *Propaganda & Persuasion*, 5th edn. Los Angeles: Sage.

Jowett, G.S. and O'Donnell, V. (2015). *Propaganda & Persuasion*, 6th edn. Los Angeles: Sage.

Juslin, P.N. and Sloboda, J.A. (2001). *Music and Emotion*. Oxford: Oxford University Press.

Kazan, Elia, dir. (1954). *On The Waterfront*. Horizon Pictures.

Keating, Ronan. (1999). 'When You Say Nothing at All.' In *Ronan* [CD]. Polydor.

The Killers. (2008). 'Human'. In *Day & Age* [CD]. Island.

The Kinks. (1968). 'Village Green'. In *The Kinks are the Village Green Preservation Society* [CD]. Sanctuary.

Koning, Lisa. (2017). 'Bruegel's dishonest woman and cuckold man make strange bedfellow; *As preparatory research for a creative piece*'

Korn. (1994). 'Daddy'. In *Korn* [CD]. Immortal/Epic.

Kravitz, Lenny. (1998). 'Fly Away'. In *5* [CD]. Virgin Records.

Lady Gaga. (2008). 'Poker Face'. In *Fame* [CD]. Streamline; Kon Live; Cherrytree; Interscope.

Larry King Now. (2013). 'Marilyn Manson: I've Been Blamed for 36 School Shootings'. https://www.youtube.com/watch?v=1JN9b47FoJM, accessed 3 July 2017.

Led Zeppelin. (1969a). 'The Lemon Song'. In *Led Zeppelin II* [CD]. Atlantic.

Led Zeppelin. (1969b). 'Ramble On'. In *Led Zeppelin II* [CD]. Atlantic.

Leith, S. (2012). *You Talking to Me?* London: Profile Books. https://www.telegraph.co.uk/comment/personal-view/3642416/Bob-Dylan-is-a-genius-but-hes-no-poet.html.

Lennon, Julian. (1991). 'Saltwater'. In *Help Yourself* [CD]. Atlantic Records.

Levitin, D. (2008). *This Is Your Brain on Music*. London: Atlantic Books.

Levitin, D. (2009). *The World in Six Songs*. London: Aurum Press.

Lewis, Tim. (2015). 'Interview: Nick Cave'. The Guardian. June 7. https://www.theguardian.com/music/2015/jun/07/nick-cave-bad-seeds-sick-bag-song-interview, accessed 1 July 2017.

The Libertines. (2002). *Up The Bracket* [CD]. Rough Trade.

Lightfoot, Gordon. (1972). 'Don Quixote'. In *Don Quixote* [CD]. Reprise.

Lil Wayne. (2010). 'Blunt Blowin'. In *Tha Carter IV* [CD]. Young Money; Cash Money; Universal Republic.

Little Big Town. (2014). 'Girl Crush'. In *Pain Killer* [CD]. Capital Nashville.

Lynn, S. (1994). *Text and Contexts: Writing about Literature with Critical Theory*. New York: Harper Collins College Publishers.

Lynrd Skynrd. (1974). 'Sweet Homa Alabama'. In *Second Helping* [CD]. MCA Records.

Lynskey, D. (2011). 'Strange Fruit: *The first great protest song*'. https://www.the-guardian.com/music/2011/feb/16/protest-songs-billie-holiday-strange-fruit, 16 February 2017, accessed 8 July 2017.

Lynskey, D. (2017). 'Q Cover Story – Ed Sheeran'. *Q Magazine*, August 2017, p. 29.

Maroon 5 featuring Christina Aguilera. (2011). 'Moves Like Jagger'. In *Hands All Over – Re-Issue* [CD]. A&M/ Octone.

Mars, Bruno. (2010). 'Just the Way You Are (Amazing)'. In *Doo-Wops and Hooligans* [CD]. Atlantic: Elektra.

Matthew 19: 23–26. Holy Bible: New International Version.

McAlpine, F. (2010). '*10 hugely famous songs that took less than 10 minutes to write*'. https://www.bbc.co.uk/music/articles/e1598eeb-14eb-4c0a-a07d-473 a1209e52f, accessed 28 June 2017.

McCartney, Paul and Linda. (1973). 'Helen Wheels'. In *Band on the Run* [CD]. Apple.

McCaw, N. (2008). *How to Read Texts*. London: Continuum.

Melrose, Andrew. (2018). 'I'm not free…' unpublished.

Miles, B. (1998). *Paul McCartney: Many Years from Now*. Vintage: London.

Milligan, Spike. (1953). 'The Ying Tong Song'. [BBC Radio Recording – The Goon Show].

Minaj, Nicki. (2010a). 'Did It on 'Em''. In *Pink Friday* [CD]. Young Money; Cash Money Universal Motown.

Minaj, Nicki. (2010b). 'I'm the Best'. In *Pink Friday* [CD]. Young Money; Cash Money Universal Motown.

Minaj, Nicki. (2010c). 'Monster'. In *Pink Friday* [CD]. Young Money; Cash Money Universal Motown.

Minaj, Nicki. (2012a). 'Pound the Alarm'. In *Pink Friday: Roman Reloaded* [CD]. Young Money; Cash Money; Universal Republic.

Minaj, Nicki. (2012b). 'Starships'. In *Pink Friday: Roman Reloaded* [CD]. Young Money; Cash Money; Universal.

Minaj, Nicki. (2012c). 'Va Va Voom'. In *Pink Friday: Roman Reloaded* [CD]. Young Money; Cash Money; Universal Republic.

Minaj, Nicki. (2014). 'Anaconda'. In *The Pinkprint* [CD]. Young Money; Cash Money; Republic.

Minaj, Nicki with will.i.am. (2010). 'Check It Out'. In *Pink Friday* [CD]. Young Money; Cash Money; Universal Motown.

Minogue, Kylie. (2001). 'Can't Get You Out Of My Head'. In *Fever* [CD]. Parlophone.

Mitchell, Joni. (1970). 'The Circle Game'. In *Ladies of the Canyon* [CD]. Reprise.

Mitchell, Joni. (1971a). 'A Case of You'. In *Blue* [CD]. Reprise.

Mitchell, Joni. (1971b). 'The Last Time I Saw Richard'. In *Blue* [CD]. Reprise.

The Monkees. (1968). 'Daydream Believer'. In *The Birds, The Bees & The Monkees* [CD]. Colgems Records.

Montgomery, M., Durant, A., Furniss, T. and Mills, S. (2013). *Ways of Reading: Advanced Reading Skills for Students of English Literature*, 2nd edn. London: Routledge.

Morrissey. (1992). 'The National Front Disco'. In *Your Arsenal* [CD]. HMV.

Morrissey. (1994). 'Now My Heart Is Full'. AllMusic Review. http://www.all-music.com/album/mw0000120863, accessed 1 July 2017.

Morrissey. (1995). 'The Operation. In *Southpaw Grammer* [CD]. RCA Victor.

Morrissey. (2004a). 'First of the Gang to Die'. In *You are the Quarry* [CD]. Sanctuary/Attack.

Morrissey. (2004b). 'The World Is Full of Crashing Bores'. In *You Are the Quarry* [CD]. Sanctuary/Attack.

Morrissey. (2006). 'Life Is a Pigsty'. In *Ringleader of the Tormentors* [CD]. Sanctuary/Attack.

Morrissey. (2014). 'I'm Not a Man. In *World Peace Is None of Your Business* [CD]. Harvest Records.

Morrison, Van. (1988). 'Carrickfergus'. In *Irish Heartbeat* [CD]. Mercury Records.

Mueller, K. (2014). '*Anaconda': Why You Should Watch Nicki's Video Again*'. http://www.huffingtonpost.com/uloop/nicki-minaj-anaconda-video-meaning_b_5766450.html, accessed 5 June 2017.

Munden, Paul. (2016). 'Research Output'. In J. Kroll, A. Melrose and J. Webb (eds), *Old and New, Tried and Untried: Creativity and Research in the 21st Century*. Champaign, IL: Common Ground Publishing.

Nannucci, Maurizio. (2003). *Changing Place, Changing Time, Changing Thoughts, Changing Future*. Peggy Guggenheim Collection, Venice, Italy. http://www.guggenheim-venice.it/inglese/collections/artisti/dettagli/opere_dett.php?id_art=178&id_opera=411, accessed 1 July 2017.

Neale, Stephen. (1980). *Genre*. BFI Publishing: London.

Newman, Randy. (1977). 'Little Criminals'. In *Little Criminals* [CD]. Warner Bros.

Nick Cave and the Bad Seeds. (2003). 'God Is in the House'. In *God Is in the House* [DVD]. Mute.

Nirvana. (1991). '1999'. In *Smells Like Teen Spirit* [CD]. The David Geffin Company.

Nirvana. (1993). 'Heart-Shaped Box'. In *In Utero* [CD]. DGC.

Nirvana. (1996). 'Aneursym'. In *From the Muddy Banks of the Wishkah* [CD]. DGC.

Noelliste, L. (2016). *'Unaware of Jamaican patois, critics blast Rihanna for speaking "gibberish" on her new single 'Work'*. https://bglh-marketplace.com/2016/02/unaware-of-jamaican-patois-critics-blast-rihanna-for-speaking-gib-berish-on-her-new-single-work/p439, accessed 10 May 2017. DOI: 10.1080/03069885.2011.621522.

O'Connor, Frank. (1957). *'The Arts of Fiction No 19'*, The Paris https://www.theparisreview.org/interviews/4847/frank-oconnor-the-art-of-fiction-no-19-frank-oconnor, accessed 18 September 2018.

Orbison, Roy. (1961). 'Only The Lonely'. [Vinyl Single]. RCA.

Osborne, J. (1978). *Look Back in Anger*. London: Faber & Faber Main Edition.

Partridge, K. (2016). *'15 Best Songs about Money'*. Billboard (May 16). http://www.billboard.com/photos/7370491/15-best-songs-about-money, accessed 12 June 2017.

Pattison, P. (2009). *Writing Better Lyrics*, 2nd edn. Ohio: Writer's Digest Books.

Parton, Dolly. (1971). 'Coat of Many Colours'. In *Both Sides of Dolly Parton* [CD]. RCA.

Parton, Dolly. (1973). 'I will always love you'. In *Jolene* [CD]. RCA.

Paxton, Tom. (2002). 'The Bravest'. In *Looking for the Moon* [CD]. Appleseed Recordings.

Perraudin, F. and Halliday, J. (2017). *'Don't Look Back in Anger Becomes Symbol of Manchester's Spirit'*. The Guardian (May 25). https://www.theguardian.com/uk-news/2017/may/25/dont-look-back-in-anger-becomes-symbol-of-manchester-spirit, accessed 3 June 2017.

Petty, Tom. (1976). 'American Girl'. In *Tom Petty and the Heartbreakers* [CD]. Shelter Records.

Petty, Tom. (1991). 'Learning to Fly'. In *Into The Great Wide Open* [CD]. MCA Records.

Pink Floyd. (1970). *Atom Heart Mother* [CD]. Harvest Records.

Pink Floyd. (1971). 'Echoes'. (1965). In *Meddle* [CD]. Harvest Records.

Pink Floyd. (1975). 'Shine On You Crazy Diamond'. In *Wish You Were Here* [CD]. Harvest Records.

Pink Floyd. (1979a). 'Another Brick in the Wall (Part 1)'. In *The Wall* [CD]. Harvest; Columbia.

Pink Floyd. (1979b). 'Another Brick in the Wall (Part 2)'. In *The Wall* [CD]. Harvest; Columbia.

Pink Floyd. (1979c). 'Another Brick in the Wall (Part 3)'. In *The Wall* [CD]. Harvest; Columbia.

Pink Floyd. (1979d). 'Don't Leave Me Now'. In *The Wall* [CD]. Harvest; Columbia.

Pink Floyd. (1979e). 'Goodbye Cruel World'. In *The Wall* [CD]. Harvest; Columbia.

Pink Floyd. (1979f). 'The Happiest Days of Our Lives'. In *The Wall* [CD]. Harvest; Columbia.

Pink Floyd. (1979g). 'Mother'. In *The Wall* [CD]. Harvest; Columbia.

Pink Floyd. (1979h). 'One of My Turns'. In *The Wall* [CD]. Harvest; Columbia.

Pink Floyd. (1979i). 'Young Lust'. In *The Wall* [CD]. Harvest; Columbia.

Plan B. (2012). 'Ill Manors'. In *Ill Manors* [CD]. Warner Bros.

The Police. (1983). 'Every Breath You Take'. In *Synchronicity* [CD]. A&M.

Presley, Elvis. (1969a). 'Are You Lonesome Tonight'. In *From Elvis to Memphis* [CD]. RCA.

Presley, Elvis. (1969b). 'In The Ghetto'. In *From Elvis to Memphis* [CD]. RCA.

Prince. (1982). '1999'. In *1999* [CD]. Warner Bros.

Prine, John. (1971). 'Hello in There'. In *John Prine* [CD]. Atlantic Records.

The Prodigy. (1997). 'Breathe'. In *The Fat of the Land* [CD]. XL Recordings.

Puff Daddy. (1997). 'I'll Be Missing You'. In *No Way Out* [CD]. Bad Boy Records.

Queen. (1975). 'Bohemian Rhapsody'. In *A Night at the Opera* [CD]. EMI; Elektra

Rachel, D. (2013). *Isle of Noises*. London: Picador.

Rage Against the Machine. (1992). 'Killing in the Name' [CD]. Epic.

Railton, D. and Watson, P. (2011). *Music Video and the Politics of Representation*. Edinburgh: Edinburgh University Press.

Reed, Lou. (1972). 'Walk on The Wild Side'. In *Transforner* [CD]. RCA Records.

REM. (1998). 'At My Most Beautiful'. In *Up* [CD]. Warner Bros.

Remnick, D. (2011). 'Introduction'. In Paul Simon (ed.), *Paul Simon: Lyrics 1964–2011*. New York: Simon & Schuster.

Rihanna. (2010). 'Only Girl (In the World)'. In *Loud* [CD]. Def Jam; SRP.

Rihanna, featuring Calvin Harris. (2011a). 'Love in a Hopeless Place'. In *Talk That Talk* [CD]. Def Jam; SRP.

Rihanna, featuring Calvin Harris. (2011b). 'We Found Love'. In *Talk That Talk* [CD]. Def Jam; SRP.

Rihanna, featuring Drake. (2016). 'Work'. In *Anti* [CD]. Roc Nation; Westbury Road.

Rihanna. (2017). 'Wild Thoughts'. In *Grateful* [CD]. Epic Records.

Ritter, Josh. (2006). 'Girl in the War'. In *Girl in the War* [CD]. V2 Records.

Roberts, W.R. (1995). 'Rhetoric'. In J. Barnes (ed.), *The Complete Works of Aristotle, The revised Oxford Translation*. Princeton: Princeton University Press.

Robinson, P. (2017). "Charli XCX'. *Q Magazine*, March 2017, p. 28.

Robinson, Smokey. (1969). 'Tracks of My Tears'. [7" single]. Motown.

Robinson, Tom. (1984). 'War Baby'. In *War Baby: Hope and Glory* [CD]. Castaway Records.

Robson and Jerome. (1995). 'Unchained Melody'. In *Robson and Jerome* [CD]. RCA Records.

The Rolling Stones. (1978). 'Some Girls'. In *Some Girls* [CD]. Rolling Stones.

Rooksby, R. (2006). *Lyrics: Writing Better Words for Your Songs*. Milwaukee: Backbeat Books.

Savage, M. (2017). 'How many people does it take to write a hit song?,' BBC. http://www.bbc.co.uk/news/entertainment-arts-39934986, accessed 4 July 2017.

Searle, J.R. and Vanderveken, D. (1985). *Foundations of Illocutionary Logic*. Cambridge: Cambridge University Press.

Seeger, Pete. (1963). 'We Shall Overcome'. In *The Complete Carnegie Hall Concert* [CD]. Columbia.

The Seekers. (1965). 'The Carnival Is Over'. In *Night of Nights: Live!* [CD]. Musicoast.

Selden, R. and Widdowson, P. (1993). *A Reader's Guide to Contemporary Literature Theory*, 3rd edn. London: Harvester Wheatsheaf.

Self, W. (2011). 'The King of Bedsit Angst Grows Up'. In P.A. Woods (ed.), *Morrissey in Conversation*. London: Plexus Publishing.

Sellers, Peter and Loren, Sophia. (1960). 'Goodness Gracious Me'. In *Peter Sellers: Best Of* [CD] One Day Music.

The Sex Pistols. (1977a). 'Bodies'. In *Never Mind the Bollocks … Here's the Sex Pistols* [Vinyl]. Virgin.

The Sex Pistols. (1977b). 'God Save the Queen'. In *Never Mind the Bollocks … Here's the Sex Pistols* [Vinyl]. Virgin.

Shabo, M. (2010). *Rhetoric, Logic, and Argumentation: A Guide for Student Writers*. Clayton: Prestwick House, Inc.

Shaggy featuring Rikrok. (2000). 'It Wasn't Me'. In *Hot Shot* [CD]. MCA; Geffen.

Shenton, Z. (2017). *'Jay Z apologises to Beyonce and references Solange lift fight and 'Becky' on honest new album'*. http://www.mirror.co.uk/3am/celebrity-news/jay-z-apologises-beyonce-references-10713338, accessed 30 June 2017.

Shenton, Z. and Wilson, J. (2015). '*Why Bad Blood Is REALLY about Katy Perry – The Complete Timeline*'. http ://www.mirror.co.uk/3am/celebrity-news/ bad-blood-really-katy-perry-5718268, accessed 8 June 2017.

Shepherd, J.E. (2015). '*Tyler, the Creator on being banned from the UK: "I'm being treated like a terrorist"'*. https://www.theguardian.com/music/music-blog/2015/sep/01/tyler-the-creator-comments-banned-uk-freedom-of-speech, accessed 4 July 2017.

Sherwin, Adam. (2017). *i Newspaper*, 15 June 2017, p. 25.

Simon Hattenstone. 2017. 'Steve Earle: 'My wife left me for a younger, skinnier, less talented singer'. https://www.theguardian.com/music/2017/jun/14/steve-earle-so-you-wanna-be-an-outlaw-interview (accessed 1st July 2018)

Simon, Paul. (2011). *Paul Simon: Lyrics 1964–2011*. New York: Simon & Schuster.

Simon, Paul. (1968). 'America'. In *Bookends* [CD]. Columbia.

Simply Red. (1991). 'Stars.' In *Stars* [CD]. EastWest Records.

Sir Mix-a-Lot. (1992). 'Baby Got Back'. In *Mack Daddy* [CD]. Def American.

Skinner, M. (2012). *The Story of the Streets*. London: Transworld Publishers.

Smith, T. (2016). '"Bad Blood" – A Blow-by-Blow Account of Taylor Swift and Katy Perry's Long-Running Beef'. NME. http://www.nme.com/blogs/nme-blogs/bad-blood-a-full-timeline-of-taylor-swift-and-katy-perrys-beef-5732, accessed 11 June 2017.

The Smiths. (1984). 'These Things Take Time'. In *Hatful of Hollow* [Vinyl]. Rough Trade.

The Smiths. (1985). 'Meat is Murder'. In *Meat is Murder* [Vinyl]. Rough Trade; Sire.

The Smiths. (1987). 'Last Night I Dreamt Somebody Loved Me'. In *Strangeways, Here We Come* [CD]. Rough Trade Records.

Sondheim, Stephen. (1973). 'Send in the Clowns'. In *A Little Light Music* [Musical].

Song Exploder podcast. (2016). 'Weezer – Summer Elaine and Drunk Dory'. http://songexploder.net/weezer, accessed 11 August 2017.

Sonny and Cher. (1965). 'I Got You Babe'. [7" single]. CBS.

Splendid Fred Records. (2016a). 'Breed'. In *This Changes Everything: 11 Songs about Climate Change* [CD]. Splendid Fred Records.

Splendid Fred Records. (2016b). 'Lost'. In *This Changes Everything: 11 Songs about Climate Change* [CD]. Splendid Fred Records.

Splendid Fred Records. (2016c). 'Some Day'. In *This Changes Everything: 11 Songs about Climate Change* [CD]. Splendid Fred Records.

Springfield, Dusty. (1964). 'Wishin' and 'Hopin'. In *A Girl Called Dusty* [CD]. Phillips.

Springfield, Tom. (1965). 'The Carnival Is Over'. [7" single]. Columbia.

Springsteen, Bruce. (1975). 'Thunder Road'. In *Born To Run* [CD]. Columbia.

Springsteen, Bruce. (1980). 'Hungry Heart'. In *The River* [CD]. Columbia.

Springsteen, Bruce. (1980). 'Stolen Car'. In *The River* [CD]. Columbia.

Springsteen, Bruce. (1984). 'Born in the USA'. In *Born in the USA* [CD]. Columbia.

Springsteen, Bruce. (1987). 'Tunnel of Love'. In *Tunnel of Love* [CD]. Columbia.

Springsteen, Bruce. (1992). 'If I Should Fall Behind'. In *Lucky Town* [CD]. Columbia.

Springsteen, Bruce. (1995). 'The Ghost of Tom Joad'. In *The Ghost of Tom Joad* [CD]. Columbia.

The Stills-Young Band. (1976). 'Long May You Run'. In *Long May You Run* [CD]. Reprise.

Strait, George. (1985). 'The Chair. [7" single]. MCA.

Stevens, Cat. (1967). 'I Love My Dog'. In *Matthew and Son* [CD]. Island Records.

Stewart, Rod. (1971). 'Maggie May'. In *Every Picture Tells a Story* [CD]. Mercury Records.

The Streets. (2004). 'Dry Your Eyes' [CD]. Locked On, 679.

Student Room Chat. (2014). 'Anyone Else Feel Jessie J Was a Hypocrite?'. https://www.thestudentroom.co.uk/showthread.php?t=3039775, accessed 12 June 2017.

Supertramp. (1978). 'Breakfast in America'. In *Breakfast in Amwerica* [CD]. A&M Records.

Swift, Taylor, featuring Kendrick Lamar. (2014). 'Bad Blood'. In *1989* [CD]. Big Machine; Republic.

Swift, Taylor. (2012a). 'All Too Well'. In *Red* [CD]. Big Machine.

Swift, Taylor. (2012b). 'We Are Never Getting Back Together'. In *Red* [CD]. Big Machine.

Tarney, Alan. (1979). 'We Don't Talk Anymore'. [7" single, *We Don't Talk Anymore*, Cliff Richard]. EMI.

Taylor, James. (1971). 'Hey Mister, That's Me Up on the Jukebox'. In *Mud Slide Slim and the Blue Horizon* [CD]. Warner Brothers.

Tears for Fears. (1985) *Songs from the Big Chair* [CD]. Mercury Records.

Ten Masked Men. (1999). 'Baby One More Time' (1965). [Download]. Bandcamp

'The 10 Best Protest Songs'. (n.d.) *The Telegraph*. http://www.telegraph.co.uk/culture/culturepicturegalleries/10495205/The-10-best-protest-songs.html, accessed 26 July 2017.

Thomas, D. (2004). 'A to Z of Chavs'. *Daily Mail*, 20 October 2004.

Thomson, G. (2008). *I Shot a Man in Reno*. London: Continuum to the Communication of Social Science Research'. *British Journal of Guidance & Counselling*, 39:5.

'The Top 40 Best-selling UK Singles of All Time'. (n.d.). *The Telegraph*, July 10. http://www.telegraph.co.uk/culture/culturepicturegalleries/10734367/In-pictures-The-UK-top-40-best-selling-singles-of-all-time.html?-frame=2867648, accessed 2 May 2017.

Thicke, Robin. (2013). 'Blurred Lines'. In *Blurred Lines* [CD]. Star Trak; Interscope.

Tilbrook, G. and Chris Difford. (1979). 'Up the Junction'. *In Cool for Cats* [CD]. A&M.

Trailblazers: Conscience Songs, 2017 [TV]. Sky Arts. 9 July 2016.

Travolta, John. (1978). 'Sandy'. In *Grease* [7" single]. Polydor.

Vengaboys. (2000). 'Forever as One'. In *The Platinum Album* [CD]. Breakin'; EMI Electrola; Jive, Groovilicious.

The Wailers. (1973). 'Get Up, Stand Up'. In *Burnin'* [CD]. Island; Tuff Gong.

Waits, Tom. (1971). 'I Hope That I Don't Fall in Love With You'. In *Tom Waites: the early years* [CD]. Manifesto Records.

Waits, Tom. (1975). 'Warm Beer and Cold Women'. In *Nighthawks at the Diner* [Vinyl]. Asylum.

Waits, Tom. (1980). 'Jersey Girl'. In *Heartattack and Vine* [CD]. Asylum.

Waits, Tom. (2011). https://www.npr.org/2011/10/31/141657227/tom-waits-the-fresh-air-interview?t=1537249343452. accessed 18 September 2018.

Walsh, B. (2017). 'The Last of the Protest Singers'. *i Newspaper*, 31 May .

Walsh, Joe. (1978). 'Life's Been Good'. In *But Seriously Folks* [CD]. Asylum.

Webb, Jen. (2017). https://theconversation.com/in-honouring-dylan-the-nobel-prize-judges-have-made-a-category-error-67049, accessed 1 July 2017.

Webb, Jen and Andrew Melrose. (2011). 'Intimacy and the Icarus Effect'. Canberra, *Axon*, Vol 1, No 1.

Webb, Jimmy. (1967). 'By the Time I Get to Phoenix. In *By the Time I Get to Phoenix*, Glenn Campbell [CD]. Capital.

Webb, Jimmy. (1968). 'Wichita Lineman'. In Glenn Campbell, *Wichita Lineman* [CD] Capital.

Webb, J. (1998). *Tunesmith*. New York: Hyperion.

Wedde, Ian. (2005). *Three Regrets and a Hymn to Beauty*. Aukland University Press.

Weezer. (2016). 'Summer Elaine and Drunk Dory'. In *Weezer* [CD]. Atlantic; Crush.

Wenner, J.S. (2000). *Lennon Remembers*. Verso: London.

West, Kanye, featuring Jay-Z, Rick Ross, Bon Iver and Nicki Minaj. (2010). 'Monster'. In *My Beautiful Dark Twisted Fantasy* [CD]. Roc-A-Fella, Def Jam.

Wet Wet Wet. (1994). 'Love Is All Around' [CD single]. PolyGram; Records Service.

Wheatus. (2000). 'Teenage Dirtbag'. In *Wheatus* [CD]. Columbia.

Williams, Pharrell. (2013). 'Happy'. In *Girl* [CD]. I Am Other; Columbia.

White, Allon and Peter Stallybrass. (1986). *The Politics and Poetics of Transgression*, Ithaca, NY: Cornell University Press.

Williams, Hank. (1953). 'Your Cheating Hears'. In *Memorial Album* [Vinyl Album]. MGM.

Williams, Pharrell. (2013). 'Happy'. In *Girl* [CD]. I Am Other; Columbia.

Williams, Pharrell and Robin Thicke. (2013). 'Blurred Lines'. In [CD]. Star Trak LLC, Interscope Records, Polydor.

Williams, Robbie. (1997). 'Angels'. In *Life Thru a Lens* [CD]. EMI.

Winwood, Steve. (1977). 'Vacant Chair'. In *Steve Winwood* [CD]. Universal-Island Records Ltd.

Wonder, Stevie. (1980). 'Master Blaster'. In *Hotter Than July* [CD]. Mowtown.

Woods, P.A. (ed.). (2011). *Morrissey in Conversation*. London: Plexus Publishing.

Yankovic, "Weird Al". (1992). 'Smells Like Nirvana'. In *Off the Deep End* [CD]. Scotti Brothers.

Young, Neil. (1970). 'When the Morning Comes'. In *After the Goldrush* [CD]. Reprise.

Young, Will. (2002). 'Evergreen'. In *From Now On* [CD]. 19; S Records; RCA; BMG.

Zollo, P. (2003). *Songwriters on Songwriting*, 4th edn. Ohio: Da Capo Press.

Zuckerkandl, V. (1973). 'The Meaning of Song'. In M. Clayton (ed.), *Music, Words and Voice: A Reader*. Manchester: Manchester University Press, 2008.

FURTHER READING

Adorno, T., Benjamin, W., Bloch, E., Brecht, B. and Lukács, G. (1977). *Aesthetics and Politics: The Key Texts of the Classic Debate within German Marxism* (transl. R. Taylor; Afterward F. Jameson). London: Verso, 68–85.

Anderson, S. (2011). '25 Most Annoying Songs Ever'. http://www.nme.com/photos/25-most-annoying-songs-ever-1405215, accessed 27 July 2017.

Dibben, N. (2009). *Bjork*. Bloomington and Indianapolis: Indiana University Press.

Earle, Steve. (2017). 'Interview'. *The Guardian*. https://www.theguardian. com/music/2017/jun/14/steve-earle-so-you-wanna-be-an-outlaw-interview, accessed 1 July 2017.

Gotye, featuring Kimbra. (2011). 'Somebody That You Used to Know'. In *Making Mirrors* [CD]. Eleven.

Leith, S. (2007). '*Bob Dylan Is a Genius, but He's No Poet*'. https://www. telegraph.co.uk/comment/personal-view/3642416/Bob-Dylan-is-a-genius-but-hes-no-poet.html , accessed 12 August 2017.

Longhurst, B. (2007). *Popular Music and Society*. Cambridge: Polity Press.

Markram, H. (2009). '*A Brain in a Supercomputer (Subtitles and Transcript)*'. TEDGlobal. https://www.ted.com/talks/henry_markram_supercomputing_ the_brain_s_secrets/transcript?language=en, accessed 13 September 2015.

McCartney, P. (2013) [Liner Notes]. In *New* [CD]. Virgin EMI.

Melrose, Andrew. (2014). *Axon: Creative Explorations*, Vol, 4, No. 1, July 2014.

Morrissey. (2009). 'Teenage Dad on His Estate'. In *Swords* [CD]. Polydor.

Page, C. (2002). '*Hope on the Horizon*'. The Bakersfield Californian (November 10). https://web.archive.org/web/20080203183126/http://ww2.bakersfield. com/2002/korn/main6.asp, accessed 19 July 2017.

Pedler, D. (2003). *Songwriting Secrets of the Beatles*. London: Omnibus Press.

Popova, Maria. (2015). 'Elizabeth Gilbert on inspiration, what Tom Waits taught her about creativity, and the most dangerous myth for artists to believe'. BrainPickings. https://www.brainpickings.org/2015/06/12/eliza-beth-gilbert-nypl/, accessed 1 July 2017.

Sharp, J. (2009). *Crap Lyrics*. London: Portico.

Stormzy. 'Not That Deep'. last.fm. https://www.last.fm/music/Stormzy/_/ Not+That+Deep, accessed 21 July 2018.

Tutu, Desmond. (2012). https://www.youtube.com/watch?v=wg49mvZ2V5U, accessed 1 July 2017.

Tyson, L. (2006). *Critical Theory Today*, 2nd edn. New York: Routledge.

Walser, R. (2008). 'Rhythm, Rhyme, and Rhetoric in the Music of Public Enemy'. In M. Clayton (ed.), *Music, Words and Voice: A Reader*. Manchester: Manchester University Press.

Index

Druck:
Canon Deutschland Business Services GmbH
im Auftrag der KNV-Gruppe
Ferdinand-Jühlke-Str. 7
99095 Erfurt